The Book of Fables

Also by W.S. Merwin

W.S. MERWIN

The BOOK *of* FABLES

COPPER CANYON PRESS

Port Townsend, Washington

Cover art: Adam Fuss, *Untitled*, 1988. Unique cibachrome photogram, 24" × 20".

Copper Canyon Press is in residence at Fort Worden State Park in Port Townsend, Washington, under the auspices of Centrum, a gathering place for artists and creative thinkers from around the world, students of all ages and backgrounds, and audiences seeking extraordinary cultural enrichment.

Originally published as *The Miner's Pale Children* (Atheneum, 1970) and *Houses and Travellers* (Atheneum, 1977).

LIBRARY OF CONGRESS CATALOGING-IN-PUBLICATION DATA

Merwin, W. S. (William Stanley), 1927–
The Book of fables / W.S. Merwin.
p. cm.
ISBN-13: 978-1-55659-256-0
(pbk.: alk. paper)
I. Title.
PS3563.E75B65 2007
813'.54 — dc22
2007001352

3 5 7 9 8 6 4 2
FIRST PRINTING

COPPER CANYON PRESS
Post Office Box 271, Port Townsend, Washington 98368
www.coppercanyonpress.org

CONTENTS

The Miner's Pale Children

Houses and Travellers

The Book of Fables

The MINER'S
PALE CHILDREN

The Dwelling

Once when I looked at myself there was nothing. I could not see any size, any shape, any color. I could tell that I was still there because I was frightened, and I could feel that. When I began to think about myself it kept coming down to that, as though that was the only thing to remember. Yes, that was the only thing I could remember about myself clearly and accurately. I was frightened. That one thing went back until I vanished with it. The point of that disappearance could be considered a kind of beginning. And now to the original dread this new fear was added: that I might forget that I was afraid, and so vanish again, entirely.

The new fear was a revelation. It was, so to speak, an addition to my life and I might well have thought of it as a reason for indulging in a moment of precarious rejoicing. But oblivion never left my side. The more I learned the more terrible the possibilities appeared. When I grew too tired to stand up I leaned against a high smooth cliff that ran along a little valley. That way I had a wall at my back. I could tell that I had come to something that was used to staying.

The cliff faced south, across a small stream. The warmth of the day's sunlight remained in the stone after the sun went down. I went back to that place again and again. Because I was frightened I pressed myself against the stone like a being who wants to hide. Sometimes I really wanted to disappear into the cliff. In that one place I thought I might be able to vanish safely. Night after night I spent pressed against the smooth stone. One morning when I woke I saw my shape on it. It stayed there even when I moved away. It was a shadowy form, like the opening of a narrow mouth. I could see my color there on the wall. A kind of shallow darkness. The discovery came to me like a new fear, but I wanted to keep it. I decided not to leave. I spent all day at the cliff wall, pressed hard against it, deepening my shape on it, in my own mind. I even allowed a little of my fear to play at being hope. I stayed there day and night. The age of my wandering without a shape through the shadowy mountains began to seem very remote. A legend. A legend about myself. One day I could feel my appearance itself stirring on the cliff face, turning as the sun went through its course. I knew that my darkness on the wall had sunk into the stone and acquired a shadow of its own. Inside it.

Oblivion came then in the form of a messenger. Sometimes he called himself time, or water. But as soon as he appeared I set him to work. Whatever he told me I answered by becoming more myself. I pressed myself deep into the cliff, where the day never reached. He followed me in. We conversed in silence. At last there were chambers in me, like a heart. And the dust was marked with prints of presences, in the total dark. Some of them were his.

One day I was sure who I was. I left most of my fear in one dark chamber and began to extend outward from the cliff. A wall was built up to the overhanging stone. Other walls rose on either side, and my darkness moved in there, to stay. That day oblivion told me that he was my heir but I told him that I had made up my mind now, I would appear before I disappeared. Even if it made it worse. And I stood there, dark all the way to the outer wall built of separate stones, and was filled with the thought of what I was, and who.

I came to live more and more in the outer room. The inner chambers were a place apart. It seemed to me that the darkness was becoming solid in there. Some of my dreams went on sleeping in there, but places were found for them in the outer room, and in the end most of them moved out and stayed with me. But my fear still spent a great deal of time in there. And I still kept my back to the cliff.

Then one night I grew my own fourth wall, of separate stones. And a roof. Where the cliff had always been. The new stones were not to protect me. To free me. As the work went on I could feel a terrible tremor under me, a remote heaving such as runs through the earth around the roots of an old tree when the wind blows very hard. All of my fear came out of the cliff and joined me, leaving only a ghost of itself in the old place. When the sun rose I stood in the light with four walls. The mountains were far away and were still receding. The cliff was already out of sight. But I could see what I was. I was alone. I was waiting. I had a shadow outside me.

The days move past me now on every side. The birds fly all around me and plunge into the new distances behind me. I have added to the sky. The fear is the same as ever. It is safe now. Even when the roof falls and the walls collapse and the cliff is not even to be thought of and the daylight floods everything and I am forgotten, the fear will survive. Even if it cannot be seen its features will be known, and its existence will be in no doubt. It will be at home everywhere, like oblivion itself. I will not have lived in vain.

The Bar

If you are at home in the bars of this country you will be at home in this one. It seems to be simply one more among so many others. No, no, this is the end of seeming. It really is simply one more among so many others.

The bar runs the full length of the room, from one wall to another, with no curve at either end for a jukebox or hat stand or telephone booth or entrance to the bar or door to a rest room. But there is nothing abnormal about that. The mirror runs all the way along the wall behind the bar, from one end to the other. The bottles are lined up against the mirror all the way, with that arrogance of slaves of an emperor, but that too is perfectly ordinary. Most of the bar stools are occupied. Lighted glass advertisements for beverages, hanging at intervals from the ceiling, revolve slowly, stroking the occupants with colored lights. Little beacons. Not real beacons, of course. And on a box in a corner an illuminated panel shows for a moment a young man and a young woman shooting rapids in a canoe, in bright sunlight. The river is very blue and they are smiling, holding up beer cans. Then the scene changes and they are leaning on ski poles, smiling and holding up beer cans. Then the scene changes again, but nobody watches. The line of backs at the bar faces outward like a ruined fortress. Perfectly normal.

Only when you have joined those on the stools will you notice at some point that at the end, where the bar arrives at the wall, the wall does not come all the way down to the bar top. There is a gap between, perhaps ten inches high, through which bottles, glasses, or other small objects could be passed. Through the opening the bar can be seen continuing beyond the wall. With drinks on it, and hands resting beside them, and little colored lights stroking them. Eventually you will manage to verify that at the other end of the room there is another such opening, with another glimpse of bar, drinks, hands, beyond it. Then you will notice that the doors marked EXIT are at either end of the room.

When someone new comes in a few of the backs straighten, and some of the heads turn. The newcomer stands for a moment embarrassed, afraid of disturbing something, silhouetted in the light of the illuminated scenes. Then he moves toward the bar as though to offer his poor services. When someone goes out through one of the doors at either end, no one pays any attention. The bar-keeper never speaks unless spoken to.

Beyond the bars on either side of this one there are others, and then others. The furnishings are the same, but the barmen have different faces. The illuminated scenes on the panels are different. People have their favorite haunts. They are conservative. To some it seems dangerous to move back and forth. And what for? The worst is having to go looking for someone else.

Within the Wardrobes

No one who was not born and brought up in them really knows of the life in the clothing drawers, and very few of those who did grow up there are willing to divulge any details of that ancient existence so close to our own, or as we like to say within our own, and yet so unfamiliar. No, they answer, everything has been taken from us from the beginning and you have given us only what you chose to, with no concern for us. What essentials remain to us, the secrets of our life, we will keep to ourselves. If our way of life is doomed as a result of yours, its secrets will die with it, and its meaning. We will not lend those to you for your masquerades.

By now scholars have tried everything to bring those secrets to the light of present-day reality, and with almost no success. Devices for opening the drawers suddenly have revealed nothing but the contents lying like the dead whom the light suddenly surprises. Cameras with flash-bulbs, left in the drawers in houses where no one was staying, and timed to go off during the darkest and most silent hours, have disclosed still more eerie vistas of inert recumbency; always the life has remained cloaked in the motionless forms. Electronic recording devices rigged in the same manner have picked up nothing but the gradual sinking into sleep of consciousness after consciousness in the house, until at last only one alien witness remained awake: the recorder was registering its own unrewarded vigil. It has been claimed that these last results, nevertheless, represent a step forward. If not a record of the life itself, at least they supply a record of the outer world from that life's point of view.

As might have been expected, most of the few sources of information on this life so turned away from our own have come from milieux in which neglect in one form or another has already advanced its work. Loose garments, tossed in unfolded, perhaps uncleaned, long ago, and abandoned to their own shapes have not always been able to conceal the evidences of a life to which they were born and which they had almost forgotten the need to hide. A darkness from their own world, and an odor of it, clings to them here and there when they are too abruptly hauled into ours. Others that once existed as pairs and have lost their consorts, stray buttons, fragments of ornamentation, demoralized and with a weakened sense of the future, perhaps, also betray at times the existence of other mores, other values, other hopes, if not those things themselves. These are not ideal witnesses, perhaps, but is there any such thing?

At any rate it is hard to sort out probability from sectarian wish-ful thinking, in the scant testimony thus gathered. The witnesses suggest that their own order of things, its darkness, its anticipation in which time plays no part, its community without sound, its dances, its dances, whatever they may be, are part of an order that is older than the cupboards and will survive them. They also infer quite calmly that the world of uses, for which they were fashioned and in which they are worn, knows almost nothing of reality.

The Basilica of the Scales

There is disagreement about the dates of each phase of the present edifice. No one can establish incontrovertibly when the first primitive chapel was constructed on this site. Parts of the crypt survive from that earliest place of worship. Massive squat squared pillars of gray stone. Medals and military decorations of a later day have been affixed to them on all sides like cloaks, and glitter in the light of the votive candles. The church has been rebuilt at least three times, incorporating the designs and proportions of successive ages. Each time it has been considerably enlarged. The facade has moved west. It is from there that we enter. From farther away. The transept has broadened like the canyon of a gray river flowing between us and the chancel. Most important of all, each time the ceiling, the ceiling has risen.

It cannot be seen. Not from anywhere in the basilica. All that meets the eye when one looks up, wherever one is, are the scales. Like leaves they hang everywhere above the worshippers and the curious. They are suspended at all heights, from those that can barely be descried through the pans and chains of others lower down, to a few which seem to be almost within reach—an illusion caused by some trick of perspective, as one discovers if one finds oneself near them. They are of all sizes, from delicate brass instruments such as apothecaries still use, to vast measures with pans that a heavy man could stand in, beams thicker than an arm and longer, and chains in proportion. And they too are of all ages. Some of them, it is said, are older, much older, than the first building itself. They were brought from far away and their origins are legendary like that of the grail. But none of them belong to our accounts any longer. No one climbs to examine them.

And it would be unthinkable to take one down. In the course of the many centuries since the last building was finished, two or three have fallen. One can imagine the terror that swept through the devout who were present when one of the silent measures suspended above them suddenly detached itself, with a sound of metal snapping and groaning, from what had seemed its everlasting equilibrium, and had crashed down through the lower choirs of chains and hammered pans, setting up a clangor of cymbals, a rocking and lamentation that left the farthest scales in the remote ceiling swinging and vibrating with dying songs. The fallen measures lay like dead supplicants on the granite floor. No one touched them. No one was sure what they meant. No one knelt to pray near them on the bare stone unless the crowd of worshippers pressed them closer than they would have chosen to be. In time iron railings were erected around the collapsed measures where they lay. Black cloth was draped from the rail and removed only between the evening of Good Friday and Easter morning. Candles—not votive lights but thick columns of wax the color of the faces of the dead—flickered perpetually at the corners of the enclosures.

As for the scales suspended above, it would be hard to say at a glance whether they are still or moving. A distant quiet hangs in the pans like dust. And yet the eye that remains fixed upon them for some time detects, or seems to detect, a scarcely perceptible motion, such as we think we see if we stare for long at the faces of the dead. And in fact the scales are at all times in motion. Often it is so slight that the unaided eye could not discern it at all if it were not that the thousands of minute swayings all cast shadows into the thickets of chains, beams, pans, and the shadows magnify the movements, giving that impression of a breathing lost in itself. Occasionally a single balance will forsake its equilibrium, without apparent warning, and one of its pans will slowly sink farther and farther as the other rises, then even more slowly right itself. The phenomenon has fostered various explanations. Some say it is due to a death. Some ascribe it to a peculiar fervor of prayer. Others declare that it is the dove descending. Or a wind. Past, present, or to come.

Tergvinder's Stone

One time my friend Tergvinder brought a large round boulder into his living room. He rolled it up the steps with the help of some two-by-fours, and when he got it out into the middle of the room, where some people have coffee tables (though he had never had one there himself) he left it. He said that was where it belonged.

It is really a plain-looking stone. Not as large as Plymouth Rock by a great deal, but then it does not have all the claims of a big shaky promotion campaign to support. That was one of the things Tergvinder said about it. He made no claims at all for it, he said. It was other people who called it Tergvinder's Stone. All he said was that according to him it belonged there.

His dog took to peeing on it, which created a problem (Tergvinder had not moved the carpet before he got the stone to where he said it belonged). Their tomcat took to squirting it, too. His wife fell over it quite often at first and it did not help their already strained marriage. Tergvinder said there was nothing to be done about it. It was in the order of things. That was a phrase he seldom employed, and never when he conceived that there was any room left for doubt.

He confided in me that he often woke in the middle of the night, troubled by the ancient, nameless ills of the planet, and got up quietly not to wake his wife, and walked through the house naked, without turning on any lights. He said that at such times he found himself listening, listening, aware of how some shapes in the darkness emitted low sounds like breathing, as they never did by day. He said he had become aware of a hole in the darkness in the middle of the living room, and out of that hole a breathing, a mournful dissatisfied sound of an absence waiting for what belonged to it, for something it had never seen and could not conceive of, but without which it could not rest. It was a sound, Tergvinder said, that touched him with fellow-feeling, and he had undertaken—oh, without saying anything to anybody—to assuage, if he could, that wordless longing that seemed always on the verge of despair. How to do it was another matter, and for months he had circled the problem, night and day, without apparently coming any closer to a solution. Then one day he had seen the stone. It had been there all the time at the bottom of his drive, he said, and he had never really seen it. Never recognized it for what it was. The nearer to the house he had got it, the more certain he had become. The stone had rolled into its present place like a lost loved one falling into arms that had long ached for it.

Tergvinder says that now on nights when he walks through the dark house he comes and stands in the living room doorway and listens to the peace in the middle of the floor. He knows its size, its weight, the touch of it, something of what is thought of it. He knows that it is peace. As he listens, some hint of that peace touches him too. Often, after a while, he steps down into the living room and goes and kneels beside the stone and they converse for hours in silence— a silence broken only by the sound of his own breathing.

The Dachau Shoe

My cousin Gene (he's really only a second cousin) has a shoe he picked up at Dachau. It's a pretty worn-out shoe. It wasn't top quality in the first place, he explained. The sole is cracked clear across and has pulled loose from the upper on both sides, and the upper is split at the ball of the foot. There's no lace and there's no heel.

He explained he didn't steal it because it must have belonged to a Jew who was dead. He explained that he wanted some little thing. He explained that the Russians looted everything. They just took anything. He explained that it wasn't top quality to begin with. He explained that the guards or the kapos would have taken it if it had been any good. He explained that he was lucky to have got anything. He explained that it wasn't wrong because the Germans were defeated. He explained that everybody was picking up something. A lot of guys wanted flags or daggers or medals or things like that, but that kind of thing didn't appeal to him so much. He kept it on the mantelpiece for a while but he explained that it wasn't a trophy.

He explained that it's no use being vindictive. He explained that he wasn't. Nobody's perfect. Actually we share a German grandfather. But he explained that this was the reason why we had to fight that war. What happened at Dachau was a crime that could not be allowed to pass. But he explained that we could not really do anything to stop it while the war was going on because we had to win the war first. He explained that we couldn't always do just what we would have liked to do. He explained that the Russians killed a lot of Jews too. After a couple of years he put the shoe away in a drawer. He explained that the dust collected in it.

Now he has it down in the cellar in a box. He explains that the central heating makes it crack worse. He'll show it to you, though, any time you ask. He explains how it looks. He explains how it's hard to take it in, even for him. He explains how it was raining, and there weren't many things left when he got there. He explains how there wasn't anything of value and you didn't want to get caught taking anything of that kind, even if there had been. He explains how everything inside smelled. He explains how it was just lying out in the mud, probably right where it had come off. He explains that he ought to keep it. A thing like that.

You really ought to go and see it. He'll show it to you. All you have to do is ask. It's not that it's really a very interesting shoe when you come right down to it but you learn a lot from his explanations.

Make This Simple Test

Blindfold yourself with some suitable object. If time permits remain still for a moment. You may feel one or more of your senses begin to swim back toward you in the darkness, singly and without their names. Meanwhile have someone else arrange the products to be used in a row in front of you. It is preferable to have them in identical containers, though that is not necessary. Where possible, perform the test by having the other person feed you a portion—a spoonful —of each of the products in turn, without comment.

Guess what each one is, and have the other person write down what you say.

Then remove the blindfold. While arranging the products the other person should have detached part of the label or container from each and placed it in front of the product it belongs to, like a title. This bit of legend must not contain the product's trade name nor its generic name, nor any suggestion of the product's taste or desirability. Or price. It should be limited to that part of the label or container which enumerates the actual components of the product in question.

Thus, for instance:

"Contains dextrinized flours, cocoa processed with alkali, non-fat dry milk solids, yeast nutrients, vegetable proteins, agar, hydrogenated vegetable oil, dried egg yolk, GUAR, sodium cyclamate, soya lecithin, imitation lemon oil, acetyl tartaric esters of mono- and diglycerides as emulsifiers, polysorbate 60, $\frac{1}{10}$ of 1% of sodium benzoate to retard spoilage."

Or:

"Contains anhydrated potatoes, powdered whey, vegetable gum, emulsifier (glycerol monostearate), invert syrup, shortening with freshness preserver, lactose, sorbic acid to retard mold growth, caramel color, natural and artificial flavors, sodium acid pyrophosphate, sodium bisulfite."

Or:

"Contains beef extract, wheat and soya derivatives, food starch-modified, dry sweet whey, calcium carageenan, vegetable oil, sodium phosphates to preserve freshness, BHA, BHT, prophylene glycol, pectin, niacinamide, artificial flavor, U.S. certified color."

There should be not less than three separate products.

Taste again, without the blindfold. Guess again and have the other person record the answers. Replace the blindfold. Have the other person change the order of the products and again feed you a spoonful of each.

Guess again what you are eating or drinking in each case (if you can make the distinction). But this time do not stop there. Guess why you are eating or drinking it. Guess what it may do for you. Guess what it was meant to do for you. By whom. When. Where. Why. Guess where in the course of evolution you took the first step toward it. Guess which of your organs recognize it. Guess whether it is welcomed to their temples. Guess how it figures in their prayers. Guess how completely you become what you eat. Guess how soon. Guess at the taste of locusts and wild honey. Guess at the taste of water. Guess what the rivers see as they die. Guess why the babies are burning. Guess why there is silence in heaven. Guess why you were ever born.

Postcards from the Maginot Line

This morning there was another one in the mail. A slightly blurred and clumsily retouched shot of some of the fortifications, massive and scarcely protruding from the enormous embankments. The guns—the few that can be seen—look silly, like wax cigars. The flag looks like a lead soldier's, with the paint put on badly. The whole thing might be a model.

But there have been the others. Many of them. For the most part seen from the exterior, from all angles—head-on, perspectives facing north and facing south, looking out from the top of the embankments, even one from above. They might all have been taken from a model, in fact, but when they are seen together that impression fades. And then there are the interiors. Officers' quarters which, the legend says, are hundreds of feet below ground. Views of apparently endless corridors into which little ramps of light descend at intervals; panels of dials of different sizes, with black patches on them that have been censored out. It was rather startling to notice a small flicker of relief at the sight of the black patches: it had seemed somehow imprudent to make public display of so much of the defenses.

A few of the cards have shown other, related subjects: a mezzotint of Maginot as a child in the 1880s, a view of the house where he grew up, with his portrait in an oval inset above it, pictures of villages near the line of fortifications, with their churches, and old men sitting under trees, and cows filing through the lanes, and monuments from other wars. They have all been marked, front and back, in heavy black letters THE MAGINOT LINE, and the legend in each case has made the relation clear. And the postmarks are all from there.

They have been coming for months, at least once a week. All signed simply "Pierre." Whoever he is. He certainly seems to know me, or know about me—referring to favorite authors, incidents from my childhood, friends I have not seen for years. He says repeatedly that he is comfortable there. He praises what he calls the tranquillity of the life. He says, as though referring to an old joke, that with my fondness for peace I would like it. He says war is unthinkable. A thing of the past. He describes the flowers in the little beds. He describes the social life. He tells what he is reading. He asks why I never write. He asks why none of us ever write. He says we have nothing to fear.

The Weight of Sleep

At the very mention of it there is one kind of person who laughs or looks away. You know at once where he is—in his life, in the story of the species, in the adventure of the planet. For the weight of sleep cannot be measured. By definition, some might say, though has it ever been defined? At least it cannot be measured by any scale known to the perspectives of waking. Presumably it might be measured one day if machines were contrived that resembled us so closely that they slept. And required sleep. But there again, can we tell how they would differ from us? How their sleep would differ from ours? There again one reaches for definitions and touches darkness.

And yet the weight of sleep is one of the only things that we know. We have been aware of it since we knew anything, since the first moment after conception. It grew with us, it grows along with us, it draws us on. Its relation to the gravity of the planet is merely one of analogy. The weight of sleep draws us back inexorably toward a unity that is entirely ours but that we cannot possess, that resembles the sky itself as much as it does the centers of the heavenly bodies.

When did it begin? With life itself? Long before? Or a little time after, when consciousness, the whole of consciousness, scarcely begun, suddenly became aware of itself like a caught breath, and was seized with panic and longing and the knowledge of travail? Yes, it was then that the weight of sleep came to it, the black angel full of promises. With different forms for each life. Different dances.

For the planet itself it was simpler. To the whole of the globe's first life as it became conscious of itself, everything seemed to have stopped in the terrible light. Everything stood in the grip of the single command: Weariness. Forever and ever. Then came the black angel.

For the planet his shape can be pictured as that of a driving wheel of a locomotive. The rim is darkness; he is always present. The spokes are darkness. They divide the light, though they disappear as they turn. They meet at the center. The hub is darkness. Across one side is a segment of solid black. There is the weight of sleep, properly speaking: its throne. There the wheel's mass preserves its motion. There its stillness dreams of falling. There what it is dreams of what it is.

Our Jailer

Our jailer is in the habit of placing a baited mouse trap in the cells of the condemned on their last night. Ours is a well-kept jail; mice are rare and not many stray into the occupied cells. The jailer watches the prisoners.

Surprisingly few, he says, remain completely indifferent to the presence of the trap throughout the whole night. A larger number become absorbed by it and sit staring at it, whether or not it occupies their thoughts consistently. A proportion which he has recorded releases the trap, either at once or after a period of varying length. He has other statistics for those who deliberately smash the trap, those who move it (presumably to a more likely spot), those who make a mark on the wall if a mouse is caught in the trap, and those who make one if none was caught, either to state the fact or to bequeath, as a tiny triumph, a lie.

Month after month, year after year, he watches them. And we watch him. And each other.

Shine On, Tottering Republic

In the last days of the presidents a new star appeared. By then the organization of fear was vast and persuasive beyond anything that could have been conceived by the founding fathers. It involved the whole economy. Every coin, changing hands, paid tribute to it. The rings of warning and defense, whether or not they were penetrable, insured that the entire planet would be pulverized in the event of an attack or the appearance of one. On the domestic front the police were their own masters, and no branch of technology was closed to them. Any window, any light bulb, any picture might be a television camera connected to the nearest precinct. No one dared to examine too closely. Those who did might be arrested a few minutes later, charged with obstruction or conspiracy. Bail no longer existed, trials came seldom, sentences were inevitable, heavy, and without appeal. On the whole, it was said, the public was relieved at the steady disappearance of disturbing elements.

Then the star appeared. On the dollar, first. On the seal, in the circular array above the motto E PLURIBUS UNUM (FROM MANY ONE) bill after bill began to show one star too many. It gave the motto new possibilities, but that was scarcely noticed. There were some arrests for counterfeiting but the scandal spread rapidly and involved several large banks. Severity was recommended as the number of bills that had to be withdrawn grew from edition to edition of the daily papers. Possession of the improper bills was harshly dealt with. Then for a few days the media were silent on the subject and only the pressure of rumor forced the government to admit at last that the offending constellation had been traced back to the mint itself. But the die that had wrought the terrible addition was not found. And when new bills were issued, within a week notes with the same serial numbers, and otherwise indistinguishable by any known techniques, contained the new star. The search for the counterfeiters surpassed any hunt in the nation's history. Suspect after suspect was seized, grilled, tried, sentenced, publicized, but the star continued to appear. At last the bill was completely withdrawn, and redesigned without the seal.

Then the star began appearing on the flag. Again it was simply embarrassing at first. No one could understand how it came to be there: one too many in one of the rows, not always the same row. It happened on flags that people had owned for years. Sometimes it seemed to occur overnight, to patriots who were accustomed to hoisting their flags every morning. Some were mortified and then frightened, at the thought that they might have flown the improper constellation for a day or even more without noticing it, and that someone else might have counted. For by then everyone counted, all the time. Less and less flags were flown.

In time there was no piece of the national insignia that did not risk the appearance of the free, illegal star. Officers' uniforms, taken from cupboards in their own homes, would prove to have acquired the shameful decoration through no agency known to the owners. Medals locked in cases displayed the unwarranted distinction when the cases were opened. Document after document affixed with the seal turned out to be of questionable validity because the new star had found them with its mark. Even on those monuments to the war dead that bore stars it appeared again and again under the final name, with a blank space after it. A few days later there would be another one. Followed by a blank. And then another. And another.

At last the flag was re-designed. With no stars at all. The seal was re-designed. Without stars. All the national insignia were re-designed without stars. All the stars were chiselled from the monuments to the war dead. And the country shook itself, not without suspicion but not without a smile, and began to recover from its shame.

Memory

In the first place is it a virtue after all? We despise those who are deficient in it, but that may be nothing but our predilection for those deceits that have hoodwinked us in particular, and our devotion to the habits into which they have led us. We pretend to think it is reasonable because it has taught us to reason. We pretend to believe that it is the guardian of wisdom, an antique ornament which it has shown us on favored occasions lying in a velvet box that we are to inherit some day if we are good.

On the other hand, like the rest of the blindfolded deities, it is a source of terrible arrogance. It persuades us that nothing of the past remains except what we remember. From there it is only a step to persuading us that the present too would be meaningless without it. And we take that step moment by moment as though the light fell nowhere else.

So to say that we would not be here, or even to ask indulgently what we would be, without it, proves nothing. Except that most of what we call our virtues have been made of necessities by processes that we later tried to forget. What does that tell us about our bondage?

See, the sailor emerges at last from the loom. He is convinced that his guide through all the weavings has been a personification of wisdom itself. And so memory, he repeats as he paces the familiar shore, has played no tricks on him. His guide had told him that things would look smaller, that the dogs would be old and the eyes milky. No, he says, due allowance having been made for the passage of time (as he has been careful to do) it is just as he remembered it. The same shadows on the same walls, the same lines and the same unimpressed absence on the hills. If he thought he detected a slight echo to his voice in the first moments it was gone by the time he listened for it. Even the unpleasant details — the screaming of one of the local hysterics, the smell of the back premises of the port, the crabbed features of a neighbor, the resumption of insoluble disputes and onerous responsibilities — were exactly as he had remembered them. He told himself that he had sweetened nothing, that he had been just.

Then why, by the third day—the day of resurrections—this bewilderment, this sense of being utterly lost, of turning, without a goal, in a great emptiness that, for all he knew, reached to the end of the world? Here was something that he had not remembered. Something that he never seemed to be able to remember. That same oppression that he had endured so often in this very place, that he had left with anguish and relief and now recognized with a stunned dread. What could he call it? His own presence in the place? The standing on the needle? The present? The blankness at the end of the story.

The Wedding March

To be honest it was really too late when we started out to look for the United Fish and Fowl Shipping Company Restaurant, and not the kind of evening that would have been best for such an expedition. The sun had gone down without calling attention to itself. The twilight had had a greenish cast to it that stayed on in the streets. The air was heavy and dank. On the sidewalk somebody said that it would be too much trouble to rain.

It seemed knowledgeable to have heard of the United Fish and Fowl Shipping Company Restaurant, to mention it casually as a possibility. It's a Japanese raw fish and chicken restaurant, very cheap. The party had been pretty dreadful but we were happy. It was quite early to be leaving a party although it was really too late to be starting out looking for the restaurant. I explained that although I had been there as a child I couldn't be said to know that part of town at all well. I should say I didn't know it at all. Some nice people were going to come with us, but in the end they didn't.

It takes quite a long time to get out there. That's one of the disadvantages. Then at last we were in the neighborhood. Empty streets. They hadn't even taken up the old streetcar tracks. Big warehouses on both sides, and a few wholesalers tucked among them, dusty and closed. All the doors looked like garage doors. I had a little map a friend had drawn for me. How to get there from the subway. It was on a side street. Nothing seemed to live there but cats. I saw a sign that looked as though it said United Fish and Fowl Shipping Company Restaurant down along the bend of the street, but wasn't sure. Before we got close enough to read it, we noticed a cop, in a car. He had drawn up to make a note. He had stopped in back of us, but I went back to ask him if he knew where the United Fish and Fowl Shipping Company Restaurant was.

Actually he had rather a pleasant face. He wasn't very old. He was polite. Though you never can tell. He was writing in a little notebook. He didn't answer or look up right away. He said yes, that was the place. Then he looked at me as though I were a high-school student and he were a high-school teacher who knew something about me. He said we didn't really want to go to that restaurant, did we? I explained that we'd been told about it. He asked who told us. I said a friend. He gave a little laugh. He said where we ought to go was the Chinese restaurant around the corner on the main street. He said we'd like that better. It would be a better place for us. Then I thought, I suppose now he'll watch to see which one we head for. But he said he was really off duty and on his way home. It was true, it was a private car. It was a big favor he'd been doing me. But that didn't mean that he owed me anything. He'd made it clear. I said good-night and he drove off.

We couldn't believe the restaurant. It looked more like a storefront church. The windows were painted on the inside, all the way up, with a little chipped black and gold frieze, probably a decal, along the top. The color of the paint must have been what they call Ivory but in that light it looked the shade of dried peas. There was a street light farther down the block, near enough so that you could read the sign, lettered in dark red, and through the chipped places in the frieze you could see that there was a bulb lit inside too. On one side of the restaurant a passage was boarded up and had another sign on it, a warning. On the other side there was a big sign about an elevator shaft. Inside the restaurant there were voices, Japanese probably, and sounds of tables or crates thudding and banging. We discussed it and decided to try the Chinese place after all.

It was quite near. The stores on the street were closed, even the drug-store, but the Chinese restaurant was still open. When we went in there was no one at the tables. A Chinese man of middle years and girth who seemed as though he might be the proprietor came from the back, smiling and greeting, smelling of soap. He said it wasn't too late, but then he went and locked the door behind us, and drew the curtains. There were other people in the kitchen or the back rooms. You could hear them banging metal around and laughing. He waited among the tables and took our order. I asked him whether he had heard of a Japanese restaurant called the United Fish and Fowl Shipping Company Restaurant and he said he had. I asked him whether it was good and he said it was. Then he left us.

He brought part of the order and then he was gone for a good while. The banging and laughing stopped in the back, there was a shuffling, the voices dropped and grew more serious. Just as he re-appeared with the rest of the order there was a sound of a clarinet or some other wood-wind instrument warming up, and a stringed instrument being tuned. He was smiling as though a great joke were being prepared and we were in on it. Or were part of it. A head popped out from the kitchen, looked at us, a hand covered its mouth to hide a giggle. Then it disappeared. He left us again.

Suddenly from the back came the music. Something from Schubert first. A bit brassy and quite loud, with more drum than usual, and a tambourine. Then the Largo from *Xerxes.* And finally the "Wedding March" from *Lohengrin,* over and over. Over and over, until we had finished, and the tea was gone, and we needed more. The man reap-peared to see how we were doing. Smiling at the same joke. As he took the tea pot I asked him if there was a wedding.

Yes, he said. There was a wedding. A wedding.

I asked him where.

He shrugged. "Somewhere," he said.

When?

"Every night," he said. "We play."

And you could see that it was true. Every night somewhere there is a wedding. The guests gather. The procession begins. The groom's party advances, and the groom. The bride's party, and the bride. They are united, they file out together, the guests crowd after them. All in silence. While the music is being played there. There in the locked Chinese restaurant, in the back room.

Spiders I Have Known

The one no bigger than the head of a pencil, that emerged from the forehead of the new dentist perhaps an inch above his left eyebrow, ran down to the eyebrow and along it and dropped from the side of his face to the little scalloped glass tray on which the dentist was selecting a drill. It then disappeared. From my sight at least. I did not wish to call the dentist's attention to it at that precise moment. Besides I recognized that it was a perfectly harmless variety.

I would have been ashamed to be afraid.

The one that I found had taken up residence in a bundle of letters only a few months old. It was smaller than the wolf spiders that live in some of the corners and do no harm at all. It was also darker than they, and heavily — beautifully — furred. Some of its children clung to it like troops of tiny dust-colored anthropoids, and others had taken up lodgings in several of the larger envelopes. I looked up the species. Its bite is not poisonous, if I identified it correctly. I devoted some time to trying to remember which letters those were, who had written them, what they had said, whether I had answered them, and how things now stood, as a result, with each of the correspondents.

I would have been afraid to be ashamed.

The one that hung in the old apple tree that spring when we returned at last to the farm by the lake with its old garden into which I had been allowed to run, alone, with only a perfunctory word of caution from my mother, a word whose real purpose had been to dispel the attention of my father. The blossoms were just opening on the tree and the air rushed past me carrying them with it as though I were on a swing, when suddenly there it was in front of me, as big as my face, against the bright sky the color and depth of the fenders of the new car. The whole web was swaying gently in the wind. The abdomen had a kind of face on it. No, not a face, a mask. In orange and yellow. I knew it was a kind that was more afraid of me than I was of it.

I was ashamed.

The one that ran across each of my footprints in turn as I was crossing the dry bit on my way back, when you were sick and we didn't know how it would go after that, but maybe it wasn't working at all. I had the medicines but not much faith in them. It came to the edge of each footprint, hesitated, and then shot across like a woman with a baby, afraid of snipers, or a good child caught in a cloudburst. I couldn't understand how it kept up with me. My hands were full. You were in pain. I didn't want to stop. It's bad luck to harm them. Poor things. Besides, the danger of that species has been greatly exaggerated.

I would have been ashamed.

The Fountain

In the forest of Morb, which means untouched, there is a fountain known as Llorndy, which means unchanging. The forest stretches for many days' ride over the plateau. Other trees must have grown there once. Now there are none but the oaks. They are immense, and everywhere. There are no clearings. The forest is so tall and dense that no birds live in it except owls and the little wren that can make her way through the unlit veins of the earth to its heart and find nourishment on the way. The bird of the goddess of wisdom, who cannot find her mistress. And the bird of the sovereign of darkness, who sings to herself. No one lives in the forest. No building will stand. Springs well up wherever one stone is placed on another, and the walls topple and sink into the earth before they can be said to be walls. No roads cross the forest. Water emerges from them before they have been laid, and they become long deepening quagmires. No paths cross the forest. Even fresh paths of deer and badgers grow old after a few yards and then vanish as though the undergrowth or the bed of leaves had never been disturbed. No one hunts here. The owl and the wren follow intruders, calling out wherever they go. There is no other voice, except their echoes. The oaks are so high that the rustling of the leaves cannot be heard from the ground, but the murmur seems to prevent any other vibration from entering. Only around the fountain of Llorndy and along its little stream of sweet water is there a continuous thread of sound.

The fountain emerges from a large rock on a gentle slope. A piece of pale gray stone, limestone, though the rocks in the forest and in the piled mounds of stone around it are granite or basalt or slate. Its pallor is startling, as though it were a faint light among the dark vegetation. It rises in a vaguely conical shape, with two columns down the front and the green stain between them where the water flows to begin the stream. The shape of an animal, seated erect, with no head. At the level of the collar the water wells out and brims over, blind, tireless, unchanging.

Once the forest was a great kingdom, rich and beautiful. Its farms were well-stocked and peaceful. Its arts were old and sure. Its borders were safe. It was on good terms with its neighbors. It was ruled by a king who was cultivated, intelligent, kind, and beloved of his subjects and of his family. But he was not happy, because he had a hard heart. He knew it. He had tried everything: women and religion, the company of children, the contemplation of flowers, the presence of animals, the sky itself, and he loved them all but he could tell that his heart was still hard. He loved them, he confessed to himself, only because he could imagine that they were his. And his heart remained as it was.

When his secret had been weighing on him for several years, the kingdom began to suffer from drought. In spring and autumn, when rain normally fell plentifully, the clouds gathered as usual but less and less rain fell every year, and in some years there was almost none. The summers lengthened and were less and less relieved by showers. The winters were moistened only by condensation and the humors remaining in the earth. New wells were dug but they ran dry almost at once. Dams were made but their water seeped away into cracked mud. The pastures grew bare; the farms were hungry. One by one, family by family, the inhabitants of the kingdom asked permission to leave. The king was kind and granted it, without exception, giving each family some present as it left, and provisions for the journey—dry provisions, and even a supply of precious water. Some were too ashamed to ask, and left without a word. The kingdom grew emptier as the months passed, and drier. The king sat in his darkened throne room. He had hung the walls with mourning. The windows were smoked, the columns and the candles were painted black. It was painful for him to converse with anyone, including his family. He knew that the kingdom was suffering this misfortune because his own heart was hard.

"And if only my heart were not as hard as it is," he said to the black columns, "I would know what to do. Should I go away? Is there any reason to imagine that that would solve the matter? As long as my heart is hard, this which is the result of it will go on. Furthermore it was here that it grew hard. Being somewhere else will not change it. If it is to be changed it had best be changed here, or else I will never be sure.

"Should I die? But what difference would that make? If I died with a hard heart would anything be changed? Everything might very well go on just as it is.

"Should I abdicate? It would make no difference. My own hard heart brought about this revulsion in nature. There is no way I can leave that behind. Even if I went and lived in a shepherd's hut, out on the plateau where the sheep have all died of starvation or thirst, my heart would be the same, and so nothing would change."

One day an animal came to see the king. He had never seen an animal like that one. It was larger than a horse, but was shaped more like a dog. Its eyes were set so deep in its head that he could not see them at all. They seemed to be nothing but holes. The animal was covered with long pale fur, almost white, and had a thick tail, and paws like a cat's. The claws clicked on the darkened stone floor of the throne room. The creature came close to the black candle burning in front of the throne although it was broad day outside, and there it greeted him.

"What can I do for you?" the king asked.

"I don't need anything," the animal said. "It's I who've come to help you."

"No one can help me," the king said.

"What do you want?" the animal asked.

"I want the rain to fall and my kingdom to be happy as it was," the king said. "And for my heart not to be hard any more."

"Why do you want those things?" the animal asked.

"Can you doubt that I want them?" the king said.

"I see no reason to believe it."

"Do you think I am indifferent to the state of the kingdom?" the king asked.

"No, I don't think that."

There was a pause. The king looked into the holes that were the animal's eyes.

"Where did you come from?" he asked.

"I used to live here," the animal answered. "Before this palace was built. Before anything was built here."

"I thought all the beasts from those days were dead," the king said.

"What do you know about death?" the animal answered.

"How do you propose to help?" the king asked.

"Here," said the animal, tearing a tuft of fur from its breast. "Take this. Give it to your elder son. Send him to the northern part of the plateau, to the driest place. Tell him to make a hole in the ground with his hands and plant this tuft of hair. When he has done that I will come back and tell you what you owe me."

The animal turned and went slowly across the throne room, with its claws clicking on the darkened stones, and out the door.

The king sat in the dark with the fur in his hand, turning it, fingering it. It was damp to the touch. It offered no explanations. He had to admit that he was afraid, and not sure why. What should he do now? He did not believe that the fur would make any difference to anything, but what if it did? What might it do? What might the animal demand in return? Though surely if he did nothing now it would seem as though he really were indifferent to the state of his kingdom. It would be a proof that his heart was growing still harder. He sat pondering the matter for the rest of the afternoon and only when night fell did he call his elder son.

The young man had too profound a respect for his father, for the throne, and for his father's unhappiness to show any surprise. He took the fur from his father's hand and left that night.

By the next night he was back, but the news had travelled ahead of him. No sooner had he planted the fur, he said, in the driest place in the northern plateau, than a spring of water welled up from the spot and spread swiftly into a wide basin, brimming over and flowing away across the plain. If it went on, the pastures would begin to inch back over the shrivelled wastes. The sun would be a blessing again. A week passed, two weeks, a month, and the water went on flowing. The king felt a deadly misgiving in his heart but he could not run it to earth. The throne room remained dark. He waited for the animal to return.

And when the month was up the animal reappeared. It came in and sat before the throne.

"Have I helped you?" it asked.

"I am not sure," the king answered.

"Has the water not come back?"

"It has."

"Is the grass not growing?"

"It is."

"Was that not what you wanted?"

"It was."

But the king knew that his own heart was as hard as ever. And yet he was ashamed to mention the fact to the animal, when the water had already made such a difference to the lives of many of his subjects. He felt that that would be selfish. It would also be difficult to explain. What do animals know about the hardness of human hearts?

"What do I owe you?" the king asked.

"I wish to be restored to my ancient office," the animal said. "I wish to be appointed Warden of the Waters, with full authority over the use of all the waters in your kingdom."

The king bowed his head and thought. Had he the right, he asked himself, to grant to an animal control over the prosperity and even the lives of his subjects, to leave their welfare and their futures in the hands of a creature he knew nothing about except that water came from its planted fur? That was the first objection he admitted to himself. Then there was another. Suppose the animal did administer the waters fairly and even magnanimously. The king's heart would remain unchanged. And it was the hardness of the king's heart, he reminded himself, that had caused the drought. If the water flowed now from some other cause, his heart might never be able to change again. And for another thing, could any relief of the drought that came from outside be regarded as trustworthy, in the circumstances, or even real?

"Ask something else," the king said. "I cannot give you that."

"You do not know what you want," the animal said. "But maybe you will find it anyway." It turned and went out of the throne room.

The next morning the elder son was found dead in his bed. And in the afternoon news came that the spring in the northern plateau had dried up. The king sat in the throne room, numb and cold.

A month passed. The drought was unchanged. Once again the animal stood before the king.

"There's no point in your coming again," the king said.

"Do you think that if your heart were to break—" the animal began.

"What?" the king asked, trying to look into the animal's eyes.

"Water would flow from the cracks, and everything else would be whole again?"

"It might be," the king answered. "But my heart will not break."

"How do you know?" the animal asked.

"It should have broken by now."

"Do you still care about your kingdom at all?"

"Would I be here otherwise?"

The animal tore out another tuft of its fur and held it out to the king.

"Give this to your other son," it said. "Tell him to take it to all the dry stream beds in the kingdom and drop a hair in each. I will come back and tell you what you owe me."

Once more, after the animal had gone, the king sat in silence pondering the tuft of fur in his hand, feeling as though he were drifting out over an abyss. In the evening he summoned his other son and told him what to do.

Day after day the news came in from the kingdom that the streams were flowing again, the lakes were filling, the old mill wheels were beginning to turn with a terrible screeching and shrieking after so long standing parched and split. There were even fish in the streams and ponds, as large as though they had been growing through the whole time of the drought. The other son came home happy, with messages of affection and presents from all parts of the kingdom, and his carriage full of pretty girls. The king was polite. But he trusted nothing. He grew, if anything, more withdrawn. Curtains were made for the throne room, because the light hurt his eyes. A month after the return of his son, the animal reappeared.

"Great king," it said. And then it sat down in front of the throne.

"Why do you call me that?" the king asked.

"Because of you the kingdom is happy again."

"I wish it were so," the king said.

"You can make it so," the animal said.

"I do not know how."

"Give me my ancient office. Appoint me Warden of the Waters of your kingdom."

Once again the king considered the matter. Yes, suppose it was true that the animal could make the springs rise and the streams flow as it willed. What other powers might it not have that could involve the country in greater miseries than any it had yet suffered, if the king were once to grant the creature a position of such authority. And if the original cause of the kingdom's disasters lay, in fact, in the king's own heart, would any change of the external circumstances be likely to last? Would it be something on which to base the future of the kingdom? Would it not simply remove all hope that the king's heart might ever change? It was true that this time the king was afraid of the animal. But could he allow his own fears, even for those near him, to influence him in his duty to the kingdom?

"I have no right to grant you that," the king said.

"You know nothing about rights," the animal said. "And you will never know anything about them. You can give me what I ask. Or you can refuse."

"I cannot give you what you ask."

"You can give me whatever you want to give me. That is what a king is," the animal answered.

"No," the king said at last, still hoping that one day his heart might undergo a change. And the animal went away. The next day the king's other son was found dead in his bed, and the news began to come in that the streams were shrinking and the ponds drying up. At the king's orders the whole country went into mourning. All the flames in the hearths were covered with ashes and gave off nothing but smoke. White bones were hung against the doors and windows and rattled in the wind. At the end of a month the animal entered the dark throne room again. The king stared at the creature with hatred and dread.

"Why have you come back?" he asked. "We have nothing to say to each other. Each of us must pursue his own nature."

"I've no quarrel with that," the animal said. "But I keep thinking that I can help you. That's part of my nature. It's never changed."

"I won't make you any promises," the king said. "I am not sure of anything any longer except one quality of my own heart."

"Its darkness?" the animal asked.

"Its hardness," the king said.

"Here," the animal said, tearing out a third tuft of fur and holding it out to the king. "I'll try once more. Take this everywhere in your kingdom. From every rock on which you lay a hair, a trickle of clear water will begin to flow. From every hillside on which you lay a piece of fur a stream will begin. Merely brush the village fountains with the ends of it and they will leap into the air. Keep the fur. It will last you as long as you need it. I will ask nothing in return. Not now. Not in the future."

The king felt the fur in his hand. He looked at the animal sitting in front of him. He looked at the empty eyes. He imagined going out with the fur, the springs flowing, the joy in the land. He thought of how he would owe all of that to this animal. And then he thought of his own heart. Nothing would ever change it again. The flocks would fatten, the people grow rich and happy and bless him. It would all be due to this beast who was really the warden of the waters. And meanwhile his heart would remain as hard as ever, and no happiness would be real, and one day, promise or no promise, the beast might return and demand—anything—. He stopped there.

There was a way out. It was hard, but it was a solution. Or at least it was a decision. It came from that very hardness of his heart. He thought of his dead sons. He thought of the possible threat to the future of his kingdom. He clutched the fur in his left hand and with his right he drew his sword, as he leapt to his feet. With one stroke he severed the animal's head from its shoulders.

And the candle went out. And the windows fell in. And the throne collapsed. And the ceiling peeled away like shavings and rolled down the crumbling walls. And from the animal's neck the fountain began to flow. The fountain of Llorndy, on its way to the salt. But the king fell back on the stones and from his heart the first of the oaks raised two tender leaves.

Being Born Again

Some days—and on occasion it lasts much longer—the oppression stirs, shifts (it may seem at first to be no more than a change of position) and I feel the labor begin again. However I move or wherever I go I cannot get outside of this travail, which in itself, of course, is a delivery from a confinement. The heaven and the earth of this predicament are nowhere that I can see. My eyes take in only the immediate world that my own body inhabits, and they try to persuade me that the old world is the only one. Because it is the only one that they have developed habits to comprehend.

Seeing, though, has nothing to do with the travail. It seems, rather, as though nothing that I had beheld up until that day were of use in the pressure and the searing desolation that come upon me. I must exist in many forms at a given time, after all, only one of which I think I am used to and have adopted as a convention. And the pressure has come from some other existence of myself, unknown to me or at least unnoticed, that has grown, curled in itself, until it can no longer be contained and is now undergoing a change in its very cosmos.

Can no longer be contained in what, it may well be asked. And I ask it, and send out all my senses like anguished balloons trying to find—what, who? The matrix, the life which is crushing me, through which and from which I am being torn. And yet the quest is hopeless, and I know it. These senses cannot enter into and look out from the life of that other who is suffering now pains of which my own are mere distant echoes. My senses cannot place that other being, nor define it. They can only learn of it by leaving it. Then the suffering will remain with them. Like a root torn out. It will have become their own. No longer simply an echo, but the first possession, the first knowledge of the new "I."

No, the new mother—there is no way of envisaging her form, her place, anything about her except her own pain, of which this pressure, this vertigo, this anguish, this dread, this ferocity, this hope, this tenderness, this hunger and this thirst are, or at least may be analogies—or growths, flowers, or echoes, as I have said. They are all beyond my control and presumably they are beyond hers. The only way that I will be able to learn more about her is by advancing through her and away from her, in the grip of this suffering which we share, which is nothing more or less than my being torn from her. It is not, once again, as though either of us had a choice. In anything except our willingness.

It is all very well to know this with what I have come to call my reason. I cannot remember it, and only memory would help me at this point, it seems to me, on my way into the new days. And the new nights. And memories do come at moments with messages, though whether to guide or to distract me I cannot tell. In the midst of a spasm which I tell myself (with a laugh) that I may not survive, I have a sudden clear and indubitable glimpse of myself lying in my mother's arms at a bay window facing south over a catalpa tree, in the sunlight. She has no age, and no one else exists, and what passes between us is a tenderness into which everything else crowds, shuffling its feet, then holding its breath, then at peace.

At other moments I hear the horses. It is not something that I could be said to remember, I suppose, because it cannot have been sent to my brain by my own body. It cannot belong to the nights that are to come. Can it? Can it be said to belong to the old ones? Can it come from the mother herself? There in front of me is darkness—a strip of torn earth with a blacker line of bushes beyond it, and a blacker canal or slow stream beyond that. I am being held up at a gate. Held up high, by a tall female figure, a very tall female figure in dark clothes that reach to the ground. Her hair is tied in a small knot on top of her head and a white collar circles her neck—the only white object. I never see her face. I feel the pulsing of her hands around my chest. It is almost in time with the sound of the hoofbeats. They are approaching from one side, galloping, thudding toward us, black circles, louder and louder. Then a black shape with a rider on it streaks past and is gone on the other side. But almost at once another rider streams past in the opposite direction. A coldness on my head, like a dark hand, may be wind. The thudding of the horses recedes, grows fainter, then approaches again. Again the riders streak past, one after the other, in their opposite directions. Again and again. A tiny sun is trying to rise in my throat. I fix my eyes on the glassy black water beyond the track. What will come down that current? I see only the paper boat which I know to be sleep, disappearing behind some willows. It had had something to tell me. It is sorry.

The whole scene comes and goes. At last, in a silence of great weariness, with a blow that I will always be expecting to feel repeated, the sun leaps into my head. The first of the new colors, like the old red, flows sadly into everything. It is naked. And the rawness that is my new heart begins to beat.

In a Dark Square

He who has lost the key to the ancient lies which everyone held in common is wandering at night, by himself, in an empty square surrounded by featureless doors, with no one to listen to how many telephone numbers he has memorized. For however far-flung and ineradicable their influence by now has become, it is there that the lies still live, in those tall dark houses with lights showing only above each of the front doors to illumine the numbers, which appear to be in a script he cannot understand, though it looks like the only one with which he can honestly claim to be familiar. Lie numbers, ha ha. All his life he thought he knew better and after all that he has said and studied and, as he put it, thought, it is inside those doors, and he knows it, that the whole of reason is lying, asleep, secure in the age of inventors and large families, dreaming placid dreams in which he never even figures as a possible future.

He remembers what he has heard of them, the great families. The Origins, for instance: to himself he admits that for years he has been able to recognize those individuals whom the stork brought, those who were found in cabbages, those who came in a black bag, those who rolled in over the doorsill wrapped in a dust devil, those who were given away on a street corner with a pound of tea. Without his acknowledging the fact, this had frequently been his only means of telling them apart. Frequently? How frequently, he asks himself, and for how long? Feeling the night turn cold at the approach of truth.

He wonders whether the doors are in fact locked. He wonders whether anyone inside would hear him. He wonders how he might appeal to any of them if they woke. He wonders whether the handle would be noisy. He knows that he would be able to find his way unlit through the hall, up the stairs, along the landing, to his own room. Maybe they would not wake at all. Maybe, on the other hand, they would only pretend that they were asleep as he crept past their door, left open a crack so that they would hear him when he came in. Maybe they never sleep but simply wait for him to come in, wait and wait, sad and bitter and too old to change. If anyone is going to change, he knows it will have to be him.

"Have they ever asked themselves," he says, glancing around to see whether the police are about, "have they ever asked themselves whether they were true to anything?"

He wonders what will happen if it starts to be day. The little lights, then, will still burn over the doors. They will grow yellow and fade as a new day brightens the lie numbers and he sees (for the first time, as he says) that each of the doors is crossed with colored ribbons, like a gift-wrapped package, complete with a huge bow and flowers. Then what? Are they really, all of them, presents sent from the old relatives whom he has never seen, the aunties, the grannies, the eyeless, the toothless, who have never seen him and yet presume to say what his whole life is to be? Will he finally (for the cold of the morning is terribly penetrating, after a night with no sleep, in the open) walk up the few steps, feeling a monument toppling inside him, and set his hand deliberately to the end of one of the ribbons, and undo the bow in the full knowledge that whatever that package contains will be his for the rest of his life?

"No," he says, thinking of the day warming up sooner or later and everything starting to resume just where it left off. "No," he says, "we have nothing to do with each other."

And though no one is listening he repeats aloud to the darkness that he will continue to put all his faith in himself.

Hope for Her

In the beginning hope for her was a large white cloth thickly covered
with embroidery, also in white, so rich that it made the cloth curl
like a board and so delicate that the sight of it would make you gasp,
and she was not yet allowed even to touch it. She did not know what
it was for. That would come some day. She certainly was not old
enough to think of using it. It would be a long time before that. And
beautiful though it was she seldom thought of it and was content
to wait.

Still early, hope for her was a white backcloth like the sheet her
mother hung against the wall for her to dance in front of when there
was company, only much bigger, so that it stretched as high as any
building and ran for a full block in either direction, and was smooth
as the marble forehead of Diana. And in front of it how she would
dance! They would hardly be able to believe it was she. And yet, yes
it was! It was, it really was she! She would start using it soon. In a
year or two.

Before long, hope for her was a pale moonish expanse, a shade of
white, but one that had been brushed with age and had learned of
the existence of parchment and bone, and of questions that she
could not make out but remembered hearing, whispered, when they
thought she was asleep. It was bare and troubling like the head of a
drum, and there was a light behind it that would not remain still. But
she did not need it yet.

One day when she actually wanted the drum, that very drum, to
lay her ear against—something that would be cool and not go away
as many things she had known better had been doing—it broke not
a foot from her head. Inside she saw that it was dark, empty, very old.
It remembered someone else whom she had never known. A few tiny
scraps of tan newspaper were stuck in the rim here and there. The
innards of a light bulb were swinging back and forth on the end of a
string. She seized the torn edges of the stiff calf-skin and tried to pull
them back together again, crying (she told herself) "as she had never

cried before." But all that that meant was that she had begun a new kind of forgetting.

For a long time after that hope for her was a calm lake in early spring, white because the sky above it was the color of milk. She knew that the lake was hers. She knew that it would remain hers as long as she never went there. It remained hers for a long time. She scarcely dared look at it very often. Just from time to time, out of the corner of her eye. She did not want to seem to be spying. Besides, she was afraid of water. Bushes grew up between her and the lake. In time she could scarcely see it at all. Sometimes, with a catch in her breath, she suddenly thought that it might have been taken away. But then she would laugh. How could anyone remove a lake? Was it really hers, though, she wondered. Could she be sure? But she told herself to be sensible. If she stopped and breathed quietly she could feel that it was still there.

At last hope for her was a glass jar in which she was standing. The air was cool. The glass was a little blue, like ice, but perfectly clear. She had room to move a little. She was not cold. Outside the jar a first snow was falling: huge soft flakes of white paper. As they came near the jar they whirled around it and some of them stuck to it, lower down, and clung. They had covered the whole of the outside of the jar with a coat of white feathers, up as far as her neck. From outside, she realized, she looked beautiful. She must never have looked so beautiful. The whole lower part of the jar was like lighted alabaster, and above the line of the feathers her head appeared inside the glass, the skin smooth and radiant, the eyes calm, clear and bright. But she knew that now it was her face inside the jar that was attracting the snow which had gradually blotted out her body. The flakes circled the jar in front of her face like white bees going home. They lit on the glass whenever she breathed. She tried not to breathe. She tried to keep one spot clear. Little by little, flake by flake, the whiteness covered everything except one small area through which one of her eyes could be seen, large and clear and beautiful. Then that too was covered and whiteness was all she had.

The Medal of Disapproval

It has, of course, two sides.

There is the side without a face. On this side the symbols are arranged like objects in the nest of a rat—fixed, neatly interrelated, but so far from their original backgrounds and purposes that it is often hard to say what they are. On the other hand it is obvious that they bespeak immeasurable age, and an authority that is on intimate terms with the order of the cosmos itself. Indeed they may be interpreted as being an extension of that order. Sometimes there is a laurel crown. Empty. Occasionally there is a lamp. Often, in fact almost always, there are numbers. This side is clearly abstract and there is no appeal to it. It is the side that is presented, in due course, to the person disapproved of.

Then there is the other side called the face. And in fact it has a head on it. The head of a ruler, a hero of some kind, a forebear. But whatever motto surrounds him, his face is turned away. It is turned away forever. There is no appeal to this side, either. It too is abstract. This is the side that is worn facing outward, by the disapproving. Then the other side is worn facing inward.

Forgetting

First you must know that the whole of the physical world floats in each of the senses at the same time. Each of them reveals to us a different aspect of the kingdom of change. But none of them reveals the unnameable stillness that unites them. At the heart of change it lies unseeing, unhearing, unfeeling, unchanging, holding within itself the beginning and the end. It is ours. It is our only possession. Yet we cannot take it into our hands, which change, nor see it with our eyes, which change, nor hear it nor taste it nor smell it. None of the senses can come to it. Except backwards.

Any more than they can come to each other.

Yet they point the way. And most authoritatively as they disappear. Was that their office, after all? Was their disappearance what they were?

At the top of a ladder each rung of which disappears as we climb, there is a little window that looks across a narrow strip of ground covered in thin grass yellowed by summer and twitching with wind in the cool light of late afternoon. The window is sealed. There is no sign of a path through the grass. Across the strip of ground there is a white wall too high for us to be able to see the top of it. Someone is pressed against it looking through a little window.

In which one can make out a narrow strip of ground covered with round pebbles spotted dark green over which water and bits of green-brown weed wash, cling, spread, hide. Instead of sea, at the other side of the strip of shore there is a granite wall with a small window in it and someone there looking through.

In the window can be seen a narrow strip of green hills with sheep and the shadows of clouds moving over them and beyond them a gray stone wall with a little window in it and someone gazing through. Into a narrow strip of night with tree branches hanging low over a river, and beyond that the foot of a wall.

Somewhere on the other side of that a voice is coming. We are the voice. But we are each of those others. Yet the voice is coming to us. That is what we are doing here. It has to pass through us. It has to pass through us in order to reach us. It has to go through us without pausing in order to be clear to us. Only in the senses can we pause because only in the senses can we move. The stillness is not in the senses but through them and the voice must come through the stillness. Each in turn we must become transparent. The voice will not change but we will. Will it reach us before we are unrecognizable? Will we be able to receive it? Will we not be in our way?

We close our eyes. Darkness unrolls over the strips of ground and the walls, over everything except the windows, and the heads gazing through them.

We listen to the sounds from the strips of ground. More strips than we could see. Each of them hears the voice, each of them repeats rumors of it but all we hear is the repetition, not the voice. One by one we come to the end of each of these sounds and replace it with a silence of the same size. The silence is not the voice but it carries echoes of it. One by one we come to the ends of the echoes.

One by one the tastes come. They have all been living in the past. They bow and pass on with their trays empty or piled with artificial fruit, and without expression, as though we were nothing to them.

The textures come, the sensations, unwinding themselves from the other senses, from time, from the darkness on which they grew, from the fear that is their mother. They fade. Now nothing can be felt in the darkness.

The odors come, the stepping-stones in the air, the clothes floating in nothing, reminding of the limbs that had worn them into endless ages. Tears pour down. The clothes dissolve.

There is still memory itself. The back of the head. The backs of the heads blocking the windows. One by one we forget them and the walls are forgotten.

Fire has gone. It is cool at last. There is no light.

Earth has gone. We float in a small boat that was once green, at an immense height on the unlit sea. No, there is no height, for the depth of the water is infinite. Good-bye height, good-bye depth. The sea is everywhere. It has no shores. Above us the air of this sea. The black space. The stars have all moved out of sight. The night extends beyond them into emptiness.

Then the water has gone and there is only the small boat floating in nothing in the dark. With it the directions have gone. There is only the boat floating in nothing, in the dark, without directions, without size. You cannot feel it. You cannot smell it. You cannot taste it. Then it has gone.

Then nothing has gone.

The voice must have come. Because it has gone.

Marietta

When you go, go up the road slowly until you first see the lake on your right. Be careful not to miss the first lane that turns off toward the water, almost as soon as the water comes into sight through the trees. You might go right past because the lane is small and has grass growing in the middle. And no mailboxes, and bushes on both sides of it.

It leads off at a slight angle and the bushes don't last for long. You look back and see that the road isn't in sight any more, and then you look ahead and see that you are coming out into open country. A pasture slopes down from the left, smoothed, and continuing beyond where you can see, catching the light. Sometimes cows, sometimes sheep, sometimes horses, sometimes nothing. You breathe the breath of pastures. You remember that the lake is very high. There are no fences, and the grazed slope, without a bush or a tree on it, continues its descent on the other side of the lane, all the way to the water where it ends here and there in ferns or reeds, or runs straight into the lake without anything. It's hard to tell how far away the shore is. The lane leads ahead—a narrow level groove on the green slope, in the gray light. At some distance, where the lane draws near to the edge of the lake, you see a building set facing the water. One end of it, the end nearer to you, appears to be a house. A little porch in front, a little porch in back, white boards, green trim. The other end, which is bigger but not so high, you can see is the store. The windows are broader and things are piled there with darkness waiting behind them. Sheets of tin with people's heads on them smiling, and names of tobaccos in the old colors, and signatures of forgotten soft drinks, are nailed to the unpainted facade. In front of the store a long boat dock runs out over the lake, very uneven, low to the water, with fishing poles stuck on it at the end, fishing.

You feel your stomach contract at the nearness of the lake.

Marietta will be coming down the lane. Almost certainly. You'll see why when you meet her. You can't imagine Marietta ever having been late for anything. When you catch sight of her she'll probably be at least two-thirds of the way from the store to where you are standing as you turn back to look ahead after your first pause to take in the whole slope running down to the lake. You will see the heavy but graceful figure, in the long dark skirt, swinging toward you, and it is only a moment before you will be standing face to face. Marietta never wears a hat. Most people who never wear hats look natural without them. Marietta usually looks as though she had just taken hers off and her head was enjoying an unaccustomed nakedness about which nothing will be said. Something of the same quality emanates from Marietta herself and immediately includes you. Her loose stride brings her up to you quickly and she stops as though she could not pause. When she talks the voice seems to come from the whole of her body. Anyone can always hear what she has to say.

And you stand there together above the lake while she tells you about how you look, which isn't bad. You can see that she's been through it. You can tell that from her face, young though it still looks, and lighting up as she talks, like a girl's. But when she laughs her calm laugh you can see that it's not in ignorance. Of anything.

Then if it's an even day she leads you back on your tracks a little way to a path worn through the pasture, running down toward the lake, but away from the store, into the woods. She talks about winters as though they were immense white visitors whom you have never met but who know about you. She talks about the spring, the fish, the coming of the summer. All the time you are in the woods full of pipestems and ferns and marshy patches that you cross on hummocks of grass, and she swings along in her torn jacket and finally falls silent, and a minute later leads you out into the little clearing by the backwater.

The place is utterly still. On the left, where you've come from, the woods are lush and green. The path goes on to the right through more woods, around the edge of the water, where it's almost dark. And in front of you there are more trees, looking as though they grew out of a black stretch of the water itself, which is connected with the lake and the light only by a narrow inlet. In the shadowy backwater a small white flat-bottomed boat will be floating. And in it a girl in a white dress, reading a book.

That's Flora. You know, she's older than you. You feel a ringing in your collar-bones and Marietta reaches down to a rope tied to a tree and pulls the boat ashore, and then smiles at you and leaves you with Flora.

You remember Flora but you're shy and don't want her to know that you are. But she doesn't seem to notice. What a nice girl. You go out in the boat for a little while. You don't need to row anywhere, but you do, a little bit. The woods turn. You can see the undersides of her thighs as she sits looking around. What a nice girl. And she likes you. You can tell quite soon that she likes you a lot. She talks to you about books, and she tells you that she likes talking to you about books, and you hear a beating in your throat and over your eyes like somebody running, and your mouth is dry and the corners are stiff. You can hardly swallow and you can't answer her without swallowing, and she keeps looking at you and smiling and doesn't seem to notice. They say she's very intelligent. And so quiet. And well-mannered. She leans forward with her elbows on her knees and you can look down inside the opening of the front of her dress into the dark cleft between her breasts and almost to the end of one full perfect pointed breast. You never know what it will look like until you see it. She sees that you're looking. She smiles, and she doesn't move at all, except a little bit from side to side. She waits for you to look up. You do. She goes on smiling. She leans farther forward and pushes your hands on the oars and you both row back to the clearing in silence.

You fumble, tying up the boat, while she waits in the back. She's a nice girl. You keep swallowing. You hear everything through glass. You step out and hold out your hand to her and she gets up and steps over the seats and onto the ground. You put your hand around her waist, just seeing if you can, but she lets you. Then she puts her arm around you and starts walking along the path into the woods. She's quite a lot older.

You come to where she's left her things, in a grassy place under the trees. A basket. More books. A blanket. You stare for a minute not knowing what you can do next and hoping that she hasn't by now forgotten that minute in the boat, or decided to pretend to forget it or that it was just your imagination and you really should be ashamed. You hear how small your voice is as you say, "Let's sit down."

She sits down and you see more of her legs. She doesn't seem to be trying to hide them. You look down her dress again, partly to make sure you can, and she catches your eyes again and smiles. You sit down beside her and put your arm back around her waist and she leans against you. You're shivering. You just sit there, wondering if you can kiss her, staring at nothing. Then you try. You have to turn her shoulders around, and it's awkward and doesn't work very well, but then she lies down full length on the blanket, with one knee a little in the air and the skirt far up her thigh, and you put both arms around each other and she starts teaching you what to do with your mouth. Very patient. And then she presses her body against you all the way down and that's something you've thought about a lot and you try it too.

When she lies back from you she throws an arm up onto the grass above her head so that the dress is stretched tight over her breast, and then after a minute she pushes off her shoes and raises her head to look down at her feet and then looks at you. The top two buttons of her dress are already unbuttoned. It's that kind of dress. Her hand drops to the next one and stays there but you still can't be quite sure that she's not pretending or that you're not mistaken and so you still don't dare put your hand on her breast, not even as though you weren't aware of what you were doing so that she can pretend she doesn't notice it. She undoes the button herself.

And then you undo a button at her waist and slide your hand in where it's warm and feels as though it were shining. You know your hand is cold, and you're shivering harder. You kiss again, and start to undo each other's clothes while you're kissing, and only stop when you have to, so that she can slip out of her dress and her bra while you watch, taking off your shirt and your shoes and pants. You look at her, and then, looking straight at you, she slowly pulls off her underpants and you pull off yours, with your throat almost closed up, and you let your eyes rest on the mound of brown hair and then lie down beside her and from there on start to act as though you knew what to do with everything. And she knows.

That's if it's an even day.

If it's an odd day Marietta asks you everything about your trip and about the winter, making it sound like a dark unpleasant building that's been bad for your health, and all the time she's leading you along toward the house and the store.

The store smells of ponds, fishing tackle, dogs, mothballs, and wet leather. She gives you some coffee at a table in the back and hangs up your things, talking all the time like a very old friend. She puts on some dance music a little out of date. She sits watching you eat a piece of cake, with coffee. She knows you don't drink coffee. She leads you into the back. The big room for dances and weddings. There's a pin-ball machine; they just got it. Nobody else is around. You've got a lot of nickels. She says she's got some more. She leaves you to it, with the music. You can stay there all day. And there are magazines. And at the far end of the room there's a door one step up that opens into some stairs, at the top of which is the bedroom of a girl named Flora who's a lot older than you and reads all the time and said she'd teach you to play cards. She's very pretty but she's a very nice girl, everybody says. She's probably up there reading all the time that you're at the pin-ball machine. Probably nobody else is coming, all afternoon. You could probably go up and see if she really would teach you to play cards. If she remembers. The music goes on and on. Your chest thumps as you walk across to the door and look up the stairs. And besides if anybody came by and asked what you were doing inside on a day like this, Marietta can be counted on to tell them never mind.

Graphology

I know nothing about it, I realize. Whose fault is that? Do I understand anything of its principles? Does it proceed on the assumption or presupposition at least that every act we make reveals everything we are, if we could learn to read it? Do I believe that? Or simply that there is nothing that we can do that is not ourselves? Is that the same thing? Do I believe that? Who is ourselves? Does ourself do anything at all? Does it hold a pencil? Is not holding a pencil already a peculiarity? Is it only peculiarities that we reveal? Is it only peculiarities that we know how to read? Is that what we are?

In the lines we make on paper to signify something else to us, the will is always involved. But how, and to what extent? Does this study ask those questions? Not the will at the moment of writing alone, but its history, perhaps, its relation to the subject of the writing, and the history of its relation to that. Does the study consider these matters relevant? Can it in the end isolate the will from what appear to be the manifestations of the will? Is such an isolation possible? If it is can this study trace the difference between the will and the will's performance as that difference changes at every moment along the course of an intricate looping line meaning something else to the person who made it—a process which he learned with great expenditure of effort and time, some years before? Yes, learned with great invocation of care over a number of years, during which he was persuaded and long believed that excellence consisted of the absence of peculiarity in producing a line that was as near as possible to being no one's.

Is this study an art? Is it a science? Which would be better at present? Is it simply a crabbed face over one's shoulder saying that it's there to help one? Spotting peculiarities? Insisting that one begin again?

As if one could. Does it take that into consideration? There is no going back over that line's loops and breaks and abrupt changes of direction. They will have to read it from what is there. Some point that is there and will never be reached again. Altogether there are not more than a few miles to any such line, and then no more. The line that tries to go back is itself going forward.

But suppose this study possesses, in fact, the often unpleasant powers of uninvited helpers. Will it not, as they frequently do, know too much from the beginning, and use its knowledge to learn more things that one does not want it to know? Will it not be able to look at a few inches of line that I have put on a page in the sequence of what I learned once to consider my mistakes, and descry all the hidden weaknesses, secret inconsistencies, carefully concealed dead patches, dishonesties, cruelties, and beneath that, and beneath that? Will it say, "He stopped here because he was weak"? Will it stop there? Why have I hidden those things? Will it disclose that?

Will it be able to take a segment of curved line and announce what exact place in the author's person produced that curve? And why? Will it become possible and desirable to consider the lines on their own, apart from their authors and their authors' wills, to think of them as having lives of their own to examine, to pick them up off the paper and hold them in your hands and listen to them breathing? Will the practice of this study become like counting? Or will it be—is it now, sometimes—like running along a path made in the snow by someone else, trying to glimpse that other while he remains just too far ahead among the trees, trying to understand his nature by tracing the strange curves of his single path? Then will your own path follow after you along the other person's? Will it be anxious to keep up with you? Will it sometimes fail? Will you ever turn and see that your own path has lost you? Will it find you at last, with all its secrets that you need? Will it lead you back? Will your own line and the line you are following become tangled? Will you look ahead to see whether their getting tangled doesn't make the other person look back? Will it? Will yours lead you back? Will you come to understand the line you are following so completely that you will be able to project it on ahead to somewhere the other person has not yet taken it, and call to him, "Be careful! Stop! Don't go on, that's out over nothing!" But be too late even so, for the line runs its course. Do I believe that? And the self—does it follow? Where? Was it the peculiarity all the time, that you could deduce but not know, trace but not alter, call out to but not save?

Will something lead you back?

Phoebe

She used to sit at a window of a big house and imagine herself when she was grown up. How beautiful she would be. And how kind. There she stood, looking down at Phoebe the child. She held out her hand to touch the child but the hand turned to air. Often she would tell Phoebe something. Oh, there was little she would not have told Phoebe, in time. How beautiful her voice was. But when the child looked at her and watched the lips moving she heard nothing. It was only later that she remembered the words, and the sound.

Phoebe tried to draw her picture but it was never like her. She tried to talk in her voice but it never sounded like her. She tried to repeat her words but when she did that she forgot them.

One day when Phoebe was sitting at the window imagining herself when she grew up, she saw that she was standing there more beautiful than ever, in gorgeous clothes, but in tears. She was trying to tell the child something. Phoebe had never tried so hard to listen, but she heard nothing. She began to cry too, but she tried not to so that she could look and listen. It was only later, when she was alone again, that she remembered the words.

They said that now that she was grown up she was going away. Someone important was coming to fetch her. That was why she was wearing those beautiful clothes. He was going to take her to his own house a long way from there. She would never come back. When she remembered the words Phoebe was too frightened to cry. Not only because she was afraid of whoever was coming. Not only because she never wanted to go away. Not only because she tried to repeat the name of the person who was coming, and of the place where he was going to take her, as she remembered them, and so had forgotten them.

She was frightened because all at once she no longer wanted to grow up, because there would be nobody there. After a while she ran down into the woods and began calling, "Phoebe, Phoebe," softly. You can hear her, but she has never been found.

Phoebe lived beside woods. She was very shy. She had reached the age when her parents had begun to talk about her getting married. But all she wanted to do was to spend her time with the birds, listening to them. All the birds knew her and would sing when she was there. She had discovered that if she really listened, each of their voices made something happen to her. When the sparrow cheeped she could feel her blood moving. When the swallows chattered she could remember things from her infancy that she had forgotten. When the crow cawed she could see the darkness in everything. There was one gray bird who was silent. She used to believe that if that bird called her name she would vanish.

One night in the house her parents were talking about her. They thought she was asleep. How old they looked, she thought. No bird she knew was ever so old. Her hands were cold. Her lips were cold. She heard nothing, except her own name coming from one or the other, in an undertone. She fell asleep. She dreamed of what their voices did to her. They took her by the hands and led her out into a place without trees. On and on they walked, the three of them, in the dark. There was not a sound. Her hands hurt. They hurt worse and worse. But when she pulled on them pieces of them came off. Her parents held her by the blood and walked on. She tried to say something to them, she tried to scream something to them, but she found that she had no voice. She looked at them and saw that their lips were moving but she heard nothing. She saw that they were getting older and older as she watched, and a grief, a fear, a coldness such as no bird voice had ever made her feel gripped her throat and her stomach so that she thought she would die of it. And they were taking her with them. Yet she did not want them to go on alone, without her, and grow older and older, while she was there alone with only pieces of her hands, bleeding. She woke. Her face was wet with tears. Day was breaking. The dream was still with her. It would not leave her. She jumped out of bed and ran to the door. The dream went with her. She flung the door open and ran into the woods. From a window of the house her mother leaned out to call after her as she disappeared.

Then suddenly the gray bird started calling, "Phoebe."

◉ ◉ ◉

When Phoebe and the young ruler had been married a year their union was blessed with a daughter. The people would have preferred a son. The young ruler would have preferred a son. But Phoebe was happy with the little girl, who was very beautiful and sweet-natured.

The people and the young ruler were prepared to wait. But year after year passed and Phoebe and the young ruler had no more children. At the end of seven years the young man consulted his mother about what to do to have a son. She said, "Either your wife must go, and you must get another. Or else the little girl must go."

The young man did not want to send his wife away so he decided that it would have to be the little girl.

"What do you mean 'she must go'?" he asked.

"She must not remain in this world," his mother said.

That same night he called in a man he could trust and told him to seize the child as she slept, cover her mouth with a sleeve, cover her eyes with a sleeve, tie her arms, and lead her far out into the forest where the animals would eat her.

And it all happened.

And in the morning Phoebe came into the child's room and found the bed empty. On the floor beside it were a few gray feathers. There were more by the door. And on the stairs. And on the stones outside. And on the road. She began to run. All the way along the road there were those same feathers. The road led into the woods. She began to call. The name of the child was Phoebe.

The Trembler

When I thought about Mr. Jameson it was, I am afraid, usually because his own situation so closely paralleled mine. We have both been working for years—for decades, to be honest—in the same building, he on the nineteenth and I on the twenty-third floor. And whatever titles our firms have given to our respective positions to dignify them in accordance with our advancing years, both of us, to designate it by its correct name, are (let me say) little other than office boys. Clearly by now we will never be anything more. On the other hand we are secure in our unchallenging positions. Both of us are employed by large, well-established, sober firms that would obviously survive any reverse short of a total collapse of the national economy. And within these firms we are taken for granted. We are among the oldest employees. Each of us has been serving his respective firm longer than the firm's president himself. In the event of a setback, even an important one, you may be sure that many younger and breezier men who are our superiors, even to some little distance up the scale, would be given notice long before we would be informed that our services were no longer required. In fact that latter contingency is virtually unimaginable. One turns to it sometimes, alone in the elevator, as something which will afford a passing sigh of relief on an otherwise uneventful day.

Over the years our calling has thrown us together not closely, you might say, but frequently, and we have come to know each other as fixtures of each other's days. Familiars, if I might put it that way, without being intimates. To be honest, the sight of Mr. Jameson troubled me slightly for years, in a fashion that at one time I would not perhaps have admitted. But advancing age has brought a certain reckless candor to my mental processes, something which, let me add, supplies a touch of exhilaration, on occasion, to my thoughts, and I now recognize without the least trouble that the consideration of Mr. Jameson is sometimes unpleasant to me simply because it is hard for me to avoid altogether seeing in him a mirror of my own circumstance and even my own gestures and person. I contend against any such identification, I limit it severely, in fact, with my reason, but who at my age can honestly entertain many illusions about the power of that desperate and over-extended faculty, I sometimes ask, considering the abyss into which we are all happily travelling.

It is within the framework of this situation that my curiosity about one aspect of Mr. Jameson's behavior, as it struck me at least, is to be viewed. I confess that it led me to indulge in a closeness of scrutiny which I now see that I disguised from myself for some time, verging, as it did, on the critical.

I cannot remember what particular detail occasioned it, but I well recall the excitement that imbued the entire day when once I admitted to myself that there seemed to me to be something about Mr. Jameson that I could only call furtive. I could give my mind to little else: the quality itself, and then of course whatever might be its real or imaginary source. Were either of these known and recognized by Mr. Jameson himself? I paid more attention to him, needless to say, from then on. In fact I watched him so closely that I was soon at some pains to conceal the eagerness of my observation. I am afraid that I undertook, more and more boldly, the role of sympathizer. My very eyes, if we found ourselves alone on the elevator together, came to infer, as nearly as I could manage it, that to know all is to forgive all, with the further implication that there was little in this mortal world that was strange to me. Whether or not my success can be laid at the door of this countenance which became, in due course, habitual with me in my meetings with Mr. Jameson, the fact is that something, and very possibly something about me, awoke in him a feeling of confidence where I was concerned. The suspicious but helpless confidence of a younger brother, perhaps, who knows that his candor will be abused, but who is irresistibly drawn, even so, to lay bare his paltry secrets one by one, grubbing down and down for deeper and perhaps more interesting ones. Gradually Mr. Jameson took to smiling at me in a peculiar draggled way like an ugly girl's from under an umbrella, and I knew that I was, as they say, making progress.

What vice could he have, I wondered, that had wrapped him to itself so tightly and so completely that his judgment had remained stunted by it—the faculty of a boy in pimples. With what vice of his had he not come to terms—or sufficiently so as to be able to brazen it out, at least—by his age? The matter seemed, to be honest, to present opportunities, and I watched, with an excitement which I will not venture to describe, the development of his smile on the occasions that permitted it. And fully prepared for it though I was—or so I imagined—it was with a marked quickening of the pulse and dryness of the mouth that I welcomed his first sudden painfully awkward lurch toward confidences.

In all the years that we had worked together and had gone down the elevator together in the evenings on our separate ways to our lodgings we had never—even when, as sometimes happened, we were leaving late at the same time—so much as invited each other to share a coffee or a drink before our leisure hours rolled open in front of us. That particular evening the elevator was crowded. Mr. Jameson gave me only a glance as he got on, and in it no sign of recognition. As though simply to make sure that I was there. All the way down his eyes remained fixed on the gray overcoat on the back of the man standing in front of him. He got off ahead of me. I was outside the main door when I found him beside me, asking me under his breath whether I wouldn't like a drink on my way home.

Of course I did what I could to make him feel at ease with regard to the disclosures upon which he had decided to embark. As might have been expected, several drinks were necessary, and at least an hour of faltering luckless talk. Then slowly it became apparent that Mr. Jameson's furtiveness was in fact the obverse, as I had suspected, of a secret arrogance stemming from a practice of which he was the sole devotee. He confessed it at last: his private inexhaustible pleasure, the exigeant delight which he himself had invented. It was trembling.

It was exclusively a private activity, he explained. By now he was sure that it would be impossible for him to tremble in any public situation, though he had fantasies of doing so which frightened him into a peculiarly exquisite form of indulgence in his secret practice. He described a few of the fears that he had drawn on in the early days of his vice—before, as he put it, he knew what he was about. Rather commonplace fears of parents, of teachers, of other boys, or girls. He described the dawning of his awareness that his vice was in itself a protection against such fears. It allowed him to welcome them as potential sources of pleasure. Of what he insisted was the subtlest and most luxurious of sensual and imaginary satisfactions.

He tried to distinguish, for my benefit, as he said, the principle forms of the pleasure itself, dividing them in a manner that was evidently clearer to him than it was to me, into physical and spiritual delights, but he confessed with a disarming frankness that the separation often seemed arbitrary and meaningless. The one question about his practice which he could not fathom at all was why no one else appeared to have discovered it. He was forced to wonder what was lacking in everyone else. Or did many others keep it secret?

He described for me the manner in which trembling, properly conceived, became what could only be called an activity of the soul, whereby every possible source of dread was imaginatively conjured from the circumstances of a given life and then taught to perform its peculiar dance in which the entire emotional being of the participant was caught up, sometimes to the point of ecstasy, of self-annihilation. Did I not see that the practice did away with the old separation of inner and outer, subjective and objective, self and environment, in one profound vibrancy? Did I not see, did I not see? The fervor was all in his voice. I looked at his face, his mouth. They were impassive. His hand on his glass was as motionless as the table.

Could I not conceive, he asked, even without any but (he requested my forgiveness) the most ordinary and natural experience of the subject, and (he took the liberty of assuming) the most conventional of attitudes toward it, could I not conceive of the joy of finding oneself alone with a new, an unexplored source of fear or mortification or uncertainty—and the more imaginary the better? They were kept as it were in the middle foreground or the near background for a while—an artful pretense of putting them out of one's mind while at the same time enjoying their presence as they grew to what appeared to be autonomous strength and at last seemed to thrust themselves upon one, eclipsing everything else. Then one could allow the trembling to begin. He described the main external forms, the trembling of the hands, of the legs, of the stomach, of the muscles of the chest, of the insides of the upper arms, of the insides of the thighs, of the viscera, of the genitalia, and the sensations that each might be said, very roughly, to produce. He described the purely artificial focussing of the activity in the eyelids, in one eyelid, in one cheek, in one finger. He told of the silence that at last entered the exhausted limb—a calm that in his view must prefigure that of the dead, when their crude shakings have ceased at last.

For it was exhausting, he admitted. And from there he went on to discourse upon the privations which his pleasures forced upon him. How could he, he asked me, spare himself any dread or anguish or prospect of uncertainty, any sleeplessness or deliberate deprivation, in the indulgence of so vast, so heavenly (it was his own word) a delight? Sometimes, he told me, he feared for his health. But he laughed as he said it.

I looked closely at my own discomfort.

But what were these privations, he went on, when each of them in turn, as he now realized, was a promise of new bliss. He had the great good fortune, he confessed, to be of a profoundly timid temperament. The very furtiveness which had been his from early youth, and which he had carefully nurtured over the years in dealing with the rest of the world until now he might almost say with some small pride that it was perhaps the distinguishing trait of his personality (he looked to me for confirmation of this statement and I am afraid I nodded), had become in itself at once an outward sign of his adherence to his secret practice and a ceaseless contribution to it.

Could I imagine, he asked me, what it meant to him to be able to confide in someone?

We drank for a moment in silence.

He told me then that he considered himself an extremely happy man. We raised our glasses.

The Animal Who Eats Numbers

One is just one. The animal eats it but apparently he makes no difference to it. Nothing does.

Two is a little girl in a starched muslin dress and patent leather shoes. She has on a red cardigan with a flower machine-embroidered on a pocket in front. Her thick dark hair is in bangs over her forehead and hangs almost to her shoulders on the sides and in back. She is good. She is never dirty. Everybody likes her. She is quiet. She always seems to be waiting and almost always smiling. Sometimes you look around—she has been pulling up her sock or something of the kind—and she has disappeared and everybody fusses and starts looking for her, but realizing of course that it couldn't be her fault. Usually it's because he has eaten her. For a little while. But it's such a nice day. Maybe her mother will let her come out again later, for a little while.

Three is a bigger boy without much to say for himself. He's big for his age and his clothes are too big for him and he has weak eyes. He's off by himself a lot but he doesn't get eaten very often. Sometimes he calls "Watch out!"—but usually he's not the one the animal wants. He's all right, though.

Four is eaten a lot. Very often she looks as though it's dark beyond her. You can hardly see her. Even when she's out she must be thinking.

Five is overweight. He laughs. The teacher doesn't like him much but he's funny and kind. He gets eaten all the time. He says he doesn't care. His clothes are all old anyway. He says he'd rather get eaten than do homework any day. He says he sits and plays cards with the animal as though he were at the firehouse.

Six is two's older sister. She wears yellow, mostly. She's good too. She hates being eaten. It doesn't happen to her very often. She thinks about going to college all the time. She thinks you don't get eaten there. Everybody respects her. She's terribly clean. When she gets eaten sometimes nobody notices, but if they do they're just quiet for a minute because they don't know what to say, and then they forget.

Seven is a quiet man in old clothes, including an overcoat and a hat. The teacher doesn't like him much but she never refers to him any more than necessary. He's often on the other side of the street and stops to look before he goes on to wherever he's going. Sometimes he has a satchel. He doesn't do any harm, but people don't like him. The animal doesn't like him either, and would only eat him if he were very hungry.

Eight is a cheerful nice lady in a flowered dress who seems to know everybody though nobody's quite sure who she is. The teacher doesn't mind what you're doing if she's around. Most of the time she doesn't seem to understand what anybody says, though. She's pretty fat. She gets eaten quite often too, but both she and the teacher like to pretend it doesn't happen. And to tell the truth nobody has ever actually seen her get eaten. It's just known.

Nine is another lady, a friend of the teacher's, thinner, with glasses, and very stern. She wears a dark red felt hat and an overcoat and carries a black patent leather pocket book. She resents very much the fact that she gets eaten sometimes. She probably fights with her elbows, but that wouldn't matter to the animal. She acts as though her being eaten were three's fault, five's fault, or seven's fault, whichever of them is handy. Three and five pretend to think she's a joke, but they don't really. Seven doesn't say anything and some people think he secretly likes her. Sometimes she's eaten for days at a time.

Ten is a very rich couple who never come near. If they go out it must be in their car. Apparently they get eaten too, though. The teacher and eight have been heard talking about it out in the hall. It was plain that they didn't really care.

The animal doesn't eat anything else, that we know of. The numbers know all about him and they don't worry. He never eats them for long and almost never if they're doing something. Besides, there are just as many of them as there ever were, and everyone says the future is theirs. It's the animal who is disappearing.

New Arrival

Yes, this is the right train. Or it looks like it. The dirt is familiar. The smell. The advertisements. The rattle. Yes, the air — the same. And the same featureless country, brushing the windows hopelessly with its leaves curled and papery at the edges from bruises got by tapping the train again and again, trying to say heaven knows what. I sometimes think he's calling off stations I don't know, that they've got onto another line, I took the one on the wrong side of the platform. No. I'm going home.

There's the little river. Hasn't changed. It always looks a little different. They put something different beside it, that's it. They move the houses a few feet one way or the other. They have dogs drinking or a man staring at the surface. Usually they don't bring out the whole thing if they don't know you're coming. Or something hasn't been put back in time. That's usual.

And we're slowing down at the right place. Everybody's standing. It's the end of the line. He doesn't bother to call out the station. Why should he? So far so good. They all pick up their things, they look at each other for the first time now that they won't be seeing each other any more. They start edging toward the front end of the car through the litter of packages, magazines, bottles, not noticing, eyes fixed on nothing, thinking about what next.

All crowded up at the end. I take my bag. Why can one not go out the other way? There's no one in the aisle to stop me. I go back that way. People turn around but nobody stops me. In the vestibule the door on the platform side is closed. But the one on the other side is open. The road-bed floats past. Black stones. Black stones. O black stones where is it that we have floated toward each other in different circumstances? They stop. We do not know each other. Everyone else is inching out, very slowly, at the far end, onto the platform. There they are going to stop in turn in front of a little window as though they had to buy tickets over again or go through customs. That's ridiculous. I know the place. If anybody stops me. This side is right on my way. I climb down. My feet feel naked on the black stones. I cross them—a filthy beach, sloping steeply. Already the air is remarkable, though. Another set of tracks, rusty, more black stones, another set, more black stones, and then grass! I stop and put down my suitcase and breathe. I will be home tonight.

Up the bank through the long growth. Late spring. A late spring evening. Top of the bank. The trees have grown. The cushion of pine needles. Among the trash. Well, they have put some kind of pond there now! No one ever told me. The sight is depressing. I would have liked a chance to get used to the idea. It wouldn't have mattered to me, after all. If I'd known. Too late now. The pond is darker than the sky. The clouds cross it into the woods as though they'd always done that. It must seem that way now. The sun is clouded. It was the pond that did it. Or could it have been my getting off as I did? And the little window they stopped at, what was that? An announcement? I look back. The train has already gone. The station has closed. I start around the pond with my suitcase, on the new path, but as I do I see, up among the buildings to the left, a flag start down from the top of the pole.

No, once again I will not be home tonight.

Unchopping a Tree

Start with the leaves, the small twigs, and the nests that have been shaken, ripped, or broken off by the fall; these must be gathered and attached once again to their respective places. It is not arduous work, unless major limbs have been smashed or mutilated. If the fall was carefully and correctly planned, the chances of anything of the kind happening will have been reduced. Again, much depends upon the size, age, shape, and species of the tree. Still, you will be lucky if you can get through this stage without having to use machinery. Even in the best of circumstances it is a labor that will make you wish often that you had won the favor of the universe of ants, the empire of mice, or at least a local tribe of squirrels, and could enlist their labors and their talents. But no, they leave you to it. They have learned, with time. This is men's work. It goes without saying that if the tree was hollow in whole or in part, and contained old nests of bird or mammal or insect, or hoards of nuts or such structures as wasps or bees build for their survival, the contents will have to be repaired where necessary, and reassembled, insofar as possible, in their original order, including the shells of nuts already opened. With spiders' webs you must simply do the best you can. We do not have the spider's weaving equipment, nor any substitute for the leaf's living bond with its point of attachment and nourishment. It is even harder to simulate the latter when the leaves have once become dry—as they are bound to do, for this is not the labor of a moment. Also it hardly needs saying that this is the time for repairing any neighboring trees or bushes or other growth that may have been damaged by the fall. The same rules apply. Where neighboring trees were of the same species it is difficult not to waste time conveying a detached leaf back to the wrong tree. Practice, practice. Put your hope in that.

Now the tackle must be put into place, or the scaffolding, depending on the surroundings and the dimensions of the tree. It is ticklish work. Almost always it involves, in itself, further damage to the area, which will have to be corrected later. But as you've heard, it can't be helped. And care now is likely to save you considerable trouble later. Be careful to grind nothing into the ground.

At last the time comes for the erecting of the trunk. By now it will scarcely be necessary to remind you of the delicacy of this huge skeleton. Every motion of the tackle, every slight upward heave of the trunk, the branches, their elaborately re-assembled panoply of leaves (now dead) will draw from you an involuntary gasp. You will watch for a leaf or a twig to be snapped off yet again. You will listen for the nuts to shift in the hollow limb and you will hear whether they are indeed falling into place or are spilling in disorder—in which case, or in the event of anything else of the kind—operations will have to cease, of course, while you correct the matter. The raising itself is no small enterprise, from the moment when the chains tighten around the old bandages until the bole hangs vertical above the stump, splinter above splinter. Now the final straightening of the splinters themselves can take place (the preliminary work is best done while the wood is still green and soft, but at times when the splinters are not badly twisted most of the straightening is left until now, when the torn ends are face to face with each other). When the splinters are perfectly complementary the appropriate fixative is applied. Again we have no duplicate of the original substance. Ours is extremely strong, but it is rigid. It is limited to surfaces, and there is no play in it. However the core is not the part of the trunk that conducted life from the roots up to the branches and back again. It was relatively inert. The fixative for this part is not the same as the one for the outer layers and the bark, and if either of these is involved in the splintered section they must receive applications of the appropriate adhesives. Apart from being incorrect and probably ineffective, the core fixative would leave a scar on the bark.

When all is ready the splintered trunk is lowered onto the splinters of the stump. This, one might say, is only the skeleton of the resurrection. Now the chips must be gathered, and the sawdust, and returned to their former positions. The fixative for the wood layers will be applied to chips and sawdust consisting only of wood. Chips and sawdust consisting of several substances will receive applications of the correct adhesives. It is as well, where possible, to shelter the materials from the elements while working. Weathering makes it harder to identify the smaller fragments. Bark sawdust in particular the earth lays claim to very quickly. You must find your own ways of coping with this problem. There is a certain beauty, you will notice at moments, in the pattern of the chips as they are fitted back into place. You will wonder to what extent it should be described as natural, to what extent man-made. It will lead you on to speculations about the parentage of beauty itself, to which you will return.

The adhesive for the chips is translucent, and not so rigid as that for the splinters. That for the bark and its subcutaneous layers is transparent and runs into the fibers on either side, partially dissolving them into each other. It does not set the sap flowing again but it does pay a kind of tribute to the preoccupations of the ancient thoroughfares. You could not roll an egg over the joints but some of the mineshafts would still be passable, no doubt. For the first exploring insect who raises its head in the tight echoless passages. The day comes when it is all restored, even to the moss (now dead) over the wound. You will sleep badly, thinking of the removal of the scaffolding that must begin the next morning. How you will hope for sun and a still day!

The removal of the scaffolding or tackle is not so dangerous, perhaps, to the surroundings, as its installation, but it presents problems. It should be taken from the spot piece by piece as it is detached, and stored at a distance. You have come to accept it there, around the tree. The sky begins to look naked as the chains and struts one by one vacate their positions. Finally the moment arrives when the last sustaining piece is removed and the tree stands again on its own. It is as though its weight for a moment stood on your heart. You listen for a thud of settlement, a warning creak deep in the intricate joinery. You cannot believe it will hold. How like something dreamed it is, standing there all by itself. How long will it stand there now? The first breeze that touches its dead leaves all seems to flow into your mouth. You are afraid the motion of the clouds will be enough to push it over. What more can you do? What more can you do?

But there is nothing more you can do.

Others are waiting.

Everything is going to have to be put back.

Ends

When a shoelace breaks during use the ends do not always indulge at once in their new-found liberty. However long the break may have been preparing—the threads wearing through one by one, the rub settling in the same place stride after stride, the tension mounting in the other strands, making them watchful, on guard against any further illusions—the release itself, whether it is accompanied by one of the many variants of the dull sound which in this world signifies the end of something, or comes to pass in silence, always seems sudden to the point of being unexpected. A few ends there are, it is true, which at this moment fling themselves into the air waving and disporting themselves, the result of an inherent want of substance, or simply a reaction to the long strain. Some go so far as to flap and dance as though they were now the ends of whole laces. They are usually rewarded by being removed at once and disposed of. But the better laces respond to the occasion in silence, and often do not move at all at first. Whatever their unfulfilled desires may have been, and however clearly they may have foreseen the inevitability of the parting, it is no pleasure to them to feel that they have failed to carry to its conclusion the undertaking for which they were made and upon which they had entered without reservations. The release of strain throughout these natures is likely to express itself in a sudden despondency, a disorientation, a sense of emptiness, rather than exhilaration. In this they will be reflecting the fact that with the loss of their use (for they are no longer laces—that self has gone) they have become something different, and have not yet discovered what it is. It is hard for them to relinquish a usefulness that was theirs without their having to think about it as long as they remained a whole. Their keen awareness of their fragmentary state is in itself a nostalgia for their lost usefulness. For they are still one, they are still whole, each of them, but they cannot feel that this is enough any longer, or that it will ever be enough, that it will ever have any worth, that there will ever be anything about themselves that they will value and be able to take for granted. Wherever they go next, it seems to them, they will forever feel in some part of them that they are fragments whose salvation depended upon remaining whole. They see nothing ahead of them but dissolution. Given a new self, they respond by feeling deprived of the possibility of ever having a self at all. It is possible that the self, after all, is not a matter of use. But they cling to the need to be useful as though it were a last cherished shred of their unbroken life, and very slowly and reluctantly they are drawn toward the holes and disappear around the first bends of their journeys.

The Giants

They were the first creatures on earth to be shod. Even those who affect to doubt their existence are silent on that point. They wrapped their feet in pieces of the world which they had made into couples shaped like their own feet, which are dedicated to The Twins, and measuring began. The statistical sense of reality, which we now live in, was their invention. As it grew they dwindled. As it took over they ceded. As it developed its voices they fell silent. As it became opaque they became invisible. As it sealed the mind they became incredible. It was their reward, it was their punishment, it was inevitable.

But it is not eternal. Give them their due, they never thought of us. They envisaged a new world, and being immortal they were aware that this is the new world, under our feet. It had to be touched in a new way. It had to be stood on differently, walked on differently. Whatever would permit this would have to be at the same time an everlasting signal of beginning, of a readiness to set out, taking its division with it. They knew they would have to give up the whole of the past.

We are still living on what they left.

But the newness of the world, where they have their home, is not only here, it keeps returning. At dawn I have seen the eastern horizon lined with pairs of immense shoes that dwarfed the mountains, waiting for the sun to fill them. They were there until I tried to count them.

Justice came later. With the bandaging of the eyes.

The Sentinel

They believe that each child is invested at birth with its particular grief which will never willingly forsake it afterwards. Something more personal than a name, something in fact for which the name is a blank symbol. Something never seen by its host or by others, yet with features, a voice, a touch, that no one could mistake, even in disguise. Something that will be inseparable, for as long as he lives, from whatever each person calls "me."

Once, they say, each man was born without his grief. He was a happy nature then, little better than the animals. He was content with the earth. He was content with his body. They echoed each other. Even death was something that he gave himself up to, in due course, with a struggle that was chiefly physical, like a foot-race. He did not suspect that there was more light than he could see. Creatures from other existences came and went, passing him, but for him they were like the birds. He was not curious. He had not conceived of heaven. He did not dream. He was not complete. Only in this last detail was he already man.

It was his grief that promised to complete him, and continually renews the promise. There are many tales of how the age of grief began—the dawn of man's longing for completeness. They all agree on one point: the covenant was irreversible. There is no returning to the ungrieved world. Now that it no longer exists it never existed. The knowledge of this truth, and the nostalgia which that knowledge engenders, have become an allegory—crude, imperfect, not to be taken literally—of the yearning for heaven, but at the same time they have consolidated the rule of grief, who by now is lord of this world's past, and of its future. Any step toward the ancient precincts and their limited but untrammelled peace at once encounters a figure of dread that is one of grief's most terrible aspects, an apparition that says, "You cannot pass me. You cannot see beyond me. Even if you could there would be no sense in your triumph, for you would no longer be yourself, nor know anything, nor would heaven any longer be open to you." Between that dread and the futile (but no less attractive on that account) longing to return, some natures, indeed many natures, wither and die. Their grief surrounds them with visions of their own incompleteness. It twines around them and through them, shutting out hope, guiding them infallibly to those paths in which, as they see with relief, there is none. Toward idylls which do not exist, which is what makes them irresistible.

And still, day by day each one's grief offers to complete him, and it does not lie. That is the original promise whose acceptance was in itself a first great step on the way to its fulfilment. In its efforts toward making him complete his grief leads him into every circumstance of his existence, into every light, every premonition, every terror, every memory, into the depths of the sea, into the dark of the earth, into the cold of space, into the emptiness of the tombs, into all his echoes. It persuades him to shun happiness as a doom that does not belong to him, that is unworthy of him. It tries to lead him to the threshold at which he will bid it farewell with his whole spirit—farewell to his grief and to all that belongs to it, and go on without it, alone, complete, into the endless present. At least for long enough so that he will know that it is possible. But only a few have ever done that, and each man's grief owns a few of their footsteps, but has made them its own. For the most part the individual severs himself from his grief only by dying. He conceives of such a parting and of his own death as the same thing, and he clings to his grief to the end as though life were nothing else. Only when he is finally dead does his grief forsake him, to enter, with undiminished hope, a child being born at that moment. For it is only the griefs of those who freed themselves in their lifetimes and attained wholeness, that are themselves free of their promise, and able to return at last to the joyful realm of their origin.

And yet each grief is no less equivocal than its host. It has hidden from him the creatures from other universes, his brothers. It has usurped or muffled their voices. It has altered or delayed their messages. It has distorted for him his sense of being alone. It has planted black flags around him and made him live in their shadows. It has covered him with its wings for fear he should see at each moment that he is already complete. Its final hold on him is to make him believe that heaven itself would be as nothing without it.

And yet his grief is a great guide through this world. Even, perhaps, the surest of the guides. As long as guides are needed. He may well be proud to remember that his grief was waiting for man as soon as man himself was made, and that in him alone it walks the earth. And which of his virtues, he asks himself, would exist for long without his grief and its promises of sadness?

But grief is merely the first, in their belief, and there is no indication that it is by any means the greatest of the guardians. And since each man has his own grief, they argue, why should he not be attended, now or in time to come, by other angels, by all the other angels, as well?

Ethel's Story

Of course it was on a Monday that she decided she must have a story.

It was on a Monday because of the emptiness, in which things are known to emerge that are covered at other times. She had so little washing to do now that she was all alone, and she had got up earlier than usual to get it done, and she had got it done earlier than usual and then she had hung it out, and then she had found herself wandering down through the different back yards in which no washing was hanging yet, from which the children had just left for school. She paused at the feet of wooden stairs and listened to the sound of washing machines whirring and sloshing and the voices raised now and then to make themselves heard above the noise of the machines and she felt as though she were deaf. No one would hear her. It made no difference, she said. She must have her story.

She waited until she was back at the foot of her own silent flight of wooden steps leading up the back of the house to the upper porch where the newspapers were piled on the old sewing machine, and then she started to tell no one about her canary.

The most interesting thing about her canary had not been anything you could see in the bird at all. It had been his effect on the room he was kept in. As soon as she opened the door and looked in she could tell what state of mind the bird was in. Partly it was just the air, her first breath of it. He kept himself so clean. But partly it was something you could actually see, or at least she could, in the walls themselves. If he was feeling serene, whether or not he had been singing, the walls were bright and splashed with sunlight. If he was dreaming happily about his homeland the walls seemed to have receded; the room looked bigger and the vines and flowers on the wallpaper were clearer and seemed to stand out and look more than usually life-like. If his confinement was weighing heavily on him the walls looked dark and the patterns in the paper were lost in the featureless shadows. She would go in there and look at the room and it was better than conversing with most people, she said, how she could understand what he was feeling in himself. And so it had been until the morning when she had opened the door and the walls looked dead. Nothing on them showed any life at all. They were neither near nor far, and the light touched them as though they were only pictures of themselves. Then she had known that Dickie was dead and had gone over to the cage and found him lying on his back, stiff, with his beak slightly open.

That was the story she told, then, and she went on telling it for a long time, when no one could hear her.

When someone could hear her she told no story at all, because what had happened was that her daughter had come home to the cold house and had moved in to the room where she had grown up and had said nothing to her mother by way of explanation or by way of affection or by way of passing the time of day. She had gone out a great deal and had come home late, and she never recounted a single detail of what she did or of what she had done before. Her silence was aggressive, and her mother had always been frightened of her, and now continued to look after her, but from a distance, careful not to disturb her. Not even when she slept beyond noon. Not even when she was sick, except to take in, very quietly, a little tray of crackers and milk to set down near the bed, which sometimes were touched, sometimes not. Not even when the curtains remained closed all day and there was no sound of anyone going to the bathroom, and then they remained closed all day the next day. When panic had finally seized her she had had to go and fetch a neighbor to come back and go into the dark room and find that the girl had left without a word two days before.

The Dark Sower

Now although we say it is spring the days of glass are assembling. Mogog the Dark Sower walks the earth once more. For him it is the time of year—but for him a year is a lapse that we have not learned to describe, since for us it has come only once. Is it three thousand, or ten thousand, or fifty thousand, or a hundred thousand years? Between sowings, as the centuries pass without his reappearance, his figure and his office are mistaken. He becomes confused with lesser and more sociable deities. He is portrayed as the gray god who mildews the grain, hence as the lord of ailment. He occurs on their altars with a face of smoke and they pray to him not to be consumed. He becomes the god of ice (more accurately) and they imagine that it is the ice they know, and they offer him fish and birds to seize and hold in his heart. They think of it as a heart. But what they know of cold is no more than the shadow of a gatehouse in his dominion. And now he has come again.

He walks at his time across the blue sky of the earth and he sows the days of glass. They do not fall immediately. They fly out from his hand like birds settling at evening, but transparent. With a tiny clinking like that of sleet they congregate at a height known beforehand, which they remember from the last time. No one has disturbed their encampment. Each time as they wait they add a few improvements. They wait. More arrive. More. What a host, what a host! What a forest in the seed! The whole of the air above them and below them flocks to their camp begging to be allowed to be their banners. The sounds of the glass smithies ring day and night. The stars laugh in anticipation.

And the earth, being of that celestial ancestry, remembers this season before its creatures do. Now if you mark their places day by day you will see that stones weighing many tons have begun to move across level fields, carving deep grooves in the out-croppings, and you may be able to hear their voices—muffled rumblings and shriekings, so that you remember tales of caverns full of beards at the end of which spirits without age slept with their crowns on the tables. The roots of the trees feel a stirring and the leaves tremble on still days.

And now when you open the door at night you will see huge animals leap away into the darkness. You will think at first that they are running from you. The eland is gone in a single bound, the white of his eye flashing like a comet. The cave bear breaks away like an ice jam on a black river. The mammoth moves as though stung, a black haystack, a night sweeping across the sky. In silence. But they will not have seen you. You are no more to them than a writing on a wall. How long will you haunt the earth together?

The catastrophe they are running from never ceases but moves through the universe, recurring in its own time, whereupon the days of glass in their millions all fall together and remain, centuries of them, in a single solid sheet many fathoms deep. The animals' flight, then, is no more than a kind of cyclic worship, a dance before the event. It may consecrate them but it can never save them. The glass days fall to the earth suddenly on a spring morning when the mammoth's mouth is full of daisies.

And what of you? Do the animals run to your right or to your left? With the motion of the earth or against it? And have you saved your skins one after the other to offer to the translucent god? Have you invoked his protection each time a knife blade touched a stone, each time a glass rang? God of bells. Do you still have your little obsidian key which will allow you to enter, barefoot, the grating corridors, to pass naked by the vast halls where the animals stand like clouds, to forget each in turn, to ease your bones and your anguish through the grinding doors at last and into the head of the glass valley and hear your first bird sing, and kill the creature which does not yet know you, and laugh at the first touch of feathers, and warm your hands around its heart, and eat?

The Death-defying Tortonis

I go out first now. It is a position that I am not used to in some hair-thin secret chamber on the inside of the calves of my legs, and there perhaps I will never be used to it. Perhaps no one capable of assuming the position and surviving would ever grow used to it in every part of himself. Still, I have hopes. But given the assumptions on which I base the rest of my life, including its defiance, as they say, of death, it behooves me to conceal this truth—of my not yet being wholly accustomed to my position—from the others. To whom in any event it could never be completely and continuously (because of course it is alive) and as it were luminously communicated, so that it would not, could not, contribute to their enlightenment but merely to their disturbance. I would do as well, in fact, to conceal it even from myself if I had not, in the course of the past months and years, learned to control this stubborn refusal to be accustomed, this irreducible reluctance to regard my naked position as the first rider as though it were a part of nature. Is it, in fact? But does nature defy death? I would do well not to ask such questions during the performance. The mind never despairs of escaping its own controls, even if the escape can take no form except death itself.

I go out first now. It has been two and a half, nearly three years. Four years since I began to rehearse the position. I roll the front wheel onto the wire eighty feet above the ground, with nothing below it except dark air. Dark in our eyes despite the floodlights. I feel the feet in their tights, on my shoulders. I feel the muscles in the arches of the feet contract a little. This helps me. More of my mind returns from somewhere to lend its shoulder, to hold us up. I go out only a foot or two. We go out, for they have all assembled behind me. Behind me and above me, but at this point I must not think of them as being above me. I am not sure why. It would not help. We go out only a foot or two, very slowly, as though the front wheel were groping its way along the wire to make sure it continued. At about the point where my foot on the pedal would be clearing the platform (I imagine, for obviously I do not look to see) and there is nothing under the pedal but that darkness of which the rubber of the pedal is in truth a reflection, I stop. Even more slowly we go back to the platform. They help, from behind me. And for most of two minutes we appear to be adjusting something, arranging something which, if we had not happened to notice it, would have meant certain death for all of us. We make a great display of maintaining outward calm, of showing nothing to the audience, of not betraying that anything is wrong. Those above do not even climb down but stand there the whole time with their poles, staring straight ahead, which has been found most fitting. An assistant appears to be busying himself about us. We make use of this—in fact very difficult—moment to breathe, deliberately but not in time, blinking our eyes at the top of each inhalation, at the bottom of each exhalation, until the moment when we must forget our breathing again and give ourselves solely to what we are doing. By that time the announcer far below us is announcing our act for the second time, his voice appearing to show a touch of concern, as though our false start were not a part of the act, but something unforeseen, unprecedented, and incalculable in its results. He is announcing us again but of course we do not hear it, for by then we are too far advanced in our act, its silence, its echoes. Again I move forward, the feet gripping my shoulders, gripping tighter as the back wheel, too, leaves the platform and the whole bicycle is out on the wire, the front wheel laying itself down inch by inch like a snail.

The wire. We call it a wire out of tradition rather than regard for accuracy. It is in fact a metal cable of about the diameter of an ordinary candle, enveloped over its whole length by a layer of soft rubber between an eighth and a quarter of an inch in thickness. The rubber layer has been specially applied by hand, for it is important that the bond between it and the cable should be perfect and should remain perfect. It must not slip. The outside of the rubber contains, not a coating but an admixture of sharp sand of different degrees of coarseness, which must be an integral part of the rubber layer for as long as the wire fills its present role. It would be better to have no sand at all than sand which might work loose and roll out. Or even just work loose. This is one of the things for which the wire is examined, inch by inch, after each performance. If a single grain of sand shows signs of independent movement, even though it may be nothing more definable than the first movements of a child's tooth, the whole wire is set aside, at least for repair. Naturally, when it is set up the wire is anchored to keep it from swaying.

And the bicycles. It seems hardly necessary to point out that they are not ordinary bicycles either, although everything (other than the fact that they are entirely covered with chrome, apart from the hand grips, pedals and seats) has been arranged to make them suggest the most commonplace of contemporary wheels—the low, balloon-tired sort that used to be won by selling magazine subscriptions door to door. But ours are almost as light as imported racing models. Even the girls carry theirs into the arena themselves, before the front wheels are hooked to a rope and one after the other the bicycles fly alone, straight up to the platform. (It must be their favorite moment in the whole act.) There they lean against their handlers and wait. Speed would be meaningless to these constructions. But the conveyance of power from the pedal to the rear wheel is far more sensitive than it is in ordinary bicycles, for one thing. For another, the tires are not completely round but are molded with a very slight longitudinal concavity, barely noticeable when the wheels are suspended or when the bicycle is standing by itself. At such moments this conformation appears as nothing more than a flatness in the crown of the tire, scored with secondary grooves, also running lengthwise, and a tertiary hatchwork in a triangular scale pattern reminiscent of a sharkskin. A recurrent pattern—but the shark, after all, is a professional survivor. It is only when the bicycle wheel is placed on the wire, on the platform, and the weight of the rider and then the additional weight of the others press the tire down onto the sanded envelope of cable, that the tire yields at the crown sufficiently to produce a groove, which runs the full length of the contact. A shallow grip. Of course each bicycle is very slightly different from the others, the result of endless adjustments, some of them conceived in the small hours of the night. None of us would be able to perform with one of the others' bicycles.

So I go out first, and the image of the front wheel laying itself down like a snail did not come to me by chance. We are used to leaving nothing to chance, insofar as possible, or so we have to believe, though of course chance, chance itself is probably not even limited by our efforts. But in any case, how often that snail has appeared to me in dreams. Since I was a child. Since the days of my first slow wheel. I watched him ("him," of course, hence the intimacy of my reservations, the ready and yet awed identification) set out calmly, as though I did not exist, as though my decisions, all the rest of me and what became of all the rest of me, were eventualities too remote for him to believe in. I have even called to him in dreams and said, "Look, it's me!" But nothing. No response. Thank heaven. For I believe now that if there had been anything of the kind he would have lost some innate certainty, or I would have come to doubt it, and we would all have plunged, long since, into the abyss that awaits us everywhere.

I have allowed my mind to run at times (but never during a performance; never, in fact, when I was even touching the bicycle) on his ability to proceed equally well along the side of a wire, or underneath it, for that matter. I have dwelt with satisfaction on the image of him climbing smooth walls, crossing ceilings, negotiating intricate joints in rafters, or elaborate knots, at a great height. I have had dreams in which he disappeared—yes, disappeared, and in the course of crossing the wire in the usual way. I was the shell, or rather the bicycle and I together were the shell, or rather the bicycle and I and all the rest of us were the shell and we were suddenly filled with a weightlessness that bore no relation to anything we had practised. There we hung, a case enclosing a coil of nothing, balancing as well as we could, now that we were deprived of movement and had nothing at our center, until a tiny upward breath swept us off into the void. Naturally I have remained silent about any such images of my own. As my fellow-performers have done with theirs, if they have any, as no doubt they do.

So I go out first but it has not always been so. I am not the oldest; no, I am in fact one of the younger members of what is known, for reasons of remote pathos, as the family. Behind me the front wheel of Claudio's bicycle follows the rear wheel of mine with only a few inches between them and nothing maintaining the distance except Claudio's foot on the pedal. Claudio is eight years older than I am and wears a dark reddish toupee for the act. Tortoni is his real name. And yet he has confided to me that if he had not been put to the act so young, as we all were, he might never have chosen it. He cannot be sure but he might never have chosen it. It was one of those confidences that was surely forgotten by the person who made it almost immediately and I am sure that the thought has seldom if ever recurred to him. Claudio says very little and buys magazines about animals and nature when we have any time in a city. He is heavier than I am, heavier than any of us, but his tights always fit with wrinkles. For years, ever since I began to practise going out first, I have tried not to listen to his breathing.

It was once suggested that Claudio should go out first, but the thought troubled him so much that the idea was dropped.

Behind Claudio's bicycle comes the carefully braked front wheel of his younger brother Rafael. Rafael married Marisa two years ago, after living with her for nearly three. He is much slighter than Claudio, blond, quicker but more nervous. He worries about money. He worries about the future of the act. He reads all the papers and discusses them at large to the rest of us, usually without anyone else entering a comment. Rafael needs an abdominal operation but we hope it will wait until the end of the season because the formation as we practise it now allows of no alternatives.

Behind Rafael's bicycle comes his cousin Marcantonio's. Marcantonio's mother was a Tortoni who tried to escape the whole world of the wire by marrying outside it. But perhaps because she had never known anyone except those who performed on the wire, she chose unfortunately. The marriage was brief and wretched; she herself returned, with her child, to the familiar circumstances. Not as a performer (she had never had the temperament) but as a dresser, old before her time, controlling her pessimism with an uncertainty that led us all to keep our distance from her. Yet allowing her son to be brought up as a cyclist—her own attempt to escape the wire had exhausted her belief in any such possibility. And Marcantonio avoided her more studiously than anyone, even to having his tights made and repaired by someone else. And though the differences between our performances are almost immeasurable, it is my opinion that Marcantonio is the most reliable and sturdy of us all.

Last comes Cesare, gaunt, wiry, and no more their brother than I am. He is the son of a trapeze artist who was killed when Cesare was very small. There was no one to train him in his father's act, but Carla Tortoni, the mother of the cyclists behind me, who died last year, brought him up as a matter of course and he was put to the wire at the same age as the rest of us. His passion is dancing and he is in love with a girl who has nothing to do with any act at all, which in itself has always been thought rather unlucky. She has never seen him perform and refuses even to read the reviews of our act in the newspapers.

The feet on my shoulders belong to Augusta, one of the younger daughters. Younger than I am, and pretty. We grew up together. For a brief time in our early adolescence we slept together, until the full gravity of what we were doing dawned on us at the same time. Then we stopped without a word and without the least ill-will. Now, years later, it is good that it happened. Neither she nor I have married. Again, one does not think of such things during the performance.

On Claudio's shoulders the feet are Alfreddo's. He is not a member of the family either, but a tumbler whom they enlisted seven or eight years ago. He is the oldest of us, married, with children whom he never sees; he is almost the same age as Claudio's own father. He reads one boxful of books over and over.

On Rafael's shoulders are Emilia's feet. Emilia lives with Claudio. She is the daughter of another wire artist, who performs alone.

On Marcantonio's shoulders, Giorgio's feet. Georgio is the youngest of the Tortonis, slight, small, homosexual, who wanted to be a clown.

On Cesare's shoulders, Anna's feet. She is the prettiest of the Tortoni girls, gentle, studious, and a singer.

The seats of the bicycles and the heights of the first row of balancers have been carefully adjusted so that their shoulders are all at the same height. This is important because when the balancers are in position a ladder is handed up to them, through which they all slip their heads. Then they lower it to their shoulders, which are padded to receive it, and the ladder provides a platform, running from Augusta in front to Anna in the rear. The balancing poles are then handed up, and then the second row of balancers can start to climb up, to stand on the ladder.

Mimi first, who was a classical dancer but required something more dangerous. She is jealous of Marisa and everyone pretends not to know.

Then Teodoro, who is little and dark like a jockey, and was a street urchin who used to play with us when we were first starting to learn, and picked up the act that way, and came with us. He is married and has five children who live with the troupe, but he is never around unless it is for some reason to do with work. He and Giorgio do not get along but everyone is careful not to pay any attention.

Then Maria, Cesare's sister, adopted at the same time he was. She is in love with Marcantonio, and it would be a good thing, but that is no concern of the front tire's.

Finally Ernesto Tortoni, short, neat, equable, the eldest of the sons, married without children, an impassioned and skilful devotee of the stock-market, at which he has been moderately successful over the years, considering that he started with nothing.

On the shoulders of these four, a second ladder. On which a chair is placed. Into which Graziella climbs, wearing a long gown, mock-royal, with a fluffy trim and spangles. And a rhinestone tiara. Graziella was also picked up on the street, an acquaintance of Teodoro's. She grew up with us. We first let her practise the act with us after watching her walk up a hawser into a ship, on a dare, when she was a little girl. I suppose it would be said that Graziella and I are engaged. Yes, that at least.

When we are half-way across we stop. The cyclists, one after the other, take their hands off the grips and hold them out like wings. Then each of the bottom row of balancers raises an arm. Then each of the second row of balancers raises an arm. Finally Graziella rises, climbs the chair, and unfurls a flag. We remain there, not hearing the rolled drums or the applause, for a moment, and then continue.

Everyone's role, as may be imagined, is difficult. But for the cyclists it is more difficult than for anyone, and our training began almost as soon as we could walk. Even before, if you will, with toy bicycles. We came early to regard these two-wheeled fabrications as though the world itself revolved around them. We thought of them day and night. Everything we learned led back to them at once or seemed pointless. At last we could ride. The fervor increased. We cared for nothing else. We learned to ride more and more slowly. We learned to ride backward. By pure force of concentration we learned to stop, to remain upright in one place. Then came the moment when an old wire was laid on the ground and we set the wheels on it and started. When that became practicable the first of the drops—an old tent canvas, painted—was spread out under the wire. It represents an arena. At the edges are the first tiers of seats, with spectators painted sitting there, life size. We soon ceased to notice them. In due course the wire was raised a few inches, just enough to clear the ground. Same canvas.

Then when we were used to the raised practise wire another canvas was spread under it. The arena was smaller. More tiers of spectators showed. They were smaller. As we grew more proficient the canvases depicted the arena and the audience farther and farther below us, until the arena looked the size of a dinner plate and the spectators the size of hat-pins. Then a black canvas, which was the hardest of all to get used to. Then we were ready to start learning the act itself.

But after all that, and even with luck, will we grow much older in the act?

The audiences are not what they were even a few years ago; our expenses are rising all the time; none of the young seem to feel that there is a future in following our exacting profession. Less and less people seem to believe in us, to say nothing of understanding our art.

But Grandfather Tortoni says that the decline of interest has nothing to do with the world, but only with ourselves. He says we are no longer of interest because in fact we are not defying anything real at all. According to him we know too much, and it is all a game. Even if we were killed we would be killed in a game. That is what they mean when they say they don't believe we're really doing what we seem to be doing. In contrast to us, the old man declares that he admired his son Tomaso, Claudio's father, just once, when he combined risk and wit and performed on the wire, at the age of eighteen, on a unicycle, on his head. And the old man is thinking (though he is too proud to mention it) of the day when he himself drove a bicycle with a huge front wheel—an ordinary high-seated penny-farthing without special tires or anything—across a city square, a hundred feet up, without rehearsal, simply because, as he once said, it got into him that he could. He watches us seldom, and with scorn, and he says we should turn to something we know nothing about if we are going to talk about defying death. The whole matter, he says, is far simpler than we have made it. It consists of nothing but being able to look straight ahead and see that there could not possibly be any other way.

The Visitor

And what about her, my lord, what about her? Is the kingdom of heaven only a step from her also and will the passions of the earth at a single movement of her heart fall back and bow their heads as she passes?

For seventeen years, my lord, she has come twice a week, well before the specified hours. Sundays and Wednesdays, in clean clothes with her face rubbed like an elbow and her basket heavy. To stand with the others on the far side of the street, looking up at the high black wall of the prison and the studded grilles of the windows through which shaved heads can be dimly made out, through which a hand occasionally flutters or flicks out to seize a bar as though its body had fallen from it and it was clinging to the last proof of mortal life—a prison bar—by itself. She stands there and smiles up and from time to time she waves. When the bell rings she goes over with the others to the little door by the drawbridge, between the guards' shelters, and in her turn approaches the guard who opens the door. From her basket she takes a bundle, carefully and attractively wrapped. If it is a month that bears flowers there are flowers tied to the string. The guard nods to her. He knows her. They all know her. She points out the name on the bundle. He nods. She asks for news, he says everything is just the same so far as he knows, but he never sees the prisoners. He is younger than she is.

Is there any chance yet of her being able to see her husband, she asks. He looks at a board and says no. Will he not place her request before his superiors, she asks. He promises. He looks at her and says that the decision has nothing to do with him. She tells him that she knows that. She goes back and stands across the street and waves again.

From the basket she takes out a man's garment that she has been working on that season and holds it up to show the progress she has made. When the bell rings again all the hands at the grille wave and then the shaved heads disappear. She waves, the last time with a handkerchief, and goes, with the others shuffling toward the side-streets.

Sometimes she returns before dusk and stands there by herself, looking up, when there is no one at the windows.

Of whose decision, made in what circumstances, is her life the consequence, my lord? Is this her first existence?

The wall by which she stands, by which she waits, is called Rumor Wall. Everyone else has heard something, whether or not it is true. Everyone else, and long ago, has heard something even about her husband but each one, my lord, and each for his own reasons, has spared himself telling her that her husband, a political suspect never in any case allowed out of his cell, was transferred to another prison some time during his fourth year and executed the following morning.

A Thing of Beauty

Sometimes where you get it they wrap it up in a clock and you take it home with you and since you want to see it it takes you the rest of your life to unwrap it trying harder and harder to be quick which only makes the bells ring more often.

The Second Person

You are the second person.

You look around for someone else to be the second person. But there is no one else. Even if there were someone else there they could not be you. You try to shelter in imagining that you are plural. It is a dream which the whole of the waking world is trying to remember. It is the orphan's mother who never lived but is longed for and has been accorded a pronoun that is an echo of your own, since she has no name. Her temple is an arrangement of mirrors. But nothing stays in it. Think how you keep your thoughts to yourself, on your rare visits there. And how quickly you leave.

You are the second person. The words come to you as though they were birds that knew you and had found you at last, but they do not look at you and you never saw them before, you have nowhere to keep them, you have nothing to feed them, they will interfere with your life, you cannot hear yourself, the little claws, meaning no harm, never let you alone, so tame, so confiding. But you know they are not yours. You know they are no one else's, either.

Sometimes between sleeping and waking you really forget that you are the second person. Once again you have embarked, you have arrived, nothing is missing, nothing. The twilight is an infinite re-union. Then a messenger enters looking everywhere for someone. For the second person. Who else?

Made in the image of The Second Person, you never see your face. Even the mirrors show it to you backwards. Dear reader at times imagining in your own defense that I am the second person, I know more about you than I know about myself, but I would not recognize you. For your part, it is true that you do not know your own story. That it has all been given away. That it lies at the bottom of a river where everything joins it but no one owns it. No one admits to it. Why this elusiveness of yours, like that which lives in an animal's eye? For you have to be found, you are found, I have found you. You make a pathetic effort to disguise yourself in all the affectations of the third person, but you know it is no use. The third person is no one. A convention.

Can you never answer happily when you are addressed? Do I want you to?

No, you insist, it is all a mistake, I am the first person. But you know how unsatisfactory that is. And how seldom it is true.

The Moles

The ants are waiting their turn. Their baggage trains are packed in the tunnels, their soldiers know no hesitations, their decisions are ready far in advance, and absolute. The discipline in each of their orders is flawless, their architecture is at once a portrait of their minds and a model of the universe with its conflicts in harmony. In their time we have almost ceased to exist. They scarcely notice us, they pause, they had forgotten that we were still here, a passing inconvenience. They move through us without individuals, without loss, without regret. Pain for them is a lantern signalling at a distance: Thieves. Even when the whole of the sea has gone the ants will not notice. When they bury us it is with a utilitarian coldness and a finality which put those qualities in ourselves to shame. The blood, the brains, the organs they pile above the spot, after changing them back into red earth. They use only the veins, gradually improving everything beyond recognition. They descended from the sun, live on fire, fear nothing else. They are farther from us, with their great heads, than any star.

But the fate of the moles is linked to our own, and to the sea's. They are not waiting for anything. They seek tirelessly for new places to ask us whether we are who we are, and if that is enough. Each time that we are led at last to lie down in green pastures they raise near us their little mounds that are models of our graves. Is this dust yours, they say? Confronted with silence they raise another one, a lost city in the twilight. Is This Yours, is its name. Is this the one you will return to? Is this the one you were made of? Is this you—the rest of you, which you left behind? If this had been taken up in the same hand, and the breath of life had breathed into it the same command, and it had come with you, would you be whole now, would you be at peace? The stars come out. New hills rise around us. More lost mothers. Once again we become part of the darkness. It is not too late. The moles, propelled by a small model of the forgotten sea, with eyes for nothing but their labors, urge their black bones forward in our endless quest.

The Islands

The islands always disappeared.

After a long time men learned to build their own islands. Then men too began to disappear. There were more and more men all the time and the faster there were more of them the faster they disappeared.

Under the sea there lived an old man bent over like a bell, who could hear pain. He could hear the pain even of those who disappeared. He could hear the pain of disappearance itself, of which night is one form and day another. He could hear the pain which those who disappear left behind. There was nothing he could do. All suffering flowed into the sea and the weight of the sea rocked on his ear-drum. His breathing made the waves. When he saw the moon he was reminded at once of how everything was and he sighed, and the tide turned once more. The worst thing was that he could not tell whether the pain he heard was from the past, the present or the future, for pain was already time's keeper.

It is because I forget, he said. If I did not forget things they would not disappear. He tried to remember. The pain grew worse. And everything, as it disappeared in the sea after all his efforts, was still crushed into one terrible syllable that sank straight toward him. It is because I know too much, he said. And he tried to forget. But the whole sea shook him to remind him, bringing the echoes.

If there is no hope for me perhaps I can help someone else, the old man said, for he was a good old man. For his own sake and for theirs he tried to find someone who knew nothing about pain. At last he gathered around himself the unborn and in a very low voice began to tell them stories about the islands.

Blue

In the deepest part of blue one of the immortals lives alone.

There is almost no light so he sits outside. His vast eyes—two moonless, starless, windless nights across which the same clouds are passing—never close. At long intervals one of them re-visits the world of the spectrum and is a night again. (The other never leaves him.) Even then the two remain one in his mind. While they are apart all dreams cease except the dreams of frogs, toads, and fish— cold dreams, like his own, full of shadows, with no future. It is only when his voyaging eye is away that he himself dreams. All that appears to him during such eclipses delights him, and his memory is composed of nothing but remnants of those nights full of the silence of antiquity.

The recurrence of one of them is announced by the darkening of a rainbow. A shadow appears on the blue edge and deepens. A line of violet, almost black, bends upward into the sky. It spreads across the iridescent path, washing each zone with blue, then darkening. Finally the almost black rainbow rises until it fills the sky. That night we lie empty of everything, dreamless, while the toads sit hypnotized by the drumming of their hearts.

There is no pity in him. Where would he have learned it? The dead drift past him in their gray boats but he never knew them.

But there is no harm in him. Over his door, where no mortal eye could read anything, it is written, WE ARE ALL CHILDREN OF THE LIGHT.

The Songs of the Icebergs

One at a time, one at a time, men have been favored with the sound, even sometimes at great distances, or at night, or in fog. In almost every case they have spent the rest of their lives cherishing their disbelief. Or so it has been at least since the invention of printing—a day, after all, in the saga of the ice. And the legends—mermaids and sirens were easier to accept, for their faces could be seen, their mirrors, their hair, their hands extended in gestures out of the dreams of men. It required consistent deliberation to deny them souls, to banish them from the plausible world door by door. The songs of the icebergs never entered it except as a cold breath. After which one of those who had felt it would be seen, perhaps, with the look of a man who is surprised to find himself in possession of an incomprehensible and inexpressible secret.

The songs have even been seen more often than they have been heard, but then it has been easy not to recognize them. They have taken the form of illuminations rising from within, toward the surfaces of the leprous cliffs, like the northern lights themselves still searching for them, or like arms and faces drowned in slow rivers, appearing and then sinking again, to reappear farther along.

Those white mountains are far from home. What can they do but sing? The water, and the habits of our own ears, distort the sound so that what usually reaches men seems to be nothing but a series of creakings, splinterings, gnashings, occasional screams—emanations to which the hearer, with the familiar door-shutting movement to which he believes he owes his very identity, hastens to deny any vestige of intention, plan, form, spirit. And yet the whales, who are imprisoned in no such rigid refusal, though they themselves have been able to catch only occasional chords from the pale submerged hillsides, have built on their recollections the whole of their rich and happy music. And from still fainter refrains the porpoises have shaped their delicate carols.

Yet the songs of the icebergs are tragic. That is why they come to men only to be turned away. Much as man wants pain, this one he knows he dare not welcome lest it prove to be his. He shuns it as though his very teeth had begun to sing and sleep had threatened never to touch him again. For this is a strain of the great singing. None is more bereft, none more lonely, none more hopeless. The icebergs, floating in a stunned peace that moves slowly toward the bright rim of the earth, are mercilessly shattered by their own destiny. All their whiteness was born of the dark, all their fires were lit by the cold at the ends of the earth. From their depths to their summits they were brought up to silence. They might have stayed there in perfect peace until time had died. But there was a flaw in the whiteness. It was in love with the light. And with unspeakable pain it set out to reach the sun, forsaking everything else forever. However the planet turned it continued its journey, gathering to itself a few ghosts, a few bones, a few echoes of bones, a few curses, a voice. Crossed by a few white creatures. Unconsolable. Breaking. That is in the songs.

The Sky Beetle

Shortly before dawn he burrows into the sky and begins to sing. One by one the stars turn to the other side to hear him, and their light leaves ours and fixes on the small black insect singing of the world that they will never see because it is on the side from which they have turned. As long as it is day here he sings to them and we do not even hear him. And as soon as our light has gone he stops and comes out and sits on the sky, having done his work, and then they turn one by one and try to see the world of which he has been singing. All night their faces burn through the darkness, empty but hoping.

The Remembering Machines of Tomorrow

The human memory is a wonderful development but its fallibility is infinite. How can it be left to men? It has forgotten even its own story—the whole of evolution. It does not recall why the spirit of man walks with a limp. It can no longer say why, through a landscape of peace, fatness, and fragrance, his for the taking, of sumptuous birthplaces with meals already set, fires already lit, welcomes prepared for no one but him, he forces his bitter mouth and his naked hands farther and farther into his hunger, his cold, his namelessness, his desolation. What triumph will he recognize, what wind will he acknowledge, what sky will he warm for long? Everywhere he dreams of a creator who remembers, and he continues the search for Him, hoping that in the end what he will find will be himself. But whenever he moves he forgets something. Whatever he adds to himself he adds at the same time to the void which gnaws at his organs—all of them. It is this gnawing, and no hunger that he shares with the rest of the creatures, that drives him from them. He listens to the gnawing as though it were a song, and goes on, forgetting even that. How could things be left in such hazard? When he has finished forgetting the past he will have no choice but to start on the future. He has started already. No, it cannot go on.

Fortunately he still has his thumb, the inventor, and even before the problem has been clearly stated (oh, long before that) he has contrived the first steps toward its solution. The distance from the first notches bruised into bark, which were the ancestors of numbers, to the air-conditioned archives of the age of history, represented only a few strides in his ignorant progress, a day in his forgetting. But once there, he noted with a certain shame that everything seemed to have left him to hide in the intricate halls, where he could not again feel that it was really his, though the halls had been designed by minds like his own. His own story had now forgotten him. No, it could not be left at that either.

Faced before with crises he had developed his other thumb, named (by him) Sacrifice. At each movement of utter risk he had held up this shell-faced totem and offered part of himself in exchange for—often that has been forgotten. What was given up was presumably given up forever, but not all at once. The payment might be spread over a long time. He gave up his legs for the wheel. He gave up the strength of his arms for the lever. He gave up power after power of his physical form. And now at last, as more and more was forgotten, he began to relinquish his memory so that something would be remembered.

Since the great primitive repositories had been impersonal, and what he took to be their codified memories seemed to have less and less to do with what he still remembered as himself, a new link was needed.

The rest of this does not allow of the past tense.

The first of the remembering machines is immense, immobile, no one's. It learns, that is true. But its learning is based on information fed into it by sophisticated procedures, consciously, voluntarily. It is constructed of fragments. Even though it can record anything about us that we can conceive of having recorded, it is still in the main a recorder, rather than a memory. But its progeny is approaching us.

The machines will become, in time, more compact. They will become the pride of smaller and smaller institutions, the playthings of more and more of the privileged. They will no longer retain mere symbols in an arbitrary system, but something which can pass, at least, for whole experiences—intellectual, sensual, visionary. The process—not so much of remembering as of confronting a memory recorded with mechanical objectivity, will be painful of course, but that has not proved an insuperable obstacle in the past and is not likely to do so in the future. It will be construed as part of the new sacrifice. And the development of the remembering machines will come to be regarded as an important next step in man's evolutionary progress—something at once inevitable and worth anything it might cost. When the machines become small enough so that every person can have—then must have—his own, the day will be celebrated as the beginning of a new age of The Individual.

The machines will retain, in flawless preservation (though the completeness of what they remember will occasion some dispute, for a time) not only what their owners experience but what their owners think they have experienced, and will sort out the one from the other.

More and more, such distinctions will be left purely to the machines. And it will be noticed that the experience to be retained is itself becoming a dwindling fauna, clung to by sentimentalists, from afar, who still lay aside their machines for days at a time and secretly yearn for the imaginary liberties of the ages of forgetting.

The simplification of private experience will be more than made up for by the rapid improvement of communication among the machines themselves. It will be possible to share more and more fully the memories of others. The memories of the dead will be available in the new repositories, and many will be privately owned. With the universal recognition of the therapeutic benefits and the practical advantages of a precise memory, children will be fitted with these devices at birth. Their pre-natal experiences will have been picked up and played into their first sets. They will be given new ones as they grow older and can use them. The stages of such use will seem to reveal a new pattern in the growth of the individual and hence of the species. What man is will seem to be on the point, once again, of harmonious emergence.

Then here and there a ghost will be seen. Someone who has lost his machine. The terror he engenders will be discussed, collated, contained. It will be comprehensible, though the ghost himself no longer is. The apparition will be accorded its place, and will not long trouble those who still have their machines—any more than if, in the old days, they had seen some mutilated creature begging in the street, in the service of his unimaginable life. Little by little it will be remarked, but with a mathematical coolness, that experience is not only flowing into the machines but that they, to an increasing extent, are becoming its source as well. Man's experience of the mechanized memory of his experience—that is what will fill more and more of his days on earth. Until, apart from the simplest bodily functions, his new life will come to revolve around nothing but the operation of the machines themselves. The memory of old risks will return, but faintly, vaguely, and so crudely that he cannot take them seriously. For perfection will seem to be in sight at last. Attached to every person like a tiny galaxy will be the whole of his past—or what he takes to be the whole of his past. His attachment to it will constitute the whole of his present—or of what he takes to be the present. The neat, almost soundless instrument will contain all of each man's hope, his innocence, his garden.

Then one by one, but with growing frequency, men will begin to lose their machines.

What We Are Named For

To say what or where we came from has nothing to do with what or where we came from. We do not come from there any more, but only from each word that proceeds out of the mouth of the unnamed.

And yet sometimes it is our only way of pointing to who we are.

The Billboard

Whenever he asks they tell him the same thing. They are going to give him something for the use of his place, once they have finished investigating his title to it. As he understands them, it won't be a lump sum. Actually he'd settle for a lump sum but he thinks it's shrewder not to admit that. It will be more like rent, dealt out to him at intervals for the rest of his life. He can see how they stand to gain by such an arrangement. At his age they might not have to go on paying for long. Still, as he reminds himself, after that it won't matter to him. And it had never occurred to him that he might end his days with a pension. Anything at all would be better than his present position. No income at all. Living on what he can find, down in the streets. Making his way back up, in the evening, to the shed, where he can shut out the dogs. Where he used to be able to shut out the dogs.

The investigation, to tell the truth, is taking longer than he'd expected from what they'd told him at first. But he's not seriously worried. He has a better title to his place than most of his neighbors, in the thousands of sheds on the hills around the city, have to theirs. He's been there longer. He's kept women there, raised children, pigs, chickens. It's probably taking them so long to investigate because it was so long ago that he came there and built the shed and brought the first of the women up to the place. It had a good view, and at that time he and she used to like to sit in the doorway and watch the lights in the city, before going in to bed. That's one thing he regrets, a little. The billboard they are putting up on his place is gradually shutting out the view of the city. But he tells himself that that's a trifle compared to ending your days with a pension. It isn't as though his eyes were much good any more, anyway. If he sat in the doorway now, even if the sign weren't there, all he'd see would be a blur. They're shutting out part of the sky, too, but with a pension he could buy a hammock and lie outside looking up.

Recently he has been inquiring more often about the progress of the investigations. Not just because the inquiry seems to be taking longer than he had expected, and he would prefer to start on his pension while he might still be able to enjoy it, but also because the construction of several of the supports for the billboard has forced the construction workers to demolish parts of his shed. Every evening when he comes back he finds that more of the building has been ripped down to make way for the beams and trusses and pits filled with concrete that are to anchor the high wooden wall in the heavy winds that sweep through the valley. The dogs get in through the wide jagged openings now, and eat or run off with whatever he leaves there. He drives them out when he comes home and barricades the openings as well as he can with the sticks and rubble that have been torn down from the walls of his shed. It would be a help if he could use some of the materials left over from the construction work. But the new materials, naturally, are locked up, and in any case they'd notice at once if he ever managed to incorporate any of those in patchwork construction of his own. And the odds and ends left over after a day's work are either burned on the spot or carted away in trucks. Whenever he asks it's explained to him that there's a law which forbids them to let him have any of those things. And they will not allow him to attach his repairs to the sign supports. Every morning they knock down anything he has built which touches or gets in the way of their construction.

And every day less remains of the shed. But he still lies in a corner at night, holding his stick to beat off the dogs, telling himself that the billboard will be a fine windbreak, and that the investigations cannot be far from completion now, because the workmen have nearly finished the enormous sign which will tell the whole of the city what to want.

The Conqueror

"It has not always been like this," he said. "At one time my performance did not call up vibrations out of the Great Fault. On the other hand I was not remembered for so long."

Here I thought of the sound of the stadium as I had approached it, when the sport had already been going on for heaven knows how long. The air had been oppressive around the walls, like a held breath, and I had been unable to tell whether the shrieking that rose from inside was an expression of the excitement and pleasure of the spectators, or the monosyllable of some ultimate terror.

"This is by no means the first time it has happened," he went on, "but so far no one has been so hypocritical as to destroy my statue or change my name on the boulevards, and they will not do so this time, never fear. Though even if they did, it would not make much difference, in the long run. As it is, look at the size of my name on the posters. Each time I take the field I am their idol. What they would all like to be, to be loved by, to know. How they smile on the little boys, who are happy to admit it. Then the anthem is sung. The adversary comes forward, all flutes, flowers, little songs. I draw my sword. The match begins. I used to have to send back reports. Everything took longer. Except the game itself.

"After the beginning, one forgets the spectators. One forgets time. One plays as well as one can, aware for the moment of nothing else. One wins, and turns in one's bloody boots to see that the spectators have changed. Everything about them looks different, and they are on their feet, shrieking, not in admiration but in disgust. They cry now for vengeance. They grieve over what I have done to please them. If only I were alive, they say, so that I might be punished! Imagine! Pretending that I am not alive!"

I said, "In my own part of the stadium it is not so much the killing they object to, as the pleasure it gives."

"They won't escape that, either," he said, "merely by building larger stadiums, with worse acoustics, as they're doing at present. The only way for anyone to get home is to go with the crowd. Those who leave before the show is over, either singly or by twos and threes, though the party were to include the president himself, are met at the gate, where they are covered with flowers, presented with flutes, and given little songs to memorize."

The Locker Room

This time no one told us anything. We do not even know where the battle was, on which our fates depended. But there is not a word of surprise as we find ourselves, at our age, being herded down those iron stairs to the pale green foyer lit with naked bulbs. Bulletin boards. Frosted glass windows and doors. One of the big windows opens, revealing several men younger than we are, in white smocks, seated or standing at desks, among filing cabinets. We are kept waiting. There are no benches. We look around to see who we know. We see a face we recognize, and we smile little wincing smiles, but then wonder whether we should indicate that we know anyone there at all, and from then on we stand still, saying nothing, feeling our stomachs like dark ships slowly sinking. We are told to take off our shoes. Keep the socks on. We stand holding our shoes, watching how the others hold theirs, without meeting eyes. Yesterday this time, or even two hours ago, we were being deferred to in positions of relative eminence. Our modesty became us. Almost certainly it became us. We deprecated. And quite genuinely: aware that the esteem in which apparently we were held exceeded our deserts. Yes, but we did not stand in our socks, with our shoes in our hands, waiting, on a cement floor that was not quite dry, smelling the shoes, the socks, the floor, something else, and beyond double frosted doors the unlit locker room. Some of us, clearly, had taken no exercise for years. Some were perspiring. Some seemed to be looking for things in their pockets. It's true that we'd been picked up without warning, and just as we were. Told we would need nothing else. Probably no one knew where we were. A clever-looking young man, growing bald already, hurried out from the room with the desks. His white smock billowed around him and he was carrying a clip-board from which sheets of paper struggled to detach themselves and fly away across pallid horizons, where they would settle quietly on vast plains, in the spring twilight, two by two. He opened the locker room doors, switched on the yellow bulbs inside, and motioned us through, checking off each of our names as we passed him, and giving each of us a little string with a tag on it, bearing a locker number.

The strings were dirty.

"Don't put the tags in your mouths," he told us, though no one seemed tempted to do so. And we filed past, holding shoes in one hand, tag in the other, and began to drift and eddy up and down the rows of lockers, a slow yellow-lit tide backing up into an old harbor. Then the sound of the first tin locker-doors. A few voices, laughing a little at having found them. Striking up new acquaintance, with an effort at jocularity, even at such a time, in such a place. And the smell of the lockers. The care with which hand after hand hesitantly sets about undoing its necktie. And there are no hangers for suits which have always had hangers. Years ago we did not have suits that were used to hangers. The ones we have come in with hang uncomfortably on the snub hooks, and at once dust seems to have begun to settle on them. Out of the corners of our eyes we see garters, and white calves, and white shirt-tails, and then shirts fluttering into the lockers like guilty things, but all we hear is an occasional creaking and snapping of joints, heavy breathing, wheezing, sniffing, a stifled moan. And the squeaking and banging of the locker doors. Pale sides of skin emerge to right and to left, bending, patting, sighing. Some of us must have had no exercise for years. Some of us plainly have had no exercise for years. Some of us obviously have revealed our birthday suits only to the bought bulbs of bathrooms, for years. The young man with the clip-board moves along the aisles, checking. He tells us to hang the tags on the locker doors when we are finished, and then close the lockers and stand with our backs to them. There is a muttering. Some are saying prayers. The smell of us grows stronger than that of the old locker room, but when I look up at the ceiling I can imagine that we are still as we once were, years ago, standing under those same yellow tiles, with no hair on our cold privates, shivering, and I cling to that image.

Almost all of the locker doors must have shut, and almost all of the abdomens must have turned slowly, the shoulders squaring a little, the eyes seeking out some spot on the locker across the aisle, when another clever-looking young man with a clip-board comes through the doors and confers with the first one. They speak together in low tones for a moment, comparing their papers. Then the first young man nods and straightens.

"As you were," he says. "Get dressed."

The sigh. The sound of bodies falling as one or two faint. The fumbling with the lockers. The underwear. Feeling tight. Feeling clammy. The shirt. Feeling dirty. And too small. The trousers. Feeling tight. And short and strange, and looking different in the light. Yes. They've grown old. Very old. As old as though we'd been standing there for years. Or as though they'd been hanging there since we were children. And the jackets. Much too small, too short in the arms. And old. With holes in some of the pockets. And in others nails. Clasp-knives. Crumpled pieces of paper which we remember but about which we say nothing. The socks. Dirty, fished from among several dirty pairs. The shoes. Sneakers. Too small. The first young man with the clip-board is going among the aisles telling us to hurry. The wallets. Almost nothing in them but our names. The sound of somebody sniffing again. And the first young man with the clip-board and the billowing smock, leading us rapidly down a green hall that echoes like an inner-tube, to the gymnasium, where samples of our blood, our urine, our hair, are collected. And then the safety doors clanking open and the cold air of the recreation ground, where we are released—yes, released—one by one and allowed to walk away in silence, past the new windows.

The Answers

You knock once more, wondering whether they will recognize you, after so long. Probably they will not know you on sight. Now what if a window flies up, farther along the narrow street, and a crabbed old woman puts her head out to ask you what you want? How will you find a few plausible words suitable for shouting to an upper window when you would, to tell the truth, prefer not to be overheard?

How can you say, "An answer"?

Then what if she asks your name, as she almost certainly will? You will pretend, for many reasons, not to have understood, and knock again?

"But they don't live there," she will call at last, indignant, just as you notice that the house is directly across the street from the police station. Adding, "And they never lived there."

It's true, there's not a sound inside and there's no name beside the door.

What if she asks, "What did you want to see them about anyway?" Can you really shout back, "That's one of the things I hoped they'd know."

But by then the night air will have started to wake and stretch in the shadows, and she will have clutched her soiled shawl around her neck and shut the window.

"And yet everything in the world," you insist as you go down the steps, "still has its door."

Tribesmen

Nothing about us impresses them. They walk into a town, emaciated, hollow-eyed, and very tall, and they look around as though they doubted whether we or anything that is ours had three dimensions. They laugh at our weapons even when they die of them. They brush our buildings with their fingertips, then they look at the fingertips, catch each other's eyes, and shrug.

They say that the only enemy worth overcoming is shame. This spirit assumes a different form, so they believe, in each generation. He is overthrown sometimes for good, sometimes for evil. He himself is neither. He is Non.

But nothing belongs to him. He is merely a guard. And a liar, like most guards. They respect no one who is his dupe or his lackey. But they revere only those who have advanced boldly and alone into the very domain he has been set to keep watch over—the country of Non—and there have seen at last, reflected in the sky, the walls of light, and have glimpsed the beginning of the crystal stairs.

Greeting to Be Addressed to the Dead on the Morning of Their Fifth Year

It is your day, patient one.

We would hardly know it was you, under the rags. Pieces from last year, a belt from the year before, remnants of boots from the year before that, even some buttons and rusted fastenings that must hark back to the ill-fitting narrative you were buried in. Everything that we have brought you year by year, please note, has been true to what you might have been, insofar as we have been able to imagine that. Look, we have brought you your new story.

The hat with the bright feathers was a gift from the king of the winds, a token of esteem and an invitation to meet and to be loved by his daughter, the most beautiful princess in the empire. You are on your way to his domains. The whole of the night is your guard. The blind are drawn up along your road. As you pass each one he sees the sunrise. These flowers, now, are to give to her when you see her. And these are to give to her the day after. And once again this ribbon which we wrap around you recounts the days of your happiness and of our hope.

You that were poor. You that were ignorant. You that were graceless and ungifted and frightened and cold of heart.

This year you will find us again in your story. In great need. Remember us. Bless us out of your superabundance. Wake us with hope. See, we leave you every colored thing we have brought with us, and turn back in our black garments to what we have inherited and call the truth. To history, the form of despair reserved for the living.

Noon

He who is wearing the helmet of Death is walking at the foot of the walls. The shadow of the enormous casque falls over his body like a bell. He lets others do his shouting for him. No one shouts, wearing the helmet of Death. He turns. He waits.

Around him the empty plain, and the dead, who have taken the form of doors, each standing by itself, locked, with no shadow. Large birds alight, bringing their own shadows to walk on, and disappear behind the doors. He is wearing the helmet of Death.

While he wears it no weapon can touch him, no sound can startle him, no sight can move him.

No one dares fight with him. The silence is his triumph.

But Death has missed the helmet.

The Daughters of Judgment

Over the door the central figure is not God, neither the Father nor the Son, but Judgment himself. Here is suffering in the stone. His eyes, one must suppose, are somewhere in the shadow under his forehead. It is not possible to say whether they are fixed on anything.

Around the portal in orderly multitudes are carved the daughters of Judgment, each of them with her deformity—one with one eye, one with none, some with no hands, some with no feet, several with no legs, many with no heads. After each of his decisions a daughter was born to him. Many, many daughters, each as far short of perfection as his decision had been.

And this is Judgment himself, for whom they were named, and from whom we are descended.

Companion

A feather has been following me all morning, like a little dog. One laughs at such moments, mumbling something about knowing what that means. Of course one does not, but it is better to suggest that one does, and has made one's arrangements. It was lying there on the rug when I got up. A small gray breast feather, curled like a lock of hair. I could see the down trembling, though I could feel nothing, myself. When I put on one of my shoes it came forward. I thought that perhaps the shoe and the feather were joined by something—a hair, or a spider's thread—and I passed my hand between them. Nothing. As I walked away the feather skimmed along behind.

It followed me down the stairs. Do I make that much wind, I wondered. I went more slowly. It did the same. It followed me back up the stairs again.

I tried to catch it. Hoping no one would ask what I was doing. That led nowhere. And I felt that I would have offended us both if I had continued.

But I did try to drop clothes over it. It knew that trick too. It followed me, when I left, over grass, across the road, among animals, through the rain. I wondered whether anyone noticed. Sooner or later, I thought, and tried to imagine how long it would be possible to laugh about it, and what would be said after that.

But it does no harm. When I sit down it settles a little way off, sometimes out of sight. When I get up it's there behind me again. Does it want anything from me? Does it know anything? Whom is it obeying, and why? Will it ever say? Has it come to help, to betray, or simply—as one hopes—to please itself?

One gets used to things, and in the end one does not want them to go.

Where Laughter Came From

Laughter was the shape the darkness took around the first appearance of the light. That was its name then: The Shape The Darkness Took Around The First Appearance Of The Light.

The light still keeps trying to touch its lips. The lips of darkness.

The light's hand rises but the darkness is not there. Only laughter.

The Cliff Dance

It is dangerous to look back down the cliff. But the cliff above is invisible until it has been touched. Below, it can never be touched again, but at least it can be seen, however distorted from this angle.

And I must look at something besides the eternal clouds, their shadows, the wings that flash past like swords in the ceaseless battle that is only occasionally comprehensible. The cries, the cries! To think that I once cried like that, and gave it up for these hands, these words, this weight and this strangeness, from which everything is made, and knowledge emerges.

Looking down I hang in my own throat like a clapper in a bell. Oh let the hour not catch me at this, nor prayers, nor fires, nor funerals. Wind, stop and think. We are all trying to do something that is beyond us.

Below me, however the rock face changes, the pattern of the holes where I have clung to it repeats itself over and over, climbing. Out of the infinite patterns available to two arms, two legs, the same star has been discovered again and again, climbing. I see the story. From the foot-holes and hand-holes to which I will never return, life and death are pouring. From one a trickle of water. From one a beam of light. From one birds coming and going to feed their young at that height. From several a thread of smoke. From many a hollow sound, groaning and whistling. From many a splash of blood.

Steps of the dance.

I am dancing.

The Barriers

Often I would wake being told that I had never been asleep, that I
had seen every red light appearing in the darkness and had called
out in time to warn the driver in his ink-blue coat which I secretly
believed was black, and the black hat which he wore to some meet-
ings and to some funerals, and which smelled of cold. My warnings
jarred the three old women nodding on the velvet seats, admiring
their circumstances in the darkness, shivering from the cold, feeling
their brooches, and one or other of them, in the beginning, was sure
to say to the driver, and then to the others, "See, he hasn't been asleep."

I was sitting, in short pants, on top of the glove box, so that I had
to bend down to see out ahead and speak up when I spotted a red
light and often I would wake being told that I had never been asleep
but had heard every word of the driver's telling the three old women
in their hats like black wedding cakes that this was the best hour for
driving, when no one was on the roads. Now was when time could
be made. The darkest hour. The hour before the dawn. The psalmist's
hour. The hour for which we were all old enough. The hour of no
music. The hour of no birds. The hour of slate, of washed slate, of
slate rising washed and drying, in which we are rising, making time.
Often I would wake shivering and dropping forward and being told
that I had never been asleep and hearing how we had made some
time already, and peering ahead to see whether there were more
lights to be discovered, and seeing the shadow of the car rise up out
of the ditch like a kidnapper in clothes that had been given to him
and totter alongside on the bank, running to keep up with his peaked
cap, and pitch forward even so, and fall full length, face down into
the ditch once more, only to rise, over and over, as often I would
wake and be told, and see ahead of us the barriers striped black and
white, sometimes hung with yellow lights, but usually with none,
and I would speak up then too, but be greeted with silence.

Then we would turn, to the sound of slowing down, and the
barrier would veer beside us, flashing black and white, and the driver

would say that that was just one more reason to travel at that hour—because we were refreshed, which was all to the good, since there was always the unforeseen but we would make time even so. I did not know any name for the barriers. Each time that was the same. They appeared again and again, but when I spoke up saying that they were there, there was no answer until they were past. Then the driver would say something about the hour again and how we would make time even so.

Often I would wake being told that I had never been asleep, and the light was seeping into the sky, the shadow of the car had stopped rising and prowling and falling, the lights were growing faint and beginning to look naked, and the board fences painted in stripes of black and white were nowhere to be seen. Already they had been caught up into the gray. No one remembered them. No one wanted to refer to them. But I would wake having seen them, having never been asleep, while the old women lurched, time was still being made, and we went on toward day.

What Happened While They Were Away

The ——s (they were quite real, they are quite real, they were well-known in that section of ——, which is the name of the town, they were even what is known as respected, even very respected, and if I do not give their name it is not because I do not know it but because on the contrary they are terribly real, and they might be hurt. More important, they might sue me.) The ——s were supposed to be away for the summer. I say they were *supposed* to be away for the summer. And they were away for the summer, but someone had been left behind. He thought there never had been such an empty afternoon. There was not a flower in the parched garden. They had all been put away. There were no passers-by to greet, naturally, because every-body had heard that the ——s were away. In the vacant lot next door the dust had its own games, but he did not know anybody there. Everybody seemed to have changed. And the whole summer stretched ahead. Meanwhile the present was empty all the way up to the sky. And then he noticed that something seemed to have hap-pened to everything he could remember. It was no longer solid. He did not dare watch. Bitterly he turned his eyes away.

Those with stronger characters may disapprove. He felt he had no choice. He made his way down into the cellar. Mr. —— always said, "Are you sure you've locked the cellar door?" but he made his way down for all that. Oh the summer light through the cobwebs on the cellar windows, resting fondly on the faded labels of the endless cans of peas bought wholesale, years before, at a discount, and on the equally faded labels of numerous larger cans of sauerkraut, bought in bulk, years before, from an acquaintance, and on the labels, faded only at the ends of the boxes, of soap flakes, bought in quantity, years before, at a saving, from an advertisement, and on the yellowing labels of dark red jars containing home-made jams—their ink now turned the color of iodine, and their labels like turned-up eyes of people lying on their sides trying to remember. So! The cupboard doors were open. This was what happened when the ——s' backs were turned! Nothing seemed to be missing (though how could he tell?) but there were signs. A person had been there. Perhaps was still there! Yes, he could see: it was an old woman. There were her overshoes. She kept them out here. There was her umbrella. Old woman's umbrella. He was on the scent now. He listened, which of course he would have done well to do in the first place. From the inner room, the boiler room, he distinctly heard sounds coming—sounds repeated over and over, like the faint rasping of a broom on a hollow paving stone, but quicker. Like a broom in sand, but quicker. More like a quiet hooting, like someone breathing all the time through a tube. Of course he went in. But he went in slowly. So that his eyes would be able to set themselves down in the darkness in there without mishap.

But it was not as dark in there as he had expected it to be. It was the boiler and the coal bins that gave the impression that it would be dark. Beyond them the light was quite good considering that no one was at home. And there—he had been absolutely right—was the foot of an old woman's bed, with the shape of an old woman's feet under the old quilt. Sitting bolt upright in the bed, with her shawl around her shoulders, was a skeleton, and sitting on two bentwood chairs beside the bed, very close to her, with their backs to him, were two skinny men, shaking and making the sound that he had heard. He stood there, and they went on making the same sound. He could not tell whether they were laughing or crying. He edged around toward the light to get a better look, to see whether he could see any tears. (He remembered that was always the first thing to do.) When he got to where he could see their faces, which were very skinny indeed, he still could not see any tears. On the other hand he still was not sure whether they were laughing or crying. They never looked up, never seemed to notice him. They were gazing the whole time at the skeleton's face. It was awkward. With the ———s away. He was not quite sure what to do next. He was not sure how far his responsibility could be said to extend. He cleared his throat. Still the two skinny men paid no attention to him, sitting there with their hands on the edge of the bed, leaning forward to look into the skeleton's face. Well, in the end he went right up to one of them and said, "Excuse me," and started to feel his pulse (which he had finally remembered is always the next thing to do).

It was only then that the skinny man turned to look at him. The other went right on watching the skeleton.

"Excuse me," said someone, "but I only wanted to see if you were all right."

The skinny man just stared at him.

"The ———s are away, you know," someone said. Still no answer. The same blank stare. The other skinny man still paying no attention, and both of them still shaking and making that sound.

Then the one whose pulse was being felt stopped making the sound. He looked at someone. "It's too late," he said.

"Yes," someone agreed. The skinny man's pulse seemed weak and rapid.

"The ———s are away," the skinny man told him in a dazed voice. What he said came from a long way off. He went on. "So we made our way down here." There were signs that another person—yes, it was an old woman—had come down ahead of them. Appeared to have moved right in. They had seen her overshoes. Old woman's overshoes. And her umbrella. Old woman's umbrella. Though it had not been raining for weeks. Then they had heard a sound in the boiler room, like a sighing. So of course they had gone in. It was not as dark as they would have expected. And there she was, a very old woman lying in the bed. She had asked them what they wanted and they had told her that the ———s were away and that they had made their way down here. She had said that she knew that the ———s were away. Well, they had told her, they would go now and not disturb her. But then she had asked them not to go, please. Please not to go. So they had stood looking at her.

Then she had asked them whether they could see all right and they had told her that they could see fine, thank you. So she had told them to bring their chairs over by the bed. They didn't have any chairs but they had found two and brought them over to the bed and sat down beside her. Then she asked them again whether the light was all right and they said it was fine. And as soon as they said that she had sat bolt upright in bed, looking past them, and out of her eyes everything that she had ever seen had begun to flow in two almost identical films that ran down her face and over the bed and onto the floor and out the door, while they sat and watched and everything became clearer and clearer.

The Eight Cakes

At a given moment in your life eight cakes are being eaten.

The first is in the very country you are in. It is a blood-colored cupcake. It is being raised from a box, on a train, by someone who is used, at last, to your absence.

The second is in another country. It is stone-colored, but iced with nuts and cherries. It is being eaten in the dining room small as an infant greenhouse, though the meals in that family are taken in the unlit kitchen. Plants are standing everywhere, veiling the huge old radio and the piles of magazines. The cake is the first admission of pleasure in that house after the most recent of many deaths. You too have eaten cake from that table but you will not sit down in that room again.

The third is in a third country. It is pale yellow. It is stale. The mice are eating it, in the light of dawn, far above the wide silent water, while in the next room someone long close to you dreams again and again that you are lost.

The fourth is white. Two pieces of it are sitting on a marble table in a crowded tea-room and have not yet been touched by two greedy old ladies, both of whom you have known, who have not seen each other for years. Neither of them will give you a thought. Why should they?

The fifth is in the same country as the second. It is green. It is being eaten by an official whose face you cannot see. He is wearing a flat tie-clasp and no jacket over his nylon shirt. Beside the plate on his desk are documents relating unfavorably to you. He does not like the cake.

The sixth is chocolate. It is being eaten by a child sitting in a chair in which you learned the meaning of "venereal." But the child and you will never meet, and the chair, like the Bourbons, learned nothing.

The seventh is pink. You are eating it yourself out of politeness and boredom, among people who have provided it themselves and whom you will almost certainly never see again.

The eighth is dark purple. The hand that is cutting it drops the knife, and the hand's owner then thinks of you.

Humble Beginning

When he had learned how to kill his brother with a rock he learned how to use a rock to begin stairs. For both of which secrets he thanked the rock.

He considered the rock further. It had always been there keeping secret what it could do. It had never so much as hinted at what it had already done. Now it was keeping all of its other secrets. He fell on his knees facing it and touched it with his forehead, his eyes, his nose, his lips, his tongue, his ears.

He thought the rock had created him. He thought that.

The Smell of Cold Soup

You know at once that it is leaking in from some other part of your life to which your eyes, and indeed all your other senses, are closed. Is it from some sector or plane that you have forgotten? Is it, in that case, from somewhere that you have been? Or from somewhere that you have not been? And if you have not been there, why not? Out of neglect? If so, how dim and gloomy it must be there by now. Smell. The abandoned cobwebs sagging with dust and grease, stretching as far as you can see in every direction. Their dead weavers rocking among them. The cold is not the cold of winter, which contains the promise of spring.

This invisible cold soup is what is fed to the invisible prisoners. It is perfectly nourishing. They do not die in the present. They are dying elsewhere. But they would do that, after all, whatever they were fed.

Gray waves shiver through the cobwebs. It is the war. Even now attempts are being made to improve the lot of the prisoners. Far out of sight a bird, a large unidentified bird, tries to bring them news, tacking and wheeling among the webs, but he is caught and hangs with his neck broken. Yet they must not despair. It may have been a false bird, with false messages. From the same direction someone is running toward them, a tiny figure, waving, shouting, but nothing can be heard. Always one can tell that one of the senses has been shut off. Is it the only one?

Would the news mean anything to them by now?

One should not allow such a question to cross one's mind (a false bird again). You know from the smell of cold soup that they would still understand if you were to break through to them—as you could if you really cared enough—and tell them that whatever else happens we have not ceased to be ourselves, and that the war is still going on somewhere.

The Cheese Seller

Everything, they say, everything that ever exists even for a moment floats on the black lake, and there at each moment what is reflected is its opposite what is reflected is. This is one of the basic truths, without which existence itself would be impossible. How can that be? Opposite in what respect? In one single aspect of the thing? If the thing is upright, for instance, the reflection is upside down. Yes, that, I say, I can see. In two aspects? If the thing is moving from its right to its left, the reflection is moving from its left to its right. I say I can follow that too. In three aspects? If the thing is black the reflection is white. All right, I say, I can go that far (though I have a moment of wondering, "What if the thing had been blue?" and I could get lost there, because I never was much good at the more abstract forms of mathematics). If the thing is only a few years from its birth then the reflection, presumably, is only a few years from its death. Well, I say, but there must come a point at which just one too many aspects of a thing are reflected as their opposites, after which the reflection is no longer recognizable, seems to bear no conceivable relation to the thing. Why must such a point come? they ask. Because I cannot imagine it otherwise, I answer. That, they say, is why the lake is black.

And so somewhere on that dark surface is the cheese seller's opposite, the opposite of that moment a long time ago, and my opposite in it. And so instead of coming from the hospital, as we were doing, probably we are going to the hospital. We? Leave that out of it. Instead of there being someone there—no, I will keep to the cheese seller's place itself, the lake is black enough. If I was a child—no, I will leave myself out of it for the moment, if I can. Except that this time I am permitted to stay and listen to him, I am allowed to go with him (do I recognize him, do I recognize anything, do I know where I am?) through the upside-down door. We make our way up, walking on the ceiling. His voice must be the same, aha! Or is only its opposite to be heard echoing over the black surface? Well, I must assume that I know it. That my opposite knows it. And there we are,

I am listening to the opposite of the interrupted discourse—the un-interrupted discourse. Instead of lamenting the gradual disappearance of the no-longer appreciated cheeses out of the past, on each of which he once laid an affectionate hand, he is extolling the sudden emergence of the highly esteemed cheeses of the future, which are ranged around him on plates, from each of which his hand rises in turn like the cover of a chafing dish, to show that the plate is empty. Instead of my heart being variously oppressed by my heart being variously oppressed by the interruption, by not being allowed to listen, the interruption, by not being allowed to listen, by the neglect of the old cheeses one by one, it is variously delighted by the untroubled encomium, the prospect of—no, I will go on leaving myself out of it.

Well, you cannot do that forever, they say. You remember that the cheese seller himself is in the past.

Far in the past, I say, wondering why the recollection ever attracted me.

Therefore his opposite, they say, his opposite—

So I will come to him one day, I suppose. No, I say, it is only my opposite who will come to him. And will find him easily, it must be, in the midst of a time of untroubled happiness, and will share without misgivings his innocent pleasure in the ethereal delicacies of tomorrow. And later even the hospital room will be empty.

At this they say nothing. They are not even there. All by myself I remember the color of the lake which I cannot see.

A Lost Tribe

It has no name. Too many tribes have been lost and there are not enough names as it is. And in the days when names were lent to them the lost tribes never gave them back. The names were never heard of again. They have been lost as well. Somewhere the lost tribes unpack them when they halt to make camp in the evening, and later turn them over beside the fire, when they have eaten, and by the dying light ponder these now almost meaningless relics of an abandoned life. They put them away before they sleep. Worn smooth.

They have left us to die alone. They have left us the whole world to die in, alone. They have left each one of us. Some did not even wait until we were born. We did not even have a chance to watch them go. We did not even have a chance to say, "Go in peace" (for we would have said that) "and we will take care of your things until the day we die." What things? They left none. And what good would it have done to mention death? A thing which does not affect them. A place they will not know.

From each of us they have set out. Each of us has lost and lost, and the tribes, when we looked, had gone. There is no tracing them. They would be harder to follow than those war parties of the Tewas who shod themselves with discs so that pursuers would not know whether they had been coming or going, or than their neighbors whose tracks were erased by friendly ants. These tribes have neither enemies nor friends. And still they leave us. Whenever we have chosen, they were the other. There is no way of calling to them.

We have clung to promises. They have marched through the Promised Land again and again and not recognized it.

This evening one of the nameless ones, one of mine, I think, has come down through a pass in the ice somewhere. Oh their hymns of arrival, which I can never hear! Before them is an empty lake sur-rounded by snow. They eat in haste, then the fires are made to blaze up and once more they start to tell the story, beginning with the an-cestor, a shadow who came to a fork. At last they sleep. Tomorrow the snow will be unmarked. Tomorrow night they will not tell of this place. They will repeat the old story about a path, the story which by now is their home, and which they believe.

The Camel Moth

There is a moth so small that it can walk through the eye of any needle and look up at the arch overhead as at the ceiling of an enormous gateway. In this world it lives on the fur of camels. It burrows into the hair at the roots and lays its eggs. The larvae dig deeper into the roots and devour them, and from this nourishment each of them spins a length of thread, fastens one end to itself, passes the other end to a neighbor, and then falls asleep. In due course the hairs drop out and blow away over the desert, bearing with them the dormant banqueters. These can survive in a state of suspended animation for centuries, for millennia, for at least as long as the hair of a camel, in the desert climate, can resist the blandishments of decay. When a hair beaches at last on some appropriate shore the sleepers wake and emerge from the minute opening at their end. They come out very slowly, in single file, linked to each other by the silken strand which they had woven before they fell asleep. They are blind. They come forth in silence, a colorless caravan, bearing their colorless thread, as though through the eye of a needle. They enter the earth or any solid object on its surface and stitch their way into it farther and farther. The fabric of their unseen journeys holds the visible world together. And they move on slowly, searching, searching, until the odor of camel hatches them out all together, with eyes open on their heads, and eyes on their wings, and they fly off to their next living mountain.

They have existed far longer than their hosts. In the eons before camels came into being this same race of moths lived on other species that have vanished without a trace.

And even these moths are part of the kingdom and numbered among its servants. But a great while before they wake in heaven where there is no devouring and no change, the camels themselves will have vanished from this world and its riches, and will have emerged in the living tapestry of paradise, naked as their tongues.

Among Mutes

Even things divulge the form of their desires, if we could read their lips. Everything that is reflected in a window or a polished surface is being judged for its likeness to a glacier. Which may never have existed.

The Travel Figment

It is one of the many unacknowledged gifts of Hermes, the God of Delusion, to those images imprisoned behind their own eyes, men. He had to deal with them. He got to know them, in the manner of dealers. He watched them dragging their shadows in ignorance— those boneless black banners that were all that was left of their wings. He watched their blood groping through their brains like the ghost of an amputated limb, looking for the sea. He was moved— not by pity, of course, to which he is eternally immune, but by an impulse to elicit from mortals a fuller admiration of his own com- mand of distance, his grasp of the elements, his ability to transmit himself instantly from world to world. He was moved by vanity, of which he is one of the lavish princes. And by his own love of idleness —he thought he might make his missions easier, by making his activity more apparently comprehensible.

He gave men the idea of travel.

Before that they had simply travelled, transporting their limbs, just as they were, from place to place in answer to specific needs as they recognized them. Men moved heavily, in comparison with many of their forebears, or with him, for example, but they were going through an awkward phase. They were changing. Something which he did not take into account, but no matter—what is done is done. He gave them the idea of travel. Or rather he fished it out of their dreams and presented it to them like a new life, which in a way it is.

And it may be said that few men have ever travelled since. Not in the old manner, slow but honest. Slow but whole. The irrevocable gift worked its way between men's minds and their journeys, widen- ing the split. From then on even the possibility of actual simple travel receded into the past, and men staggered and sank under the influences of a new freedom balanced by a new slavery. Now they could envisage travelling—that was the freedom. They could sit or lie still, at home, and watch the ports fall astern, the waves part, the clouds slip from them; they could hear the shouting in outlandish marketplaces, and attend while the exotic streamed forward bowing to each of their senses. And they could summon in luminous detail the remotest places in which they had found themselves in the past. They could revisit them again and again. They could establish a living contact with them. They could evolve a conception of a coherent world in every part of which they could move freely. In their minds.

But by contrast what they referred to now as travel was a poor paralyzed state. Energetic vehicles containing their mortal limbs continued, it is true, to depart and arrive, reaching farther, providing greater comfort, assuring greater safety, realizing greater speed. But it became evident that all they were doing was killing distance, killing time, turning the one into the other and removing the corpses of both. Often the bodies of men were not even carried from one genuine place to another genuine place, but were merely hauled past the bodies of other men, between interchangeable settings. Meanwhile the individuals being transported saw an arrangement of objects moving, but they sat still. Everything that was rushing past them was outside them. Cut off from them, and cutting itself off from them farther and farther. It was displaying its unreality to the travellers, who were not there where it was, but inside themselves, sitting still, looking out. They could not touch what was passing—their "travel." Only rarely and confusedly could they be touched by it, by fragments of it, and often what they chose to mistake, in the poverty of the moment, for actual travel, was merely their sedentary contact with other travellers, strangers passing through a synchronous remoteness and absence. Almost the only occasions that from time to time restored reality to travel were those in which it was suddenly invaded by "accident"—by disaster, which is presided over by gods even greater than Hermes.

But once the travellers arrived, once they had again acquiesced to their unchanging circumstance, and had sat down in some room or other that would never move except to fall, then travel, the habitual figment, could embrace even those meaningless itineraries which they had just exhausted. And the solid walls around them, the local air, could be made to yield up all the experiences which the travellers might have had on their vacant journeys, and which in fact they may really have glimpsed, but not tasted, not believed, not made theirs, as they passed. Or those same soon-familiar walls might remove themselves entirely, making way once more for the unsubstantial places where the travellers now might be.

But the wish on which the travel figment was fed never forsook them. It was a wish that, in its true form, no god would have understood. If only, it kept saying, we could set out now, just as we are, and leave ourselves.

The Baptist's Singers

Each time the varnish of the carriage fills me with a profound but
unexpected delight such as rises from the sudden recollection of
something loved in childhood and long forgotten. The luster of the
varnish is so deep that it appears to have its own source of light,
which moves under the surface, approaches, fades, divides and
comes together and disappears according to a pleasure of its own.
The motions of the light bear witness to something in the nature of
the carriage, and to some appearances of the world that it passes, but
however closely they are watched, their play looks as though it were
independent of both. And I realize each time, when it is too late, that
the motions of the light in the varnish have so captivated me that I
cannot say with any certainty what color the varnish is. I know it is
dark. Some opalescent shade scarcely distinguished from black. But
not black. And on the side of the carriage, in an arc like a rainbow's,
are the words THE SINGERS, in blue letters edged with little flames
of green and gold, and under them is a painting of John the Baptist
standing thigh-deep in the sky-blue Jordan.

The horses are dark too, but not black, and their wine-red harness,
and the carriage itself, stream with white ribbons tied in little bows.

In the carriage the four singers face each other: two women, one
young and pale, the other with a darker complexion and heavy fea-
tures, both of them in the wide bonnets of another time, both of
them in long gloves, with which they hold their stringed instruments.
They are riding backwards. Across from them a portly man in a tall
hat and a ginger coat, and a boy in black velvet, are sitting, the boy
holding a flute. All four of them appear to be laughing merrily at
their own conversation. Their heads nod, but nothing can be heard.

The footman raises the long coach horn but if he blows it I can-
not hear it. The coachman in his dark coat drives on, slowly, and the
carriage moves on as smoothly as a barge. The blue wheels turn on
the glassy surface of the road, where rain has just fallen. The carriage
glides along on its reflection, the blue wheels spinning above and
below, making no mark where they touch, and then very slowly the

wheels begin to sink into their reflections. The rims disappear. The wheels above and below share a lost segment that grows like the rising of an invisible sun. And now the footman is surely blowing his long gleaming horn, but there is not a sound to be heard as the carriage sinks into itself, and the feet of John the Baptist meet, stand on each other, and are washed away, and the Jordan is swallowed up in the Jordan, and the singers in the singers. Only a piercing silence rises from both coach horns, and continues to echo long after they themselves are out of sight.

The Roofs

There are woods close to our village. Thin at the edges, but you can-
not see far into them. They are broken here and there by tracts of
empty plain that stretch all the way to the horizon. The birds that
approach and recede above the dark woods are not the same as those
that rise and dip over the treeless spaces between. The birds of the
woods reflect darkness. Those of the open ground flash like signals
of light. It is beyond these signals, across one of the tracts of open
country, to the east, that the roofs of the other village can be seen
above the horizon. Only the roofs—the steeples, the peaks of gables,
the smoke from chimneys. When the sun sets on our village the
roofs of the other are already a part of night.

No messages come from there. None are sent there. No one from
our village ever went there, or would admit to having gone. The very
subject is frowned upon, and the elders answer all questions about
the other village with an abrupt and unyielding silence. But it is only
the very young children who ever ask such questions, and they sel-
dom persist beyond the second or the third time. Then they begin to
wonder whether the roofs on the horizon are not something which
only they see. As for the idea of going to the other village, by the
time we can walk any such notion seems as remote from possibility
as does that of flying by flapping our arms.

But I dreamed of the other village. It was a dream that returned
at intervals over several years, always essentially the same, but always
in greater detail. Gradually I came to know the other village in those
dreams: the corners of lanes, the massive stone portals, the doors
open into courtyards, the smells of cow barns and of meals cooking
over fires fed with some unfamiliar wood, the backs of women van-
ishing into kitchen doors, leaving their fresh-hung laundry behind
them—it's true I never saw their faces. And I never heard anything as
I walked through the winding streets which at last joined each other
like sections of a jig-saw puzzle, forming an image through which I
could find my way from one place to another, with no blanks at all.
But only outside: I never saw the interiors of the houses, except for

an occasional glimpse through an open window of a fly on an empty table, or a plate standing on edge. Still, the image was as complete as any map, and once that was so I began to be possessed by a wish to visit the other village. I knew I could tell no one of this desire, and the sense of the folly of such a wish grew with the wish itself, but could not prevent it or even diminish it. I was appalled to find that I was beginning to lay plans.

There are no roads over the plain between our village and the other. And even if there were, how could I have set out to walk there in full view of my neighbors? I would have to take one of the paths into the woods, and then turn aside once I was out of sight, hoping that I would not lose my bearings. I would go in the morning, when every man in the village left for the day's work on some piece of land or other that belonged to him. I would leave earlier than the others so that I would not have to lie. I would carry an axe as though I were going to cut wood. As others would be doing, for it was August.

And from the path I turned north and made my way to the edge of the woods, where I could see both our village and the roofs of the other, and I started toward the roofs, keeping among the trees. I soon realized that the other village was much farther than I had grown to believe. I crossed broad hollows from which even the steeple was not visible. The sun was almost at the zenith when I came to the top of a gradual rise and saw in front of me, close at hand, the steeple, the gabled roofs, the smoking chimneys, down as far as I had always seen them, and below that point nothing. Air. The plain, going on, with birds flashing across it, in silence. The roofs did not even cast shadows on the ground.

It may be that I should have turned back then. But I walked on, down the long slope, and took my first step among the roofs. And my second. Looking up. I recognized where I was, from the dreams, though the walls of the first storeys, the doorways, the windows were not there, and I was walking on the unmarked plain. I passed the steeple. I looked up into its darkness and saw long ropes emerging from the black and then dissolving at the same height at which everything else dissolved, but swaying as though they ended far below. I reached out to see if I could feel a wall where I could see none; I walked on, that way, groping in the daylight, but I could feel nothing. In the dormer window of one of the largest houses I saw a face, in the shadow of a shawl, watching me. It turned away at once and I saw the shawl descending stairs, and then reappearing at another window, turning again, going down more stairs, coming—as I thought—to meet me. But the stairs never emerged below the horizon line, and I stood watching the empty windows. I wanted to call. What could I call? I waited a long time. Then I turned back. At the line of trees I looked around and the horizon had risen again to support the roofs.

But now it's my own village that eludes me. Suddenly I look up and above a certain line I see nothing but air, and through it, far away, the birds of the woods. Members of my own family climb stairs and vanish, headfirst, step by step, and I want to call, but what could I call? And night after night I am still staring up into darkness when the sun, no doubt, is already playing among the doors of the other village.

The Abyss

On occasions whose return—more and more frequent—obeys some law that I perceive only dimly, if at all, I open my eyes, and instead of the world where the days have names and belong to weeks, I see that I am really still hanging by my breath, high in space, with night already advanced and no prospect of a morning.

Here I am, tilted far forward as though I were swimming, yet I dare not risk a swimmer's gestures to his element. I hardly dare move at all. I ease my breath out, I draw it back cautiously. The slightest jar would dislodge me from here, where I am suspended. Then I would drop through the darkness as though a hand had let me go. For I am held up by nothing but a transparent film like the skin of a bubble, which stretches across the darkness from side to side. Above it my head. Below it everything else. It fits close around my breath, as long as I breathe in and out very slowly so as not to break the seal. And I am trying to move forward.

Below me, far below me, the light is a little clearer, but it is sealed away from my eyes, and only in that condition can it shine. After all, it is the same way with the filaments in bulbs. Below me a faint glow, made possible by the membrane in which I am hanging, cautiously looking down. There is a house I know, I am sure, there by the river like a line of paint, the vein of the valley. There's the little path behind it, climbing the ridge. I remember how it twists its way into the first high village, and arrives at the fountain. I must not follow it. I must not be drawn down from my breath. If the seal breaks, the bubble will vanish, and the lights will go out below as I begin to fall.

The film in which I am trying to move forward may be stretched from the horizons, but I cannot see that far. I catch reflections, at moments, from its surface, but whether from the upper or the lower side I cannot tell. It seems to be waving up and down very slowly, like sea swells in a calm, or like another breath. I see my body just beneath the film, like the limbs of a doll twin in a toy bath tub, there under the transparent surface. What can I do? I long to move forward. But I dare not reach out or grasp—there is nothing to grasp. I dare not call. To whom would I call? Silently, watching the shadowy valley rise and sink below me, I say to my breath once again, little breath come from in front of me, go away behind me, row me quietly now, as far as you can, for I am an abyss that I am trying to cross.

Knives

Around us hangs a curtain like rain. Around us, spirits of salt waiting for our griefs to release us. We cannot touch the curtain. It hangs in front of the days and nights, the sun and the earth. It wears us away but we believe we would be nothing without it. Or if not nothing, then naked. Our spirits scarcely speak. Could they pass through the curtain without us? Have we no others? We look out and see nothing, through the curtain, but uses.

We look at the knives, those gentle creatures, many of them older than we are. We see only the service we ask of them — separation, separation, and pain. Without which, as we say, we would be nothing. So we never see those meek faces themselves, moving in a world upon which they open no eyes at all, about which they know nothing, and of whose savageries they have become a symbol. They who eat nothing, who do not even defend themselves against the dew, against rust, against any of the bearers of loss, and who make no sound, except an occasional clear note like the calling of a bird, when they have been struck, or abraded with a stone. They who will obey any guide.

Through the curtain we look at them shining quietly on the wall and we are nudged by a vision of a bloody shore.

The Hours of a Bridge

When the black.

When the lamps fill, when the lamps empty. When a prayer. With no one praying it. Oh yes there is someone but they are hanging back, hanging back. All through the darkness. In the daytime they are nothing but a long gasp. When a prayer they let the prayer go ahead by itself and they hang back and become deserted. When a prayer again. No shoes running after it with a limp. Or is that the prayer? No stars. Above or below. And still long long before.

When a rat. When a flag. A long flag.

When the battle will cross. But that will be by its own light. Between the smug statues.

When the sins of the night, in a butcher's cart. The same cart that is used for the plagues. A dog painted on the side. A dog walking under it. Mist walking on each side. The wheels and the cart and the dogs and the mist and the sins all unaware of each other.

When the man with the red hood that looks black. Going home.

When the battle will cross again, coming back. When the statues will all become statues of the death of the air.

When the dawn's cat. Sits right down. By a coat, getting light.

When the coat is disturbed water runs out of it. Old water. Old old water.

But the best thing for us, we believe, is to go on for as long as we can, living upstream, tending our instruments by night. On the one bank.

Tracks

O summer-faced patience, how long you have waited, and nothing
must have seemed certain. But I know at last. I see that we will come
after all, you and I, to a white house at the top of a long street. It sits
there waiting for us, empty. Every morning the yellow sunlight
streams in through the windows which face out on the other side,
away from the street that climbs the hill, just as it will stream in on
the morning when we will be shown into the house, through the
bright airy rooms, with my mother patting the cushions, opening the
big cupboards, my father fingering the cord of a blind at a shining
window, everyone brimming with recent knowledge, with revelation,
with arrival, with peace. The house stands in a row with several others
along the top of the hill. It is quiet up there: no traffic, no sounds
from the other houses when the windows are opened and the spring
air flows in. On the other side of the house—the front—the railroad
track runs past the door, as in so many of the towns through which
the history of my family has been threaded. But here the track—a
single line—gives off silence. It is beginning to rust, even though it is
almost new. Grass is starting to grow between the ties. Beyond the
track the cliff falls away abruptly. It is a sheer drop of several hun-
dred feet, and at the bottom the details of the landscape emerge only
partially, here and there, from the gray mist.

In front of the porch, in the middle of the tracks, an upright stake
of angle-iron is fixed into the crushed rock of the road-bed; it is
painted black and yellow; other stakes of the same kind can be seen
at intervals, every few ties, for some fifty feet in either direction. The
tracks are not to be used. No trains will pass the house, making it
tremble. My father will lead me—as he has never done—across the
tracks themselves, as though they belonged to the family at last. He
will point to the bends in either direction and explain that although
trains might conceivably come that far still, they would not continue.
Just the same, he will show me the source of his worry: the place
almost across from the house, where the tracks ran until recently

when the top of the cliff gave way under a coal train and the loco-motive and the cars poured like an iron waterfall onto the misty rocks far below. It will seem, as he tells it, as though echoes of the crash were still rising from the gray valley. The new tracks have been set farther back from the edge, and blocked with painted spikes on which the paint is kept fresh, and my father knows and approves of the man in charge, and for the time being no trains will come past the bends, but my father's worry will not sleep. In a low voice, so that no one else will hear, in a few words, he will let me know his fear that the edge of the cliff will continue to collapse. At some hour when we do not expect it the new tracks will sag and snap and swing down over nothing, as though through water, groping, and the house will plunge after them, shrieking and ripping, into the gray abyss. He will inform me that none of the houses on either side is lived in at present.

But I will laugh and say that his fears are exaggerated, that what the place needs is to have us living in it, us, with what we know now, with the sunlight and its welcome, with the sense that the house is ours and has been waiting for us, and that no evil can befall us there. I will tell him all that, quietly, calmly, smiling, as to a child, and with-out believing a word I say.

Memorials

One after the other, if they are not wholly lost, our intentions, unless they started that way, turn into legends. On the other side of their effects we walk on, thinking we know. And they, whom we continue to address and refer to as though their presence were something that we understood perfectly and could take for granted, leave us without our so much as noticing. Yes, sometimes most of them will be gone at a time, while our activities continue without them. And then they will return across great distances, like the influences of planets, and even when they are reborn in something very like the old forms it is probable that we will not recognize them, any more than we did the last time. It is this aspect of existence that—without our meaning it —our monuments commemorate.

After each war the men from the memorial companies tour the little towns. On their arrival the custodians of the locally accepted intentions welcome them. These neighborhood officials, thoroughly rehearsed, impress themselves once again, in a manner that has acquired its own rough ritual, with the superstitions that they now believe were the intentions (including their own) underlying the recent conflict, and with the feelings which, in consequence, they had encouraged themselves to profess. They are scrupulously mindful of what they take to be the intentions of their neighbors, hereby to be commemorated—the grief of widows and bereaved mothers, the proud and vengeful wrath of fathers, the as yet undeveloped but indubitable gratitude of children. Insofar as their combined means will allow—and this is not something over which any of them would wish to be sparing, or would admit to such a wish if he felt it—they want an object that will express all of these things clearly, changelessly, and in perpetuity. In this spirit they approach the latest catalogues.

Also they have piously in mind what they take to have been the intentions of the young men who went away and died. Quite as much—more so—than the actual features of their faces (though they have not ruled out a hope, of course, of finding a happy resemblance, and with this in view, rather than trust their pathetic memories they come provided with photographs collected from the bereaved but supposedly proud households). Furthermore, the intentions with which these youths are presumed to have faced the fatal conflict, or confronted death itself when it stood before them, must also be represented. The catalogues are limited, naturally, and such individual matters are now beyond verification. Something at last is chosen which is felt to be, within the practical limitations, suitably sad and suitably noble, to commemorate all of these fictions.

And the result, for heaven knows how many years afterwards, graces the little square in all weathers, with the names on its base and the war in which they were called meaning less and less to more and more people. Familiarity and the symmetry of its surroundings before long set about making the object itself grow dim. What it evokes, in a while, to many of those who see it, both natives and strangers, is the boredom of the square, the elusiveness of meaning, the anonymity in which the names, even of the living, are ghosts, the delusions of others, at times even a shifty levity, and at times an uncomprehended and unmentioned fear.

The Permanent Collection

In a rich provincial city there is a museum as imposing and quite as
large as any in the capital. The facade is immense and the portico
dwarfs the visitor, seeming to fill the space between his usual size
and his shrunken self with an echo. The style of the building is not
obviously contemporary, though it could have been produced by no
other age. It manages to suggest, with its general proportions, high
columned halls, and open airy courts surrounded by enormous
arcades, an entire classical tradition in which temple and palace are
never completely distinguishable from each other. The approach to
the building is lined on either side with marble pedestals, each of
them empty. Across the top of the main portal there is a large panel
for a name or inscription. It is blank.

The museum is referred to, in the literature supplied by the
chamber of commerce, as The Permanent Collection—the gift of
an anonymous donor. The terms of the donor's will stipulated that
there should be no other designation. But publications for which the
city administration cannot be held accountable reveal that the mu-
seum was the bequest of a local millionaire whose forebears, through
several generations, had played a dominant role in the exploitation
of that region. The name is common in those parts, on streets, banks,
office buildings, bridges, housing developments, foundations. But
the family—at least the direct line for which these have all been
named—has died out. The last of the line was the builder and donor
of the museum.

In his youth, according to the local historians, he had fallen in
love with the daughter of another wealthy household, at a northern
resort where both dynasties had summer houses. Only one portrait
of her is known to have survived. It shows the girl at the time when
they first met—already beautiful: slender, dark-haired, her expres-
sion gentle, delicate, remote. She had pretended not to notice his
early, clumsy suit. During the first winters her name was coupled
with one boy after another from the same schools which he at-
tended. But one summer, perhaps out of mere indolence, she had

paid him more attention, or at least had spent more time in his company than before, and their families had come to take the relation between them for granted—though neither of the young people did so. They were spoken of for a winter or so almost as though they were engaged. Between the assumption, which he met on all hands, of his future with her, and the secret barrenness of his hopes, he became aware of an abyss that would swallow everything he knew.

During college he had seen as much as possible of a succession of other girls. He had even formed attachments with several of them, lasting for a matter of months. But she was the one whom he tried not to want, and the longing for her grew with him. He proposed to her before he left college and she listened to him quietly and told him she wanted to wait. Then she had gone abroad with her family and he was not surprised when, shortly after their return, he received an announcement of her engagement to someone else.

They had continued to see each other, occasionally. She had had a daughter. He too had married—twice, once hilariously, both times disastrously. He had had no children.

Her marriage too had ended in divorce, after fifteen years. Her husband spent his summers on his own estate, and her daughter was sent to be with him in June. She herself had returned to visit her family, in the northern resort. There she had seen her former suitor again. There had been a second courtship, to which he deliberately imparted an air of casual urbanity that was as contrived—on his part—as the stillness of the breath above a trigger-finger. It worked. They were married during the following winter. Nothing is known of their life together. Outwardly it was placid. She died a year later, while swimming.

The entrance to the museum is guarded by wardens in plain dark uniforms without metal buttons or insignia of any kind. Inside the main portal is a vast hall, with another marble pedestal in the center, catching the light. It is empty, like those outside. In the walls on either side are tall niches, also containing nothing. Guards in the same featureless uniforms stand in pairs at each doorway, and at intervals along the corridors and in the arcades. There is a prescribed order for visiting the rooms, and the guards point the way. And in each room there are more of the large pedestals, without statues or names. In some, besides, there are glass display cases, of different shapes and sizes, empty, and picture frames containing blank canvas on the walls. All along the arcades there are empty niches and pedestals, alternating, and in each of the courtyards there is an empty fountain. No one talks. It takes well over an hour to make the tour of the rooms and step out into the world again on the same side as the entrance but farther along. From there one leaves by another walk flanked by empty pedestals. The donor lived to see the building completed, but the public was admitted only after his death.

Why did he want the visitors at all? Could he have foreseen those who come out from the building with a sigh of relief and a joke, or with a burst of indignation at the abuse of wealth or at the enormity of his egoism or with a yawn, a glance at a watch, a suggestion about eating? Could he have foreseen those who emerge from time to time in silence, with their faces shining?

The June Couple

If we could afford it, he says, we have often said that we would have a little place beside the water. He enjoys saying *little place* even more than *beside the water. Beside the water* comes to him like an old pleasure which is becoming increasingly a matter of memory. The water is forever darkening. It always seems farther away. By now it might be dark glass. With artificial reeds growing through it, and life-like ducks among them. But *little place* announces his firm hold on the world of men, and his aspirations in it, even those he would not otherwise admit to.

Yes, she says, we've imagined from the beginning how we'd love to have a place of our own somewhere by the water. When she says *from the beginning* she can actually feel the air near the water, and the water itself, which is only slightly cooler, and moving slowly, a quiet stream passing through a meadow under old trees.

One day maybe we'll take a house by a lake, he says. *One day maybe. Take a small house.* By the age at which he imagined such a thing might be possible he would phrase the suggestion with a wink.

She sighs and says, it was one of the first things we realized we agreed about. We love to imagine standing watching the water flow quietly by.

Needn't be anything elaborate, he says. A simple cottage, after all. Envisaging a lake-side construction covered with tan imitation-brick shingle, with a screened porch all along each end.

It's all I ever want, she says. Her eye filling, as so often, with a picture of a low stone building, one tiny dormer in its thatch roof open toward the breathing sounds of the trees over the stream. And there they both stand, between the door and the water, on the soft grass, with a family of ducks threading past them, and her cat at her feet. Her husband is wearing a top hat and a white dress uniform with gold frogs and she is most becomingly dressed as a shepherdess. Both of them in Sevres.

He sees them standing outside the screen-porch to be photographed.

No one is watching. Her parents are out. She puts her tongue (as she has been strictly forbidden to do) to both of the figures. It is just as she had imagined. Sugar. Like all secrets. The cottage is sugar too, and the pink and white clouds. And at the edge of the sky, beyond the little crooked fence, there is a round window with little roses all around it, and an eye filling the whole window.

Yes, he says, looking out over the first few feet of still water, at the black camera occupying the middle foreground, with the sun on its shoulder. He has recognized the eye filling the whole of the lens.

Yes, he says proudly. Mine.

Yes, she sighs, in utter agreement, recognizing the eye filling the window at the end of the sugar sky. Mine.

The Wives of the Shipbreakers

No. The wives of the new shipbreakers. The distinction must be made at once, and they help to make it. They do more than help. Properly observed, they would be enough by themselves to make the distinction clear. To make it clear, first, and in a short time to make it seem inevitable. Is this surprising, after all? It certainly does not surprise everyone. There were cool heads that foresaw it in the earliest stages of the planning, and among them were those who urged most insistently that the new shipbreakers should remain celibate. But irony triumphed, and they were overruled on the ill-defined grounds of humanity.

It might almost be said that the distinction, in some sense, is made clear only by the wives of the new shipbreakers. The new shipbreakers themselves, after all, are never seen by the world at large. It is scarcely just to reproach their wives for keeping together, as they tend to do. Yet some people naturally resent any such behavior in others, since it bespeaks a secret—something in the order of a different language, sometimes a pain from which those who watch are excluded. And everything from which they are excluded and to which others cling they suspect of being a privilege, a real one, which reminds them that their own (which they praise and defend, therefore, with new fierceness) are substitutes.

It may be that the wives of the new shipbreakers do, in fact, keep together more exclusively than is necessary. But how can we judge? What do we know of their reasons, of the persistency and discomfort of their need on the one hand to remain apart from all who do not share the peculiar knowledge and questions of their existence, and on the other to seek what reassurance may be found in the company of those who may be called their colleagues? Some of their neighbors even find grounds for resentment in the fact that all of the wives of the new shipbreakers may be presumed to be in their present condition voluntarily. A few of them married new shipbreakers after the men had decided to enter upon that irrevocable calling. Others had been free (as the neighbors put it) to leave their husbands, if they could not dissuade them, when the men first suggested such employment. It is interesting that very few observers imagine that the extra pay, in itself, could provide the incentive for either the husbands or the wives to embrace such a decision.

It is already possible to recognize one of the wives when she is alone on the street. The complexion, for one thing. No worse, perhaps, than that of many of her compatriots. But as though it had already abandoned the wish to remain skin. A glimpse of earth under artificial light. Then the jaundiced eyes. The teeth, thinning, appearing translucent, flaking. The nails, easily chipped and split. A slackness in the thin legs. Without exception the wives smoke heavily. Pregnancy is rare and so far has miscarried in every instance, though in theory there is no reason why childbirth should not be possible. It is too early to tell—or to predict the effects on any eventual offspring.

Remember that the vocation of the new shipbreakers is not surrounded with honor. Rather, their practice is shrouded, and mention of it slurred over in public. The new shipbreakers themselves are allowed to know only a little about what they are called upon to do. And yet some sleepless attraction, some consuming exhilaration or unspeakable contentment, the furthest reflections of which remain an exasperation to many who presumably benefit by it, day by day causes the profession to grow. As it must, while the new ships in increasing numbers continue to return.

From a Mammon Card

Those who work, as they say, for a living, are not to calculate how much they make an hour and then consider what they claim to own, remembering that there was a time when they made less per hour, and then consider that what they claim to own is perhaps all that remains of what they sold that many hours of their life for, and then try to imagine the hours coming again.

The Uncle

Yes, but to fall heir in the middle of some night to this huge blistered
edifice with its once-white clapboard here and there swinging loose
in the ceaseless wind of the prairie and knocking on the walls like
boats. And so to wake one morning in front of a box-shaped facade
facing north on the edge of a small town, with a broad level expanse
of cinders in front of it where trucks could pull in, where the tracks
of a long-disused trolley line still run, where puddles are spread out
like a cold day's laundry, and the weeds are moving in. To stand in
front of it under its own unrepeatable clouds and to hear the silence
coming from the building coming from the building coming from
the building as a whole and dwarfing the voices of the local worthies
in their darkest suits emerging ahead of you and around you from
their dark cars drawn up on the edge of the cinders as on the edge of
a beach. The silence coming from the building and drowning the
notes of their car doors slamming, of their affable weightless ex-
changes. The tones of undifferentiated and unexamined respect with
which they approach, continuing explanations of a life that is theirs
but which they persist in describing as though it were a complex
habit which you must surely remember, suddenly, and embrace with
joyful tears, and resume. Their behavior is not all of a piece. The
manner which they present to you matches the dark clothes and gray
faces with rimless spectacles which they have worn for this solemn
but singular occasion, but the side of each of them that is turned
away from you might well be wearing gaudy sport clothes of some
shiny synthetic, which they flash at their clambakes as they spill their
beer. It is no surprise that a pair of them, brothers, furniture whole-
salers and retailers, prove to be also the leading funeral directors,
who had supervised the elaborate ceremonies surrounding the final
disposition of your uncle's remains, details of which they keep relay-
ing to you with unfeigned pride as you proceed together across the
cinders toward the building. They assure you that nothing that
might conceivably have been done had been neglected. That your
uncle's wishes, with which they had been thoroughly familiar, had

162

been respected to the letter and indeed far beyond it, far beyond it. That not one of the orders, lodges, fraternities and civic organizations which your uncle had served so selflessly, so unforgettably, and with such distinction in his lifetime (every one of which was represented by some member of the deputation here this morning) had failed to contribute to the memorial services, each with its own most solemn rites and honors and with the presence of all of its most sacred panoplies and paraphernalia, to say nothing of the wreaths. Never in the memory of the town had there been such a show. The attorney and his assistant walk along with the funeral brothers, and the rest take their tone from these.

And in this company to approach the porch running all the way along the front of the building, its gray-painted floor raised only a few inches above the cinders, its high roof sagging just a little between each of the slender iron uprights topped with its cast pineapple still bearing the vertical ridges of the mold. To hear the feet, one by one, step onto the hollow porch, not without a certain ephemeral reverence despite their familiarity with the place, and to recognize in that momentary unaccustomed self-consciousness and restraint the influence of the period between that moment and the removal of the uncle's body—an interim during which the building had stood alone like a tomb. To notice that all the windows had been whitened from inside.

Then to watch the attorney step to the door, face the others, draw from two pockets his black kid gloves, deliberately put them on, smoothing one finger at a time, draw from a third pocket the will, open it to the relevant page, re-read the passage relating to the building, the land around it, and all their contents, then draw from still another pocket a pair of scissors with which he cuts the black ribbon stretched across the door from side to side and sealing it shut. Whereupon his assistant produces the key to the door and one by one you enter.

To see the enormous center hall with its cobwebbed ceiling. To glance, in passing, into the dusty wooden caverns of the flour mill, through a door to the left, and the corresponding caverns where the sacks were piled, through a door on the right, and into offices beyond, observing the shrouded machines and closed roll-top desks in each. To climb, in that black-suited company, the cobwebbed unpainted

stairs with their oft-repaired banisters, and find those who had pre-
ceded you drawn up in front of another ribboned door, named for
one of the local lodges, and to watch the representative of that lodge
take a pair of scissors from his pocket and cut the ribbon and produce
a key and show you a room with some flags standing in a corner,
chairs folded along one wall, and a paper bell hanging from the light
globe. To have that ritual repeated in room after room of that wind-
ing hall, to a continuo of coughs, shuffling feet, wheezing, whispers,
smothered laughs. To be shown a door marked with a sign saying
LADIES and to see it opened to display a wall covered with pages of
ancient fashion magazines and piles of boxes.

To accompany the representatives of the lodges and orders to the
top of the stairs and thank each in turn and shake his hand, and re-
turn with the attorney and the funeral brothers to a ladder fixed to
the wall and climb with them through a trap door to the living
quarters above. There to see the immense front bedroom with its
shrouded bed the color of dust, its faded green Chinese rug, its massive
furniture from the days of the famous blizzards, its gray water-light.
The long dining-room, along the east, with its draped table double-
ended like a ferry, and its dark ceiling over the china cabinets and
the mirrored mantelpiece, on which a black marble clock had
stopped promptly at two. To emerge at last in the sanctum itself—
the room at the back of the building, facing south, with its wooden
ceiling and heavy square table, and its roll-top desk by a dusty window,
and its tiers of shelves lined with books and ledgers, and its dirty
coffee cup. Here to be given the keys, to be given the papers, to be
given all the addresses, to be given all the written instructions, to be
shown the safe, to be given the combination, to be shown the little
stained bathroom, to be shown the door to the back stairs leading
down to the mill and the loading platform and the siding, visible
from one window, on which a few empty freight cars are still standing.
To notice, instead of listening, the patterned glass of the lamp-shades.
To be shown the uncle's diplomas, honors, citations, framed on the
walls, and to be left alone at last in that room, looking out of one of
the dusty south windows, onto the black-rimmed arm of the lake,
the color of steel, in which black barges are sinking all the way to the
horizon. A window at which your uncle (on your mother's side) had

stood often, imagining the heir who would never know him, who would enter at last, and stand there alone, looking out, thinking of him. It makes you wonder which of you has died.

The Approved

This one I was allowed to know. His face was a triangle standing on its point, hiding a parade of hollows. He was allowed to know other schoolfellows. And I was allowed to know him. Sometimes we pretended to a liking which neither of us felt, because it was approved. But no one could walk far on that surface.

He was respectable. At that age. His conduct at school was indeed better than mine, who was allowed to know only him. I with my one-legged japes, ill-timed, the delight of no one, like irrelevant misquotations from a foreign language. Little shames for which I was not otherwise punished because of some undefinable privilege that hedged me around, like a correspondence between a parent and the authorities, which is a great pointer of fingers. But he made no awkward sallies, played the games, was not considered the most cowardly, in fact excelled at catching a ball, and in class answered as well as I did, with the hollows prompting him.

For he too had a source of privilege. It was not his mother alone, who worked all day at a notions counter, suffered with her feet, and heaved herself up on Sundays in the choir to take solo parts in the anthems, her voice like an empty powder box. She was married to his privilege, she was its daughter as well, and while I knew her she became its mother.

I was allowed to visit their house. He was allowed to go where he pleased and I was allowed to visit him in the dark sagging unpainted building smelling of cats, where the grandmother sat in the kitchen year after year, clutching herself and crying, clinging to the privilege. For they were Death's family. No one contested it. Death visited other dwellings in other streets but that was all in a day's work, and he came back to them to sleep.

Death was the grandmother's father, born in the old country, and she clung to him and showed his picture and told of the food he liked and of how he missed his home. Then Death was the grandmother's husband, also born in the old country, and she showed his picture, so like the other, one man at two different ages, both of them clearly

Death, both of them forms of the same presence, the same exaltation. It had brought the old country with it, a weight in a locked trunk on its back, and at night it stretched its legs in the house and the windows rattled and the cats clawed silently at the doors. And Death was the mother's husband, as she had not understood until too late. She never showed his picture. She brought up his two sons and struggled to turn them into repetitions of him. And so it transpired with the elder, who of the two seemed less like him, but who was still a child when he lay in Death's bed like his father and his grandfather and all the other males of the family except the one whom I was allowed to know, and the privilege washed over him like an arm of the sea. In Death's room in which he himself had reverently suspended from the ceiling the paper airplanes which he had made with tireless care. They turned slowly above him—pieces of his memory. In Death's room with its pictures of Death at all ages, and its lace from the old country, and its gray wallpaper.

I was allowed to know the youngest because it was a nice family. And because of the privilege. Sometimes we imagined that we liked each other, because it was approved. But we never came to trust each other, to laugh, to be content. He was not Death, but one of Death's only sons.

A Garden

You are a garden into which a bomb once fell and did not explode,
during a war that happened before you can remember. It came down
at night. It screamed, but there were so many screams. It was heard,
but it was forgotten. It buried itself. It was searched for but it was
given up. So much else had been buried alive.

Other bombs fell near it and exploded. You grew older. It slept
among the roots of your trees, which fell around it like nets around a
fish that supposedly had long since become extinct. In you the rain
fell. In your earth the water found the dark egg with its little wings
and inquired, but receiving no answer made camp beside it as beside
the lightless stones. The ants came to decorate it with their tunnels.
In time the grubs slept, leaning against it, and hatched out, hard and
iridescent, and climbed away. You grew older, learning from the days
and nights.

The tines of forks struck at it from above, and probed, in igno-
rance. You suffered. You suffer. You renew yourself. Friends gather
and are made to feel at home. Babies are left, in their carriages, in
your quiet shade. Children play on your grass and lovers lie there in
the summer evenings. You grow older, with your seasons. You have
become a haven. And one day when a child has been playing in you
all afternoon, the pressure of a root or the nose of a mouse or the
sleepless hunger of rust will be enough, suddenly, to obliterate all
these years of peace, leaving in your place nothing but a crater rapidly
filling with time. Then in vain will they look for your reason.

The Bandage

They told you, remember, that one day it would come to seem natural. And so it has. You have forgotten their saying it, perhaps, because they were right—the bandage has become so natural to you that you have forgotten its presence. Never notice it. Never realize that your first question, upon waking, is whether it has slipped. Whether it has slipped, you see, not whether it is there. And you know with the lightest of touches whether or not it has slipped, wherever it may be at that moment. You know it even though the bandage wraps a different place every day. That doesn't confuse you. And it doesn't lead you to ponder the shifts of misfortune. No, a slipped bandage is a slipped bandage, wherever it is to be found on waking. It belongs where it is, only more securely.

Yesterday on a leg, today on an ear or an eye—on whatever surface or appendage of your anatomy it is performing its office when you wake, you remember why it is there. And you remember also enough of the accident so that you know you don't want to think of what the bandage mercifully conceals, so that you would never peer under the bandage at the black landscape sunk in its fate. You recall with a lurch of nausea how it happened, what you did wrong. You always think of that when it's too late. Only the bandage, now, can help to make things right—or as right as they can be. Better than before, sometimes, as you know. Whatever the bandage cradles you will have to try to use again as soon as you can, just as you did before. The thought appalls you. The broken, appalled by thoughts of the whole. But every day another part of you reappears, is restored to you again almost as it was, and you never notice. You take it for granted. You forget which limb it was. You grope, delicately, breathlessly, not for the scar, but for the bandage. Where are you? You murmur. How is it with you? And with fingers perfected in humility you tighten it so that you can begin the day.

The Diver's Vision

Every season we who have his welfare at heart say again that the champion diver should retire while he is unbeaten. It would be terrible to see someone younger come along and—

Though it is impossible to conceive of anyone else approaching him in one respect. At the top of his dive. At the top of his dive he stops. The rest of his diving is superb but is clearly within the province of what flesh and blood can accomplish, given exceptional physical gifts and the best training. But at the top of his dive he seems no longer to be one of us. So we honor him. And we hope that we will be able to go on doing so. But each season we are afraid.

The top of his dive seems no less miraculous now that he has explained it. When he reaches that point he looks down. On the water far below him he sees the little slick where he will enter it. A shifting apparition, its edges tattered and melting in a slow film of colorless flames. He waits, hanging in the air, staring down at it, and beholds his own face appear as a veil in the middle of that bit of surface. His own face shifting, tattered and melting, but clearly his, and at moments filled with a blinding radiance that always seems to belong to an instant just past or just about to occur, rather than to the present. Still he waits, and then around the face he catches a glimpse of a perspective which he can never describe afterwards, a landscape leading into other worlds, their love, their silence, the sight of it filling him with a tenderness sudden as lightning, and with a joy that would turn to terror unless he moved at once toward his vision. And so he falls. And as he does it disappears. It fades from his eyes, from his lungs. Not altogether from his memory. Not so completely that he does not know that it will be waiting for him the next time, however the interval is measured.

He will not retire because secretly he wants to go on until the day when he finds in himself the power to hang there at the top of his dive while the terror comes and goes. And then, he believes, the veil of his face will vanish but the vision beyond it will wait for him, clear and unwavering, at least as long as he falls.

The Clover

Well, I would say at last, when I had come in from that day's mountain, I will go out now and mow a little patch of that clover, this evening, for the beast. And I would take my scythe and sharpen it, with a sound like the strokes of a dissolving bell. At that hour the heat would have begun to leave the air. The shadows would have groped a long way toward the ruined east. A coolness would be seeping through the stems of the clover, near the ground at first, but beginning to rise. The moles would have heard it. The mice would be running through it, small gray teeth from no combs. And the leaves themselves would be starting to put aside the gray mask they turn to the sun. They would be rising like green skies, each stamped with one print of the same horse, each marked with a single broken orbit, each mourning a short-lived star. The dew would have just begun to come home to them from the sky, where it had been hiding. Well, I would say after a while, I will go out and cut an armload of that good clover for the beast.

The beast would watch me sharpening the scythe by the water trough, in whose surface the first lamp was not yet lit. It would watch me take down from the peg the folded square of old sacking for carrying home the clover. I would look at the eyes of the beast and see that the night was already there, and I would go out, with the folded sacking on my shoulder and the gray blade glinting.

And there would be the clover, stretching before me, the nation of shadow. I would go along the mossed wall to the stone gate and step through into the field. And step into the secret breathing of the clover, with my scythe. And there, the patch that I had thought to mow, the same, the very patch that I had seen in the late day of my mind—someone would have mown it before me. Someone would have already mown it. The same scythe-shaped segment, the same broken orbit, the same silent smile. Someone else had come and made them. And taken that clover. I would stand there in the little sudden breeze of twilight like a third gate-post. And no one would come. No one would pass. No one would tell me anything.

Evening after evening it would happen and at first I would cut some other place—what I had thought of as some other evening's clover, or I would take something else back for the beast. To no purpose. What I put in the manger was never touched. I watched the beast carefully, the deep fireless eyes, the nose like a rock out of a waterfall. Nothing seemed wrong. The breath as sweet as ever, the movements as placid, the coat as smooth. The udder as heavy, or heavier. I would pull up the three-legged stool and start milking. At the time I was living on little but that milk. And it was as sweet and rich and plentiful as ever. Who was feeding the beast? And better than I?

When I had drunk I would lean back in the straw, against the wall by the door, and watch my own thin blade set behind me, in the shadow. I would sit and watch the black clover growing in the sky. I would watch.

An Awakening

All day the wintry sun had hung in the same place. It went out slowly, there behind its curtains. It was gone then, and I was on the hill just as so often before, walking on, and nothing had changed. A gradual climb but a long one. Lit by memory, at that hour: the gray visibility addressing me from little stones, from the tracks of the road, from the bushes and trees holding themselves up like newspapers being read from the other side.

How many days had I been on the way there? How many days since the last time? Far be it from me to pretend I could answer. Far be it from me, I might have said, to pretend to measure the present in terms of the recurring past, but such a reply might not have been acceptable. Fortunately those questions were not put. No, but it was not to be as I remembered it. I could see that before I had gone far at all. Not something new, then, but something that I was only this time coming to see, though it had been there all the time. It must have been there, now that I consider it, and I must have stared at it again and again; gazed—with vacant eyes. No use reproaching myself: our time had come and it was beginning to appear to me at last. Like the lighting of a light. Three lights. Three figures coming toward me, stepping down, with baskets on their shoulders.

The first was a child with a basket of leaves. Gold light rose from them like the glow of a lantern, and as silent. The swarming leaves stirred as they rode, and the light rose out of them like breath. And the boy must have been there whenever I had been. Perhaps even before me, to judge by his clothes, which looked like those of boys in paintings from before my grandfather was born.

The next was a man with a basket of apples that gave off the same light. To think that I could have seen him and seen him (his clothes too from a generation long before mine) and never known. Perhaps because the glow from his basket was hard to distinguish from the fire in the sky behind him as he stepped toward me.

The last was an old man—how could I have missed such evidence of years combined with such strength? He was the tallest of the three, dressed for Sunday, and carrying a basket full of flames. Far down among them I could see a face lying. It would have been looking upward if its eyes had been open. Even among the flames its color still showed something of the old memory-gray. It might have been my own face which until then had seen nothing, being borne away.

When I looked up the night was over. There beside the road, as the sky whitened, I could make out the three baskets. No one was carrying them. A little smoke rose out of each of them. And a faint singing, dying away. In the smoke of the last basket I could see the same face, with its eyes closed, that had been lying in the flames. Its lips now were forming words to the song, but I could not make them out, though I drew close, and put my ear to the smoke, and shut my eyes. When I opened them to see where the music had gone, because I wanted to keep it, and form the words to it, there was the pale sun once more hanging in a new place, for it will not be winter forever.

The Egg

Filled with joyful longing I ran across the echoing flagstone terrace and down the broad dressed-stone steps, gradual as a beach, patterned with frost. The sky was an immeasurable shell of shadow. The darkness of the mid-winter season, when the sun never rises but the land never goes out entirely, lay ahead of me, and the empty plains, with thoughts rising out of the sleeping snow, turning to look, reeling, running a few steps, falling again. Far beyond them, the Orphans' Gate. I carried the egg in my left hand, inside the glove, keeping it warm. It meant that I had only one hand to do everything. To hold on. To wave. To fight. To balance. It meant that I would have to let one thing go before I could take up another. I had given up half of myself to hold the egg. And the other half to the journey.

At the foot of the stairs, barely stirring in the twilight, the dog teams were waiting, scores of them, lying in harness, curled on the packed snow. Beside each of them was the driver's round skin tent, and the driver himself, walking up and down to keep warm. Here and there, to what looked like a great distance, fires were fluttering in silence, like votive lights in a cathedral, with dark furred figures huddled near them. As I approached a team its driver would step toward me, grinning fiercely to show what a formidable personage he was, waving his arms to make me realize how he cracked his whip, how he terrified his dogs, how his sled flew on, how the Tooth Spirits, the Eye Spirits, the Hand Spirits, the Bear Evils, the Wolf Evils, the Crow Evils, the Knife-Carrying Ghosts, the Ice-Hollow Ghosts, the Sinew Ghosts, the robbers, and the very stars of wrong courses fled from him. He would open his mouth to show how his voice went out ahead of him to tear into his team like the heat of a building burning behind them. The whips were cracked only in gesture and no voices came from the drivers' mouths, for fear of waking the dogs. I passed driver after driver, each more awesome than the last, each offering me, on his palm, the little bell that was his life—mine for the journey, to return to him only if he brought me safely to the Gate. But I knew not to choose any of these. Ages ago when the first of my kind gave

up part of his balance, forever, to pick up a stone, which at once be-
gan to be something else, he was rewarded with knowledge. I looked
through the crowd until I found, at the edge of the camp, a team of
skinny dogs piled in a heap, and a crippled driver limping beside his
famished tent.

I stopped there and he hobbled up to me. Nothing about him
was ingratiating. Besides being a cripple he had only one eye—his
left. And the bell he offered me in his twisted palm was a piece of ice.
His sled itself was built with one side different from the other. As I
was, now. I nodded my head and he gave a little whistle and the dogs
began to stir. And as they did I thought I could feel a stirring in the
egg, in my palm—a turning inside it, or even the first faint vibrations
of a cry. And once again in my mind I saw—but more clearly than
before—the towering columns and the low door of the Orphans'
Gate, where no one would know me, but where they would recognize
the egg that my mother (who was an orphan) had given to me, and
would let me pass through to where it would hatch out and fly
before me, pausing, hovering, calling its icy song.

The Herald

After his death the herald was led into a place of stone, as he could tell from the texture of the cold on the soles of his feet, by the brushing of the cold against his cheeks and his forehead, by the taste of the cold, and by the smell of water that had turned to stone—a smell that he remembered, and with pleasure, out of some sunny morning at the beginning of his childhood, though he could not remember what it had been doing there. He had been lying alone, wrapped in white, in a bright room filled with breezes and with silent birds of reflected light. These had shimmered on the cool whiteness that was folded around him and still contained the presence of the hands that had tucked him in and had caressed his forehead, before leaving like part of a shadow. And the birds of light had shimmered on the cool whiteness that formed the next shell around him, which was made up of the walls and ceiling of the airy room. They joined the concentric spheres. It had been a moment of happiness, in which the smell of water turned to stone had passed like a white fish, never looking at him, and he had laughed to himself, without even knowing that he was born.

So after his death he was led into a place of stone, as he could tell by the fingers of cold, and by the long clothes of the cold passing near him, and by the breath of the cold in his ears, and by many other signs at once, and the blindfold was removed. He was standing in a huge hall of stone. The shallow vaults of the ceiling looked so low that he imagined he could touch them, but he felt that to do so, even to raise his arm, would be a terrible act. He turned slowly. The echo of the last crashing note of a trumpet kept dying away, dying away. The hall appeared to be an enormous circle, but he could not see whether the vaults and the floor ever met. As he turned he saw that stairs led up out of the hall at intervals, all the way around: curving stone staircases, and on each of them the shadow of a man blowing a trumpet was just disappearing around the corner as he looked. He turned more quickly, in order to look behind him, and it was the same. But the dying echo came from none of the stairs. It came from the stones. He stopped turning and at once the whole of the hall was visible to him, on all sides. The echo faded out. The black shadow flag hanging from the black shadow trumpet disappeared from all the stairs. Then the hall filled with a rush of silent birds of light, and among them the herald floated like a white fish borne up by distant laughter. He floated there without moving, at last, and was the will of the king.

The First Time

It was the first time. So it was terribly windy. And of course he had no clothes. If you see someone with clothes you know it is not the first time.

So he stood there in that time with no clothes and he was not complaining because how should he complain: he did not know that anything else was possible. The wind tore the tears from his eyes. If he had not been naked there would have been no light at all. A long moan streamed from him but there was no way of telling whether it came from his mouth or was a sound made by the wind falling from him like a climber from a cliff. As for him he shivered with cold. He trembled with fear, for like most mortal creatures he could tell that the abyss was never more than a step from him. He shook as we all do when we are leaves.

Then she said to him, "It is a place of passage."

Then she said to him, "In places of passage it is always terribly windy."

Then she said to him, "When you are in the places of passage stop trembling and the wind will wait outside."

At last he slept. It was the first time that he slept in that form, with all the forms behind him still waiting, and all the forms ahead of him still waiting, each in its own way, silent, and untouched by wind. And the wind slept at his feet like a garment he did not need. The whole sky slept at his feet like a black garment. Like a garment he did not need for the first time.

She never left him.

But each time he sleeps he wakes missing something else for the first time, some limb, some knowledge, some part of him, and he sets out in a place of passage, looking for it for the first time, naked, not even knowing what it is, unable to see for darkness and tears. And the wind is terrible. And again he will have to sleep in order to find what is missing.

The Fragments

I am beginning at last to have moments when something tells me of the miracle. I can be no more specific than that. Not yet.

I suppose I could be called grateful. Things were worse before. Before there were any such intimations. I can't take credit for the difference. I don't think I can take credit for it.

Certainly it was worse when I first came into the high room and found, in the middle of the table, the hand. All by itself. Palm up. Clean. Empty. Apparently. Like one of my own but without the scars. As I noticed in due course. Motionless but otherwise with nothing to indicate death. Warm. As I learned in due course. No sign of violence: no blood or bruise. Where it ended, where one would suppose that it had joined a wrist, after the manner of its kind, there was no garish explosion of reds, blues, yellows, no jumble of bared bone, of tubing severed in mid-syllable, of sinews shrinking. None of that. An oval segment of some colorless background, as it were of a foggy winter day in which one cannot make out details but only the day itself. I did not touch it.

It offered no explanation. Well, a hand does not offer explanations. For being a hand. Even when one knows how much is at stake. Thinks one knows. What is all that, all that is at stake from our point of view, to hands when they are on their own? But I had never thought of that. So I stood there convinced that I understood nothing, which was a help for a while. I watched it, sure that it knew something. Something, therefore, which I didn't know. Many things which I didn't know. My assumptions about the nature of knowledge, I realized, were being shaken.

What was it for? Yes, I realized after a time that this was the question I had been asking since the beginning. No, not asking: embodying. Once I recognized that, things became a little clearer. I saw that the hand was not still, as I had at first imagined. For I had thought at first, in my self-centered way, that the hand was motionless whereas I, by contrast, was moving. Now it seemed to me that I was standing as a single spot in a progression too vast for me to even imagine more than a section of it, a progression which represented the story of the hand, the destiny in whose service the hand had come to decision after decision, millions of years before I had been heard of, in order to lie, for however long, where it now lay, in its present form. Then I saw it as a path on which I was allowed to take only one step. A path which knew its origins, its end, its purpose between them — or at least more of these than I could guess.

Night fell. I let it fall around the hand, and I left. The next day the place was empty and I embarked on the usual doubts, as I still do. There was no proof. Nothing else seemed to have changed.

So things went on in the old way until the day when I came in as before and in the same place found the ear. Empty. As far as I could tell. But I was careful to make no noise. Detached like the hand. Same reflections in my mind. Turning around how much it knew, apart from me, if such a thing were conceivable. What decisions of its own were leading it past me, even as I watched? I began to think of myself as an instance. And the ear — what was it on its way to hear?

Then the ankle, the hair, the tongue. What am I but a caravanserai whose very walls belong to the camel drivers?

Five thousand had come to hear him, and some had travelled a long way and were hungry. What was there for them to eat? One of those who were with him said, "There is a boy here with five loaves and two little fish, but what are they among so many?" But he said, "Let them be given to everyone who is hungry." And when everyone had eaten his fill the fragments were gathered up and they filled twelve baskets.

I mentioned this because when I found the tongue it came to me for the first time that the miracle was not the matter of quantity but the fact that the event had never left the present. Parts of it keep appearing. I have begun to have glimpses of what I am doing, crossing the place where they have all been satisfied, and still finding fragment after fragment.

Dawn Comes to Its Mountain in the Brain

There the east, the rim, is somewhere in the center, an area like another, in appearance. But in appearance it is all in the dark. In appearance it is all imprisoned in a night without stars. Nothing is more silent than those valleys that are the cradles of the voices. Nothing is more oppressive than their sky.

Then on the slope that contains the east there is a stirring. In appearance it would be said to dilate, break, scatter slowly, sinking, dwindling, reappearing, like the spots of color on the skin of a dying squid. But the spots do not die. They become more intense, they merge. All in utter darkness.

Now in the valley beyond, under the eyes of invisible horsemen, long baggage trains are trickling away, the drivers hastily lashing down the covers of the wagons as they go. Those tribesmen will never have names. Some of them will return. None will be forgotten. In the valley beyond that one, unseen herds vanish among the rocks, without a sound.

The stain deepens on the slope. It gathers. Settles. Like the playing of lights. But all this in a darkness like the darkness in wires through which a message is flowing. Like the darkness around the queen in a hive to which a message is coming. Like the darkness in which justice is shown her palaces. And in a silence like that around a wire through which a message is passing.

It is only inside that slope that the trumpets sound, the processions and their watchful horsemen are seen departing, the last echoes of the herds fade out, and the sun rises with its message: Sun.

The west is in the same place.

HOUSES *and* TRAVELLERS

The Nest

A pair of pigeons once discovered an open umbrella hanging by its handle from a beam, in an empty shed where a shepherd had left it. It was spring. They built their nest in the black web. The wind under the drafty roof rocked the umbrella, but nothing else disturbed them, nor their eggs, nor their firstborn.

The first pair of young learned to fly, and circled farther and farther over the countryside, and met with no mishap, until one day, when they were out by themselves, it rained. Between them and their home a dozen umbrellas opened. Suddenly it seemed to them that they were flying upside-down. They were terrified, as though they had learned all at once that they were on the wrong side of the light. They tried to fly on their backs, but they were dashed against the earth, where they were caught and eaten by the animals that were walking there all the time with their heads up, watching for something to fall.

The next pair of pigeons raised in the same nest met with the same fate, in the same way. And the next, and all the generations that followed. At last the parents grew too old to produce more young.

"Well," they said, "the nest won't be good much longer anyway." Over the years the accumulated crust of straw and droppings had rotted the fabric and it hung in tatters from the ribs.

"But not one of them ever came back," one of the parents said.

"That's natural, I suppose," the other answered. "They had to raise families of their own. This is the only nest here."

"Yes," said the first, "and they may have had to fly a long way to find another one like this."

Nothing Began as It Is

Everything has its story. The story of the small black beetles, unable to fly, with a red bar on the upper half of each useless wing, is that they are the soldiers of Pharaoh, still following the chosen people everywhere, with the Red Sea above their heads.

The story of the rough stone basin of the oldest fountain in the city is that it was once the oldest miser in the city, but the mercy of the world found him painful to look at, and changed him into a form which would permit him to say, "I receive everything, I keep nothing," until he himself was completely worn away.

The story of the one-legged messenger is that his other leg is walking on the far side of death. "What seems to be over there?" they ask him. "Just emptiness?" "No," he says. "Something before that, with no name."

The story of the hinge is that it is learning to fly. "No hinge has ever flown," the locks tell it again and again. "That is why we are learning," it answers, "and then we will teach the doors."

Some things try to steal the stories of others. They have thieves' stories.

The story of each stone leads back to a mountain.

The locks say that it is possible for a thing to be separated from its story and never find it again in this world.

The First Moon

A pebble is rolling along a road. It cannot see anyone. There is no one there to see it. So it rolls on. It cannot hear anyone. It rolls on all by itself under the sun. It thinks of the sun as one part of itself, some of the time, or—more exactly—as a feeling that recurs in one part of itself, hardly perceptible, at first, and then more intense, then much more intense, and then weaker and weaker until it is gone. While the feeling is there the pebble tries to carry as much of itself as possible into that part, dragging itself up from one side where it has become loose as though it had been uprooted. All of itself that it drags up on one side slides down the other, so as long as it feels the sun, the pebble rolls on and on, and it can feel itself moving faster, too, but it believes that its speed is the result of its growing lightness, which is caused by lifting more and more of itself off the ground.

All this time its shadow runs along under it like a friend trying to make it listen. And indeed the shadow is in constant fear, constant fear, striking against every irregularity in the road, knocked out of shape again and again, stretched, snatched at and caught by cracks and by all the bigger shadows along the way, and escaping from them all each time as though by miracle. "Stop, stop," it keeps calling. "Let us find somewhere of our own before night." The stone rolls on.

But it comes to roll more slowly. Not because it has listened to its shadow (it never listens) but because it has been thinking about a permanent place for the feeling of the sun. It has been considering turning into an eye. By the time it has decided, the day is over. The pebble rolls off the road into a wood, and stops. Its shadow falls asleep at once. The stone looks up. Clouds draw back. The eye opens. Night. Then deep in the stone the first moon rises.

The Broken

The spiders started out to go with the wind on its pilgrimage. At that time they were honored among the invisibles—more sensitive than glass, lighter than water, purer than ice. Even the lightning spoke well of them, and it seemed as though they could go anywhere. But as they were travelling between cold and heat, cracks appeared in them, appeared in their limbs, and they stopped, it seemed they had to stop, had to leave the company of the wind for a while and stay in one place until they got better, moving carefully, hiding, trusting to nothing. It was not long before they gave up trying to become whole again, and instead undertook to mend the air. Neither life nor death, they said, would slip through it any more.

After that they were numbered among the dust—makers of ghosts. The wind never missed them. There were still the clouds.

Sand

An ant was born in an hourglass. Before it hatched out there was nothing to notice—and who would have looked, who would have suspected that one instant in each measure of time was an egg? And after the ant had emerged, it was too late to ask whether the birth was a mistake. Anyway, there was no one to ask, except those nameless hosts, his brothers, at once much older and much younger than he was, who nudged and ground past him, rustling toward the neck of the glass, and fell, and lay blind, deaf, and dreamless in the mountain made of each other, and would never hatch, though the mountain itself turned over again and again and sent them smoking down from its tip like souls into time. Besides, it never occurred to him that there was a question to ask. He did not know that things ever had been or ever could be any different, and whatever capacity for speech he may have been born with slept on inside him like a grain of sand.

There was nothing to eat. But he had never been told about hunger, and ants, particularly those of his species, can subsist for long periods, sometimes for generations, without consuming other life of any kind. The same was true of thirst, dry though that place surely was, made of nothing but those rocks his family. Whatever discomfort he may have become aware of, arising from either hunger or thirst, seemed to him to be like something that we would no doubt call a memory, returning inexplicably to trouble him in a new life, and certain to fade. It stirred in him like some ghost from his days as a grain of sand, but he could not remember what use it had been to him then. And he would hold it to him and save it for a while, as though there was danger of losing it. He would hold it, trying to understand it, not knowing that it was pain. Something of the kind was true also of breathing. He was breathing. But he knew nothing of breath. What, after all, reached him through the glass? The light. The darkness. Sounds. Gravity. The desire to climb. What reached the grains of sand? Light. Darkness. Vibrations. Gravity. No one knows what else.

His brothers tried to crush him. He tried to count them. He could see that they were not infinite. But he could never start at the beginning. He would count them as they edged past him faster and faster. He had no names for numbers, but he tried to count the brothers even so, as he was borne along with them, as he climbed on their shoulders, as he swam on their heads, falling with them. He tried to count them as they fell on him and rolled after him to the foot of the next mountain, to the glass. He would start to the top again at once, trying to count them as they slipped under his feet. He would climb, counting, till the mountain turned over, and then he would begin again. Each time the mountain flowed out from under him he delayed the falling for an instant, and a measure of time paused while he clung to the neck of the glass, climbing on sand. Then everything went on just the same.

No one had told him about time. He did not know why he was trying to count. He did not know what a number, a final sum, would tell him, what use it would be to him, what he would call it, where he would put it. He did not know that they were not his real brothers. He thought he was a grain of sand.

He did not know that he was alone.

The Lonely Child

The lonely child arranges all his toys in front of him.

"Come, play with me," he says to everyone who comes near. "Come and see all the toys I have."

But they go away.

So he smashes the first of the toys.

Then other children come to watch and help, and to fight over who can break his toys.

If a lonely child has no toys, he makes them.

The Salt Peddler

A man leading a horse was walking inland from the sea. The horse
was loaded with sacks of salt which the man intended to sell in the
city. It was summer and the salt peddler stopped to drink and to
water his horse at every spring and stream he found on the way.
When they had been travelling most of a day they came to a spring
and stopped. The man drank, and then turned to draw the horse
toward the water, but to his surprise the animal showed no sign of
thirst, and refused. At this point the man noticed that one of the
sacks had been torn or worn through, and that a thread of glittering
white crystals was draining away onto the ground. The leak was so
small as to be almost unnoticeable. On the other hand, it would be
virtually impossible to mend it while the sack was full and on the
horse's back. The man felt the sack to see whether much salt had
been lost, and though it seemed to be as hard as ever, he traced the
trail of salt a few steps back along the way he had come, wetting his
fingers, touching the crystals he could see, putting the mixed salt and
dust to the tip of his tongue, trying to guess how far back they led.
When he looked up he saw that his horse had started to go on with-
out him. Again the animal's behavior surprised him: the old horse
had always been patient and dependable. He started after it, calling.
Then he saw that there was a hand holding the reins, leading the
horse. He could see the hand but nothing with it: no arm, no body,
no garment. He continued to follow the horse, from a distance. And
he stopped calling.

They went on in this way, uphill, downhill. Hours passed. The man
had forgotten his thirst. He began to get used to his fear. He remem-
bered the leak in the sack and began to worry about his load. He
bent down to see whether he could still detect the trail of salt, and
whether the salt was draining away faster or more slowly than before.
There it was, visible here and there on the ground: a misty path of
white crystals. No one else would have noticed it. He wet a finger
again and touched the crystals and put the finger to his tongue and
at the mixed taste of salt and dust he felt both anguish and relief.

When he looked up he saw that there was another man near him, also examining the dust of the path. The other man straightened, and their eyes met. They walked on together. It turned out that they were both going to the city. The other man did not at first say why he was going there, and the salt peddler felt ashamed to tell how he had allowed his horse to get away from him. They went forward in silence for a while. The salt peddler watched his horse, but as casually as he could. Finally he asked the other whether he was going to the city with something to sell. Yes, the other said. He explained that he was on his way there with a load of spices. He added, as though the salt peddler might not have heard of such things, that spices were worth more than their weight in gold. The salt peddler wanted to ask where the other man's load was, but before he had a chance to, the other man asked him whether he too was taking something to sell in the city. The peddler was ashamed to admit that the load with which he was travelling such a distance was nothing but plain salt. He answered that his wares consisted of precious stones. "Small precious stones," he added at once, deprecating them. "Mere dust of precious stones, in fact." As he said that, he felt that he was keeping closer to the truth. But even so, he explained, they too were worth far more than their weight in gold.

Then the two walked in silence for a while again, with the salt peddler stealing glances at the ground and at his horse, far ahead, with the hand still leading it. Finally the other man said that he had been wondering how much the small jewels and the jewel-dust were worth by the ounce, and whether the salt peddler would consider trading a certain quantity of jewel-dust for its value in spices. The salt peddler congratulated himself on having described his load as "mere dust of precious stones"—the phrase seemed to him even more honest than before. And he told himself that if he were a bit quick and a bit lucky, he should be able to trade some of his salt for spices worth more than their weight in gold, and get away before the other discovered the trick. The two started to bargain about the values of their respective wares. The salt peddler felt that he could afford to be generous, though not so generous as to excite suspicion. They agreed at last on terms that made the salt peddler's heart pound with anticipation. He asked where the load of spices was.

The other man sighed and said that when he had stopped, earlier in the day, for a drink of water, his horse had escaped from him and was by now some distance ahead. The salt peddler looked ahead but saw only his own horse, and a large bank of cloud or mist lying across the path, into which his horse disappeared as he watched. The path could be seen emerging again on the other side of the cloud, but the disappearance of the horse troubled him, and he quickened his steps.

"Where is your load?" the other asked him, keeping up with him.

He explained that his horse too had escaped, and that he had just lost sight of it.

"I can't see mine any longer, either," the other man said.

They hurried on to the bank of cloud. The salt peddler shivered, and stepped in. It was cold inside the cloud, and dark like a winter day, and there was a sound of rushing water. The peddler heard his companion's footsteps and breath beside him. He felt the cloud condense on his face and run down into his clothes. He worried about the salt in the sacks.

At last he and the other man came to the edge of a small cliff above a stream. Down beside the water he saw his horse.

"There he is!" the salt peddler said.

"I see mine too," the other said.

"There's only one horse that I can see," the peddler said.

"It's true. I see only one," the other answered.

"Well, that one's my horse," the salt peddler said, raising his voice.

"He's mine!" the other answered, laughing, but raising his voice too. And they both slipped and scrambled down the steep slope toward the stream. The hand was still leading the horse, and kept it well ahead of them. They followed it along the water. After they had gone a little way, the salt peddler saw, to his distress, that the horse was being led across the stream, going in deeper at every step. The animal sank to its shoulders and began to swim. The peddler groaned to think of the remaining salt in the sacks. He wondered whether any would be left at all. He and the other man plunged into the stream and floundered through the salty water. On the other side, the horse led them on toward a figure sitting in the mist farther up the stream. As they drew nearer, the salt peddler saw that it was an old man with what appeared to be water running from one hand. The other hand was missing. Then the peddler saw the hand that was leading the horse go up to the old man's wrist and join it, and the old man looked up.

"Welcome," he said. "Is this your horse?"

"Yes," the salt peddler said.

"Yes," the other man said.

"Where were you going with it?" the old man asked.

And they both told him that they were on their way to the city. The old man looked at them both, then at one, then at the other.

"Long ago," he said, "two brothers set out to found that city. Before they began it, one brother killed the other. I was the one who was killed. There is my city, beyond me."

The peddler looked past him and saw a forest of towers and spires gleaming with bright metals and jewels.

"My brother has not been seen for centuries in his city," the old man continued, "but I have never left mine. And yet I cannot say that I am happy here. No one is happy here. I was never able to forget the life that I had hoped to go on with. Age after age I cherished the hope that I might do something for the living. Finally I was granted the task of making tears."

He held up his left hand, from which the drops continued to fall.

"I thought that the labor would make me happy, or at least resigned," he said, "but here, at least, what is given with one hand is taken away with the other. The tears that I made were tasteless. Up until that time people had wept, as they had done everything else, with ease of heart. Weeping was a pleasure like any other. But once their tears came from me, their weeping was insipid, and those who wept were condemned to supply the savor themselves, to which end grief and bitterness were born. After that, even when people wept for joy their joy contained the reminder and the taste of anguish. But I have not been able to forget the time when it was not so, and I long, age after age, to obtain salt, to spare them their pain. I know it is still there, I call out to it, I send my own hand away into the world to try to lead it to me. I would give anything for it. What were you taking to the other city?"

"Salt," the other man answered.

"Then the horse must be yours," the old man said. "But the salt itself never reaches me. Just the same, if you wish to, you may fill the sacks with jewels."

He held out the reins to the other man.

"But the horse is mine!" the salt peddler said.

"Your horse was already loaded with jewels," the other man said, and took the reins.

"He's mine, he's mine!" the salt peddler shouted, and he picked up a large stone and struck the other on the head, and saw him fall.

"Now he can stay here," the old man said. "You may as well take his horse." And the salt peddler felt the reins in his hand once more, and felt his eyes fill with tears so that he could see nothing, and he fell to his knees beside the body, and sobbed. When he wiped his eyes and looked up again there was no one else to be seen. The city had disappeared. The cloud was blowing away. And he stood up and turned the horse's head and started back toward the sea with his empty sacks.

The Water Clock

It is said that the first victim who fell to the armed men as they emerged from the wooden horse on the last night of Troy was a young man leaning over the stone lip of a water clock in the city square. There had long been a legend among the inhabitants that the city would never fall without being warned by the water clock. The young man was the hereditary keeper of the clock, and came to visit it at the end of each watch. As he crossed the square that night he thought he heard a hollow sound coming from the horse. He stopped in the middle of the square and waited, and then he heard the same sound—and recognized it—coming from his own heart. At the same time he heard the water clock whispering, and he went to it, and set his torch in a socket, and leaned over the rim. He saw—as he had seen all his life—the carved faces on the stone buckets, and their reflections in each of the surfaces of the water, forming a series that included the reflection of his own face, and went on, upwards and downwards, until it passed out of sight, and each of the dripping stone faces, and its reflection, was whispering, "Listen, listen, listen." So he listened, and heard the echo of his own heart, and within it the echo of feet running. Then the spear found him.

When the survivors of Troy built their city, they too set a water clock in the main square, and modelled it as closely as they could on the one they remembered, but they no longer believed in the legend.

·

The Taste

There is a drink which only the old ever taste. Everyone knows that the day is full of rocks, some large, some small, which move. They are all invisible and no one mentions them, but everyone knows that they are rocks. No one knows how to get past them, or to enter them, or to see what is inside them. They are said to contain the treasure of Age, which no one has ever looked on—a black treasure.

At night when only the old are awake, black springs rise in some of the rocks and begin to flow toward some of the old. The slow streams seldom choose for destinations the old who are nearest to them. The rocks in which they rise have all moved. The withered body toward which a stream starts to make its way may have passed the source years before and not have known it. How wide the world is now! How empty! How far a stream may have to flow! Meanwhile the old are dying.

As a stream passes through the dark meadows, birds that are standing there turn to look. Each time they think it is Memory once more. But it is not Memory. Each of the birds was a color, once, and this is where they go.

When at last a stream lies on the tongue it set out for, it rests. There is a moment of trembling. Tears come out and sit in the night. After a while the stream gets up and goes to its boat and loads the old person into it and they drift away together toward the valley. In the morning the body that has been visited can no longer stand, no longer speak. It swallows and swallows as though trying to remember tasting water for the first time.

A Conversation

There is a wind that when it turns I hear the garden and the desert discussing things with each other. Sometimes in the garden, sometimes in the desert, day or night. Mud walls, stone walls, no walls, limestone, sheep far away, howling, birds singing, hissing, trickling, silence, dry smells, watered smells, moons, stars, flowers that are keys between them.

They tell their dreams to each other, the garden and the desert. They dream above all of each other. The desert dreams of the garden inside it. It loves the garden. It embraces the garden. It wants to turn it into desert. The garden lives within itself. It dreams of the desert all around it, and of its difference from the desert, which it knows is as frail as feeling.

It must be a long time since I first heard them talking. I must have heard them when I was two. I must have heard them when I was one, and so on. Perhaps before I was born. Or anyone was born. Or any roundness became an egg. Or the water was born, cooling on a high rock, prophesying tears, prophesying eyes.

I must have heard them even before the rocks were born moving in the colored night. Probably I have heard them ever since the light began looking for something to write on, flying on, white, with the colors hidden inside it and the darkness around it, forgetting nothing from the beginning, prophesying the end of knowledge, prophesying the wilderness, prophesying the garden, prophesying the wilderness dreaming that it was a garden. And the garden. And the wilderness.

The River of Fires

Far in the north, where trees are thin and scarce, there is a wide river along whose banks every hour a fire is lighted farther upstream. This happens in the summer, when the days never end, and the smoke rises from fire after invisible fire, all the way out to the sky. And in the winter, when the blazing points can often be seen for great distances, as though the sky were beginning to flatten out, and new planets were set in it, glowing red because they were rising horizontally; and then whoever looks, sooner or later is overtaken with a sense of being the darkness fleeing before them. It happens in the fogs in the spring and fall, when even fires cannot be seen at a slight distance, and then suddenly they emerge in a gleaming cloud. And so time is constantly moving upstream. As it must, they feel in that country, if they are to live. And on the last night of the year the last fire is allowed to go out, by a clear stream in the mountains to the south, and on the first morning of the year, in the minutes after midnight, a fire is lit on the ice where the river flows into the frozen sea, on the west bank, and is carried across the river-mouth to the east bank and there built higher and higher, into a vast and desperate steaming conflagration, to help the sun to rise through the ice. And then hour by hour they go ahead, guiding him up the river under the ice, until he rises at last, and then until he never sets, and until after he has gone. They never reach the source. They believe that they would drown, or be frozen into the glacier, still facing south, like some of the heroes of their legends. They bury their dead beyond the last ashes, where the river is always cold and no one has ever explored the mountains.

At One of the Ends of the World

A girl is walking down the thousands of winding steps in front of the palace, carrying a bucket of water. The long pink light flicks open and shut between her feet.

Meanwhile a herd of horses is massed at the eastern gate, which appears to be open. Beyond the gate is the night without stars. Those horses have been captured again and again, and have escaped again and again, after each battle, leaving their riders dead on the field, and have found their way to the gate looking for their true master, from whose black meadow they were stolen, unbroken.

Each of the horses is a drop of water in the bucket she is carrying. Whenever a little bit splashes onto the stairs or onto her feet, a knot of horses plunges through the gate and is swallowed up in the darkness as in sand.

The life of each horse is an eon of sunlight. As each horse vanishes, the death of the sun moves millions of years closer to us. She is carrying in that bucket the whole age of the sun, from the beginning, from long before us, when there was only the black meadow and the silent fountain. If the bucket were to fall, nothing would ever have been.

The horses are crowded against the open gateway. Far below her there is a single tree dying of drought. But her eyes are not on the tree, nor on the stairs, nor on anything in front of her. She is thinking of her lover, whom she has never seen because he comes to her only by dark.

The Reaper

The harvest was over. Even the scythe had not been mine. I had nowhere to go.

In the evening I found a young woman lying on the ground like a sheaf of wheat, radiant and silent. When I bent over her she was watching me, smiling.

I carried her into an empty house among the trees. Next to the kitchen there was a room with a bed and a colored quilt. I put her there and stood between two sources of light, and the room was brighter than the day outside.

She is helpless. She cannot speak. I will take care of her.

It is her house. I learned that from a woman who came to the door almost at once, and called to her, and tried to trick me, charm me, frighten me, get rid of me. Old and poisonous. When at last she went away, she left, under the bushes by the house, a rabbit from the mown fields, that pretends to be dead, to be half-skinned, to have no eyelids, so that it can watch what I do.

It has watched me before. I will not leave.

When I shut my eyes I see the wheat.

The Bride of the East

A girl fell in love with the East and said she would marry no other. When her father heard of this he went to talk with her. He described to her all the kingdoms of the earth. He told her of the pleasures of the south, he was eloquent in praise of the glories of the north, he lifted a corner of the horizon to let her catch a single glimpse of the west. But she would not look and would not listen.

"Why the East?" her father said.

"Everything comes from him," she answered.

"But the East cannot marry you," her father said, as gently as he could. She sat still, at the window.

"The East cannot even come to you," her father went on.

"He can," she said.

"You would not be here," her father said. "You would be far away, to the west of here."

"He would see me," she answered.

"Even if you were still visible you would be too far to recognize: a very small black figure sitting in a frame full of darkness, travelling backwards into a mountain."

"I will not have gone," she said. "I will have waited."

"You can't wait," he answered.

"Why not?"

"Even now you're going."

"It's not true."

"Each time you sleep you wake up farther away."

"Farther from where?"

"From here."

"I don't care."

"Farther from the East."

"I've stopped sleeping." And it was true. Ever since she had fallen in love she had sat awake all night, every night, looking out of the east window.

"Each time you blink your eyes, when you open them you are farther."

"Only from here," she said.

"From the East," he insisted.

"No," she said. "He can go faster."

"Nothing is faster than you when you close your eyes."

"He'd be there."

"He wouldn't stay."

"And I've stopped closing them." It was true. As she sat looking out of the window, her eyes never blinked, day or night.

"I want you to go to sleep now, and tomorrow we can talk about other things," her father said.

"I don't want to sleep," she said. "You just don't want me to marry the East. Why don't you want me to marry the East?"

"I want you to marry someone from here."

"I don't want anybody from here."

"You will."

"I can't even see them. I look at their faces and all I see is holes."

"That's because your head is full of the East. But it will be different in the morning, you'll see."

"Besides, I've stopped looking at them." It was true. All she looked at now was the sky beyond the frame of the window facing east, which was then growing dark.

"I suppose that when you look at my face you see nothing but a hole too," he said. It was a trick to make her turn and look at him, but she was used to his tricks, and never took her eyes from the window. "But we're all becoming that way. You too," he said. "We're fading away so that we can't be seen at all. We're beginning to look just like air, so that even if he could come here he wouldn't be able to find you."

It was another trick to make her look, but she knew it.

"He's already found me," she said. At this her father was startled, for a moment. Then he grew angry, which is not always an aid to illumination.

"I don't believe you," he said—harshly, because it was not wholly true.

"And you will never marry him," he added, with deliberate cruelty.

"I'm already his bride," she said.

"It's impossible," he insisted. But nothing would change her thoughts nor turn her gaze from the window.

"Very well," her father said. "Wait for him." And he sent for men to brick up the east window. But she was still there the next morning. She was still there when the bells rang for Sunday, and she was still there when they rang for Easter. She was still there when they rang for her brother's wedding and when they tolled for her mother's passing, and when they rang for her father's burial, and for her brother's death, and others' deaths, and fires in the city, and storms in summer, and sieges and victories and griefs, and when the walls fell behind her because the place had stood uninhabited and untended for so long, the roof letting in until the beams rotted and then moss rooted along them and led the way down and the light followed and she was still there sitting by the bricked-up east window from which not a single brick had fallen, because scar tissue holds longer than the original. But she noticed nothing until they took down the east wall too, finally, because it was unsafe, and because they wanted the stones from the window-frame, and the space in which to put something else, and then of course the bricks fell at her feet, and she stood up and held out her hands toward the east, and feeling nothing there, took a step forward.

It is one of her withered hands that you feel occasionally on your arm, a second at a time, in an episode that must surely last for more than one life. Often it is dark when her finger touches you, and so you may not at first notice that she is blind, and is groping with both hands in one direction. She is looking for the brick wall beyond which is the East, whose image is still in her breast, but the bricks have gone, and while they were there she had lost her ability to see anything except the darkness of the East, which looks like other darkness. But once she touches you she seems to know where she is going, and she leads you through the dark tree-lined square to an unlit doorway. It appears to you that there is a scorpion on one side of the doorway and a worm on the other side. They are bowing to each other, but straighten as you approach, and are heard saying to each other, as you pass through,

"My old friend." (This is the scorpion.)

"My very old friend." (This is the worm, answering.)

"I never wanted bones."

"Neither did I." (The worm again.)

"I'm better off without them."

"That's what I say to myself. If I say anything."

"You should consider having eyes, though."

"What would I want with eyes?"

"You'd see."

"Who needs to see?"

"The bride of the East."

"What for? Only the East can pass through this door and live."

But you are not the East. You are subject to every wind that blows. And as you turn to tell her, she is not there.

The Footstep

Noon, then, is the name of the ninth angel, where he falls, where he was always going to fall, where he plummets into our world as surely and as regularly as the sun rises. Outside the books and the histories, the name was always going to mean no one, none, nothing.

And the world knows it. Everywhere it can tell that he is coming, that he is falling. The animals move into the shade of trees, and watch, hardly breathing. The birds find a little darkness, and pause. A film like dust veils the shining leaves. In the unlit hives the bees dance more slowly and come to a stop. Silence leaks into the dreams of the bats. The breeze dies. You shiver. He strikes. He is there.

At that point in time and space all directions are burned away. Where he touches, there is no promise of continuing, no reason nor direction to follow—or so it seems. But he is also one of the angels of turning, and we turn, and the air springs up again, and the day goes on, leaving behind it one more empty footstep, the place and the mark of no one.

Even among the waves, every ninth one is his, and when it reaches the shore those that follow it recede.

You know that he is one of the seals of death. But you can see, too, if your eyes can bear it, that he is an angel, one of the falling angels, who in his splendor aspires to rule heaven himself—which is why he falls. Some go so far as to insist that his beauty exceeds that of all the sons of morning.

August

In August many, even of those who will not leave, turn idle, seek out each other's company, and rove together in restless bands, aimlessly but impatiently, as though somewhere else a place were being made ready for them. Voices of things unattached, of shutters, of dead ivy, and nesting warnings of birds, go on because they forget to stop. Bells feel their age. There is gray in the grass, and the verbs stand still at unmarked crossroads.

In August names dangle, more or less, the wheat rattles, its time has come, plums prepare to fall, hands go out by themselves, far from the heart and the spring. It is hard to remember any of these days later. If ever one reappears it is without a shape of its own—a phase of an interval, a face bending over a dry pond.

In August even the cries urging dogs to bring in the cows meet and fly together, circling higher and higher in the evening sky, and a widow forgets everything and runs out calling a dog that has been dead for years. The coolness after sudden showers already belongs to autumn, although the water in the stone basins is still warm as blood. Loosestrife, and the acanthus stained with mourning. Few things are begun, lest they be overtaken.

In August the rumors grow into hay. It is a time that has been given many gods, but none of them stayed, and none returned. It was named at last for an emperor who they pretended was one of the immortals, who ruled an empire which they pretended was eternal, its provinces the colors of straw, sand, dry leaves. An empire the color of honey, without the taste. A realm of yellow glass. It too was named for him, and they called it Peace, and his, and they said it was the whole of the world, and that beyond it there was nothing but darkness. But even at the time there were gossip-mongers who insisted that they remembered him for whom it was all named, shaken with a fit of rage in the very doors of the senate, seizing a senator, and with his own fingers tearing out both of the man's eyes.

The Fly and the Milk

A fly may be waiting for the milk every day. The milk changes but it's the same fly.

The milk that the fly has drunk turns into the same fly, and from then on it stays the same, while the rest of the milk goes on changing.

So one hand puts a big white stone in the milk place.

The fly wants to fly away after stopping to drink white stone, but it isn't a fly any more. It doesn't have the soul of a fly. It's a stone with no color. A small dry stone in a desert, from then on, with sand children. Children that are not even real children. Even when they fall into milk they don't know it.

From then on there is no fly, and the milk stays the same.

The Devil's Pig

The devil's pig cannot be killed. And you too are happy to hear it—
quite as happy as anyone else. Not because pigs are the most intelli-
gent of domestic animals. Is intelligence grounds for mercy? Humans
have never been certain that it is not in itself a crime. Yet they feel
obligated to it, they depend on it, and so they pass laws declaring
that it is a virtue. But they are still hungry. And pigs in numbers like
the stars of heaven have not been fattened for their virtue but for
their flesh: to bleed at the eyes, to wear the blue rind and the color-
less wounds, never to know age, but to fill with the jellied waters of
silence, and be sundered and pass, fiber by fiber, through the mouths
of humans. But not the devil's pig.

Of course he is beautiful. He is reared by a family who become
fond of him, and display him to visitors, and the children scratch
him and ride him, and everyone says it is a pity, and when the time
comes and he is held down, and the neighbor who always does the
job holds the knife at the stretched throat and pushes, suddenly the
neighbor is kneeling at the edge of a kite, with a glue-brush in his
hand, trying to mend a gash that he himself had made, while every-
one watches in silence, for it is a kite that everyone in the village loved.
And the neighbor works for a long time, without a word, while the
family stands over him, and at the end he bends forward and breathes
on the patched place to make it whole, and then stands and gives the
mended kite to the children, and goes home afterward as though he
had been to a funeral all by himself.

Sometimes the devil's pig takes all the prizes and is the sire of a
famous progeny, and a center of envy and scheming, and is stolen,
and is the pretext for murder and imprisonment and despair, and is
returned to his owner, and survives him, and they say he will be al-
lowed to die of old age, but before the first sign of it he disappears,
and after that no one in that part of the country trusts anyone else,
day or night, for generations.

He lives with a saint and is a model of obedience, and tramples
on snakes, and is given away, but never forgotten.

He rides in the truck with the others, and climbs the ramp with them, and at the top the man with the stunner sees the little dog from home running up the ramp with the pigs, and the man shuts the gate and stops the braid of backs, and picks up the little dog and takes him out and sends him home with a pat and never sees him again.

Can you imagine killing him? Can you envisage what it would do to you? Can you think how the devil would treat you after that— your sleep, what you would hear at table, who would pray with your lips? But you do not wish to kill the devil's pig.

He has become the pride of the emperor, and his statue has been carved, and armies, after victories, have the right to carry his image on a banner. He fears neither fire nor water. He loves everyone. Why should he not? His master is the lord of this world.

Iron

In the age of iron they learned to make filings. They were led to the lodestone and their names for it drifted closer to the words for loving, but were never the same. They discovered how to induce the lodestone to impart its paradoxical virtues to the shoe of a horse, and they taught themselves how to make paper, and make it white. Onto the lodestone-inspired shoe of an unseen horse, in time they laid an empty white leaf of paper and onto the paper they threw the filings they themselves had made, and what they saw then was the rose of the world, with its two eyes and two hearts. One day they set it adrift in a boat, and the iron rose of the world went sailing, the whole world following after. But its north always varied from the true north, and in itself it was never sure by how much.

The horseshoe was made for holding the virtues of the lodestone long before the first horse was domesticated, and from having the horseshoe they conceived of having the horse. Generations of blacksmiths died in ignorance of the drift of destiny, before the first of them was led to the lodestone. But the horse for which the first horseshoe was made is still unbroken. From the very beginning you could hang up the sacred horseshoe from a tree and strike it once anywhere with an iron stick and all its virtue would fly out of it in a single cascading bird-note, one beat of the galloping horse, after which it will lie still on the ground and let the filings rest over it evenly like dust or snow, itself still nailed to the horse's footprint. And you could do it all again.

They made a drawing of the rose and laid the horseshoe at the edge of it and set them adrift, and the picture sailed away with the horse at its prow, and its tiers of oarless petals, but its north was not the true north, in the sky. Instead, its north turned in varying circles, wandering through infinite outer worlds, at inconceivable distances from the still beam at its true center. How long ago it began! Before the first blacksmith was born, whales sleeping in calm water would swing slowly to face north, the position in which they gave birth.

The north of the horse, and of iron, and of iron's rose. The north of
the file and of blood, and of ambition and the amber of commerce.
Not the axis close beside it, turning in each of them.

He Who Made the Houses

He was a man whose age nobody knew, and nobody could remember what he did before. All that time he had lived alone. He had lived simply. He looked like wax, but somewhere he was burning. He was always bent at his labor, even when he seemed to be looking at you. His eyes were always on his love, which was the work of his life. He made all kinds of houses, complete with the tools, habits, passages, hiding places, traps, cupboards, pictures, furry corridors, ice chimneys, rotted stairs, laid tables, smells, and bone-filled dens, of lives. Out of everything he could find, beg, borrow, or take away until he could try it first, he made these houses, of all sizes, opening onto every prospect, or dug into the ground. Everywhere that he could persuade someone to let him use the space and let him alone there for a while, he made these houses. He made them on some of the oldest, and on some of the poorest places, and on many others.

At least once a year—he would explain, when you could get him to answer you—all the words fly up from the places where they have been discontented. For a moment so small that you do not notice it, they leave their comfortless and insecure lodgings altogether, and fly through the air like a swarm of bees. Some people can hear them. He, for instance, could hear them. During those moments which even to him seemed indescribably short, the words manage to travel great distances. Each time it happens that some of them never get back, or end up in other places and nobody knows it, and after that, more people do not understand something, many things, each other, themselves, or all of these, and they believe that they and what they do not understand are being represented by the same words, when they are not even using words that live in the same places any more.

But if each of the words had the house that was right for it, it would go on living there, or if it did go away for a while it would want to come back to the same place. He had always suspected this, and had discovered that it was in fact so, because he had made a study of words, and ever since then he had been making houses for each one of them. Because he knew their ways he could describe how they would come, on a certain day, like bees indeed, like bees, closer and closer, having caught a glimpse of their true homes.

"Are they all like insects, then?" you might ask.

"You know they are not," he would answer. "Some are like shrews, some are like birds, some are like water, or friends of various kinds, some are like old aunts, some are like lights, some are like feet walking without bodies in a hall lined with everything any of us remembers, and so forth. They are like us. Each of them has to have been offered its rightful abode if we are to be able to speak from one day to the next and know what we mean."

He was far advanced in his task when the barbarians arrived with their axes.

Remorse

He had told the young woman about the old man, his hero, who had taught him more than anyone else. A man of great reserve, absolute independence, integrity, lucidity, charity, calm, and genius, living alone after a life of attachments. It is always hard to meet a hero again, nevertheless the young man had been happy when he, the young woman, and the old man were invited to the same gathering at a place in the country. It was at the edge of a little village with stone houses. The light was green and rainy.

But they were there for several days, and after a while he began to feel that they would never get away from the old man—not so old now as he remembered him—who seemed to be everywhere, sat with them at table, and talked and talked, always brilliantly, marvellously, quietly. The younger man watched him grow shorter, and broader, and pinker, and limper. Then he imagined, with intricate disappointment, that the older man was attracted to the young woman.

He and she went out after lunch; he hurried her out right after the coffee, in nothing but her white dress, although it was raining a little. She was very patient. They walked in the lane. It wasn't raining hard. It was warm. She asked him why he was in a hurry. He said, "To get away from him for a little," and he laughed. But she didn't. So then he was more serious, a little irritated with her too, saying that the man was becoming excessive, and she urged him to be patient, which annoyed him. There was a well in the middle of the lane, with an arch of black iron over it, from which a bucket hung, and as they were walking around it he saw that the older man was following them.

He said to her, "Don't look now, he's following us."

"Maybe not," she said.

"Yes, he is," he said. "He's by himself."

"Oh," she said.

He said, "If we don't catch his eye, maybe he'll turn back."

"Don't do that," she said.

"Yes," he said. "I want some time to ourselves," he said. He saw that the older man was waving, but pretended not to see. He thought of the older man watching him lead her out through the rain, and perhaps wondering whether he was taking proper care of her, she looked so young, and coming along to be protective in some way. Holding hands, he led her along to a stone tower on the lane, that was part of the grounds, an annex of the main house. He drew her into the tower, as though to get out of the rain.

"No, don't do that," she said. "Be kind to him."

When he was safely in the dark he looked back, and the older man was at the well. "Let's go upstairs," he said, knowing the place. "We can't not have seen him and then seem to be waiting for him." She agreed, and they went up. The tower room was furnished as it had always been. They sat on the bed. They weren't very wet. They weren't cold. They were listening. They were even laughing a little.

"He's coming," she said.

He said, "Be quiet."

"If he comes in we'll have to call to him," she said. "He'll know we can hear him, and if we don't call we'll seem to be hiding."

"He doesn't know that we know who it is," he said.

"What if he comes up and finds us," she said.

"He won't want to come up the stairs," he said. "He'll understand that we want to be by ourselves."

"No," she said, "I don't want him to think we're hiding from him."

They said nothing for a while, and listened. A long time, sitting on the foot of the bed.

"He's not coming," she said. Then they heard him, scraping his feet on the stones outside.

"If he comes in, I'll go out and look down," she said.

"No, I will," he said. They heard the older man step inside, and the young man went out and looked down and said, "Oh hello."

"I brought something to show you," the older man said, after a moment of just standing there looking up. "This is as good a place as any," he added.

From above, he looked still shorter and pinker, with the wet head much larger than the rest of him, and the face hanging in folds. He turned to the stairs and started up slowly, and the younger man had to stand and watch, and apologize for having brought him out in the rain, while the older man said nothing, all the way up the stairs, and seemed to be in no hurry. He went through the door first, and then they all three stood facing each other, saying nothing, and gave a little laugh together.

Then the older man started to talk, and talked about lunch, and afterthoughts, and then he said he had something to show the younger man — to show them both. He said he wanted to show these things to someone, after all, and it sounded as though he had never shown them to anyone. He asked their permission. He drew from under his coat a folder and laid it on the four-poster bed, and began to spread out drawings and paintings that he had done. Some of them were in white on black or dark colored paper, but most of them were in color. In the colored ones the sky was invariably a solid blue, the earth was almost always a uniform shade of tan, and on the tan earth pieces of architecture stood in monolithic isolation, some of them with a single window, with a face in it. Perfect curves, in black, connected the tops of the buildings with each other, and on each black line, or path, like a single bead, was a planet, in which a landscape appeared, rising through a face. The white paintings on darker paper depicted animals, in such a way that their shapes looked like skeletons of further bodies.

She made a few exclamations, but the older man seemed to pay no attention. The younger man said they were very powerful. There were little poems written on some of them, a few lines each. He bent to read the poems in their small careful script, and later could not remember any. He repeated the few things he had said before. And he said he knew someone who would be interested in seeing them.

Then the older man said that he imagined they would like to be by themselves for a bit, and he gathered up the paintings deliberately, and seemed about to give them to the younger man, but didn't. They all three started down the stairs together, with the older man herding them in front. At the bottom of the stairs the older man insisted on going back alone the way he had come, while they continued their walk, since it had stopped raining. They left by another door, and the young man did not want to look at her at all.

The Element

Lying on the floor of the veranda, in the dark, he considered the fact that he had never in his life been so far off the ground. He had known it would be so today, but he had not thought about it that way. He had not thought about it in so many words. The fourth floor. At each floor, on the way up, he had seen a double door without a handle, that looked like a sliding lid. Each double door had a sign over it saying ELEVATOR, and on the door there was an orange paper pasted, on which the same hand had printed the words OUT OF ORDER. He had seen all that in the daylight, in the early afternoon, as he had climbed.

He had wondered what time to come. The professor's note from the capital had said simply to come on the ninth. Why don't you come on the ninth. Why don't you come on the ninth. That was all it said, and he had tried to extract more information, just from the wording, but without success. It was written on university stationery, with a city address. He had never been to the city, but now was the time. He knew the day but not the hour. So he planned to arrive in the morning.

He took the night train, which got you into the city in the early hours when the sky was just growing light and the carts and trucks were rolling through the outskirts, converging on the marketplace, the wet stones, the waiting cats. He could see the cats in the first gray light as the train entered the station, where everybody got off and became a crowd, hurrying definitely, mingling with other hurrying streams of people. Inside the station they began to swirl and go off in different directions, and the current dissipated itself, died out at counters where tickets, food, or magazines were for sale. The sound of feet everywhere. The people standing in backwaters were closed in on themselves, busy thinking of tickets, or else eating, or buying or counting money, not looking at him drifting among them. He asked a small old man in a dark suit the way to the university, but the old man stared at him and did not answer. He asked a heavy man in a cap with a polished black visor, who said, "Out there," and pointed, and walked away.

He went out through the door the man had pointed to. The noise of the city struck him in waves. A woman selling fruit told him what street to follow. She said it was a long way.

It was a few miles, through the sound of traffic. But the day was Saturday, and almost no one was at the university. The doors seemed to be locked. A young man with a bicycle told him how to find the architecture building. The glass doors at the front would not open, and no one came when he knocked, but a smaller door, on the side, opened when he pulled it, and he went in and walked along the reverberating marble halls until a man in a uniform appeared around a corner and asked what he wanted.

When he said he wanted to see the professor, the man was unwelcoming. Said it was not possible to see the professor. The professor wasn't there.

The young man asked him if he knew the professor, and the man said of course he did. He said he was the superintendent of the building. "Today's Saturday," he said.

"Yes," the young man said.

"And anyway, you need an appointment," the man said. "Not just anybody can walk in." He stepped forward and took the young man by the arm.

The young man said that the professor had told him to come.

"What for?"

"To see him."

"What about?"

"I wrote him a letter."

"You can't just go walking around through the building," the superintendent said, and began to turn him around.

"He told me to come," the young man repeated.

"Not today," the superintendent said.

"Yes, today," the young man said. "The ninth."

"Come along," the superintendent said.

"The ninth," the young man said again.

"Didn't you hear me, today's Saturday," the superintendent said. "He's never here on Saturday, unless it's to work, and then he won't see anybody."

"But he said today," the young man said.

"He isn't here," the superintendent said, growing taller as he said it, and pleased.

The young man dug the letter out of an inside pocket, and said, "Look. 'Why don't you come on the ninth.'" He read the words out distinctly, pointing at each one with his finger. Then there was a pause.

"That's different," the superintendent said. He passed his fingers over his head as though he had just lifted a hat off, and said, "That's for the party, of course." He patted the young man on the shoulder. "But that's not here."

"Where is it?"

"It's not now, either. It's later on."

"Where will it be?"

"Some of the students are giving it."

"Where?"

"You'd never find them," the superintendent said. "I know they had a number of things planned. But they were all for later on."

"But where?"

"Then they were going back to his place afterward. The way they always do," the superintendent said, and he was glad to show he knew it.

"I'll go there, then," the young man said.

"Not now," the superintendent said.

"When?"

"I'll call up his apartment house," the superintendent said. "Wait here." And he went off down the hall and left the young man standing there. When he came back he said that in the professor's building they did not know the professor's plans.

"Can't you telephone to him?" the young man asked.

"No, no. Can't do that. But I know you can't go out there in the morning. I know that."

And the superintendent told the young man the address and how to get there, in exchange for a promise not to go until the afternoon. He did not say what time in the afternoon, and the young man thought about it as he went. The streets grew quieter.

The address was in a neighborhood of buildings several storeys high, all of which the professor and his students had designed, so the superintendent had told him. There were courtyards between them,

with flowerbeds enclosed by low walls. It was a sunny afternoon. He
felt too warm in his long overcoat, which was never warm enough
when he wore it on Sundays, at home in the country. He found the
entry. He waited until he heard two o'clock strike, and then he rang
the downstairs bell, but nothing happened. He opened the door and
went to the elevator, read the orange paper, and started to climb the
stairs. Each flight turned on itself, and at the top gave onto a wide,
long veranda overlooking the courtyard. An apartment door opened
off each veranda. Benches, ivy gardens furnished the verandas, and
flowers were planted along the balustrades. Quiet. People walking on
verandas across the courtyard flickered through shadows. He heard
their footsteps but they said nothing. After he had climbed three
flights he came to the door, the right number. He rang the bell there,
and heard it ring inside, like a real bell, but nobody answered. He
went to a bench and sat down to wait.

He felt hungry. He had been feeling hungry for a while, but it had
seemed important to come to the apartment before he ate. He had
had no breakfast, and he was used to eating the main meal of the day
at noon. When he had waited for several hours, getting up occasion-
ally to look into the courtyard, he walked back down the stairs and
began to look among the buildings for somewhere to eat. The only
place he found with a restaurant sign was already closed. Too late for
the midday meal, too early for the evening meal. He walked around
the group of buildings. There were new shops, looking as though
they had not yet sold anything. He went back up to the fourth-floor
veranda.

He had slept badly on the train, sitting up all night, and now he
felt tired. He wanted to lie down on the bench and sleep. But that
would be taking liberties, he thought. He had not even met the pro-
fessor yet. He sat on the floor, in his overcoat, and leaned against the
bench. Nobody came to tell him to get up, so after a while he lay down.
In the summer, at home, he used to lie in the hay in the afternoon
and read popular-science magazines until he fell asleep, if he was
working alone on a job, as was often the case during the years he had
been a roofer's assistant. That was before he had taken over the farm,
which was already behind in its taxes and barely fed them, the way
things had got. Even as recently as his own childhood, things had
been different. Cleaner, brighter, better off. And yet even these days

he would go fishing—wet flies in the daytime, and at night poaching in the dark, shallow, fast-running river, setting nets too small to be legal, at the edges of backwaters, in parts of the current he had known all his life. He could sell the catch in the hotels. He worked without a light, because of the police. They all knew him, though they came from other parts of the country. They got to know everything along the river. If they caught him on the bank, or outside his barn, with the nets and fish, they would ask him to open the nets, and when they found the fish below legal size, they would fine him. Depending on who was on duty, and how heavy the catch was, they might fine him more, or less. Sometimes nothing. If there was a new man or they had been told to crack down, they might fine him for possessing a net too fine to be legal. Once they had confiscated a net, but it was an old one, and he had managed to buy it back later, very cheap, through a friend. They never looked into the rusted metal barn, if he could once get the nets in there. Then he could stand in the dark and listen to the dripping, and to the voices in the kitchen, where his mother would be pouring drinks for the inspectors, and watch through the murky window, while the fish flipped their tails in the trickling net behind him. Until the men left, and then he would get out the light and shade it, and start taking the fish out of the net.

He read about fish in the magazines. He thought about their lives. There was an article about their hearing. He read it many times. The author said that fish heard with their whole bodies. Their element conveyed a continuous message to them. They were all shaped like sound waves. All waves were echoes of each other: waves in the sea and in the air; sound waves, brain waves.

He looked at a leaf, one day, and considered its spine, like that of a fish, and he thought of how the whole leaf vibrated in the wind. Each leaf must turn the waves of the air into a kind of sound, though he could not hear it, any more than he could hear what the fish heard, in the water. The author of the article referred to the element in which human beings spent their lives—whatever it might be called.

The young man had wondered why we did not hear our element, whatever it was, with our whole bodies. He felt certain that the shapes of fish were very important in understanding the whole matter. He built a boat shaped like a fish, with ribs laid like fish spines, and he lay in it listening to the current. If you could live that way, he decided, if you could keep those shapes around you all the time, maybe you would begin to be able to recognize the sound of the element in which you were living, passing through you. He made drawings of buildings with spines like fish spines, and curved walls and windows like scales. He used photographs from the magazines of groups of buildings in cities, and he drew pictures of them shaped like fish, schools of fish.

"But I have to be practical," he said to himself. 'What use would it be?' they will ask. Hospitals and schools for the deaf, first. Start with normal hearing, which everyone agrees about. Try that, first." His designs grew more elaborate. Centers for the Deaf, shaped like fish.

Then he saw an article about a famous architect, living at present in the capital, teaching at the university, a professor who spoke of using in his buildings the shapes found in nature. There were pictures of important buildings that exemplified the architect's theories, and beside them drawings and photographs of natural objects whose shapes he had adapted: shells, grains in pieces of wood, nests. His latest building, as it happened, had been an aquarium, into which he had built the shapes of waves, which he had gathered from different places. The young man had decided to write to the professor about his theory concerning the importance of the fish shape, and his idea for a Center for the Deaf. He had sent a few drawings, to make certain things clear. Why the buildings were arranged as they were, in relation to each other, in a current. "Dear Sir," he began his letter, but the title on the envelope, of course, was "Professor."

He had thought he would fall asleep, but he had lain there in his overcoat, thinking about his plans, wide awake. Maybe the restaurant would be open now, he thought finally, and it came to him for the first time, like the recollection of something funny, that he was farther above the ground than he had ever been. He had known from the article that the professor lived in a tall building like this, which he had designed himself. The young man tried to see what kind of natural form was echoed in the shapes of the balustrades, but he could not recognize anything. The professor had said that mathematics, too, was an expression of nature, and perhaps the tiers of shadowy verandas were mathematically harmonious. The young man made his way back down to the restaurant. Lights were on now, inside. It was later than he had thought. It was hard to tell how a day was passing, in a city. He went in. There was a counter to sit at. No one else was in the restaurant. He imagined the buildings around him shaped like fish, in the gathering dusk. A woman came and gave him a menu, in silence, and he ordered a fish to eat, to see what it would be like here. It was all right. The woman who served him left the radio on in the next room, and stayed in there while he ate, but she came back out as he was finishing, and he paid her, and went out into the lighted spaces curving around the new buildings, and up to the veranda. One small light was burning by the door. He lay down again, beside the bench.

He began to think about his letter—whether he had made it sound clear and correct, what impression it had made. He had heard nothing for several weeks, but he had seen in a paper that the professor had been away for the opening of a building in another country. Then the note came saying, "Why don't you come on the ninth." The young man had imagined many kinds of meetings, and he lay and worried in the dark, thinking, "Why should I worry?"

Then he heard them coming, a group, on the stairs. Young men, young women, laughing and talking. He remembered where he was. A big dog came running up to him, and sniffed him all over, lying there by the bench. Didn't even bark at him. Wagged his tail and went to the door. And the people he had heard on the stairs began to spill onto the veranda, and along to the door, without even noticing the young man, at first. When they did, they looked startled, and stared at him. Not one of them was wearing an overcoat. Shirts, blouses. Some of them carrying jackets. He recognized the professor, from pictures. But taller than he had imagined. The professor did not look as old as he must be, talking fast with all the young people, who must be the students the superintendent had spoken about. The young man stepped forward and told the professor who he was, his name.

The professor looked as though he had forgotten. The young man said his name again.

"Oh yes," the professor said, with no sound of recognition in his voice.

"You said why didn't I come on the ninth."

"You— Oh, are you the—the fish shapes?" The young man nodded.

"Come in. Come in. Too bad you weren't with us earlier. Have you been waiting long?"

The professor had his key ready, and opened the door without waiting for an answer. The students moved into the apartment as though they were coming home. They turned on the lights, established themselves here and there among the furniture, went on out into other rooms, picked up half-empty wine bottles, found glasses; one opened a guitar case and took out a guitar.

"Let's see what we can find," the professor said, turning to his new guest. "Have you eaten?"

The young man nodded.

"Something to drink," the professor said, and held up his hand as he walked toward the door that probably led to the kitchen. "This is the young man with the fish designs," he said, and left the room. The dog, lying on a sofa, watched him go out, and got up and followed him.

The students all looked at the young man, but nobody spoke. The walls of the apartment were of brick painted white. There was a large fireplace, wide and deep, raised above the floor. One student, who was lighting a fire, had turned to look at him, like the others. A big painting, over the fireplace. The young man tried to make out what it was a picture of. He felt it was much too warm in the room, which had been closed all day. He missed the air of the veranda. He was sure he would not know the answer, when the professor came back with glasses and a question. Where and when would they have a chance to talk, he wondered. He felt certain that he would find nothing to say, and would pass out after a few drinks, but he stood waiting. Some of the students were talking to each other, again. He stood looking at the picture, and at the walls with lights shining onto them, and the large windows in which the lighted windows of other buildings could be seen. He imagined himself as the professor, and at once it seemed to him that he could not hear anyone in the room.

Language

Certain words now in our knowledge we will not use again, and we
will never forget them. We need them. Like the back of the picture.
Like our marrow, and the color in our veins. We shine the lantern
of our sleep on them, to make sure, and there they are, trembling
already for the day of witness. They will be buried with us, and rise
with the rest.

The Great Union

There was an old woman who lived by herself, up the hill, on Garfield somewhere, or Taylor, near where the paving had not reached, and made shirts that took a long time, so that people laughed about it. They were good shirts, though, it had to be said, and they ought to be. By hand. Like the ones she had made for her husband. There were people who said they remembered him, but if those who said they did asked the others who were present, it would turn out that they themselves were the only ones there who would say they had actually known him, so that it was half way to his not having existed. Surely she must have had pictures of him. If there were any children they were long gone. Sometimes she came if the women's circle was having a sewing meeting, and it was always a surprise, and then it was told about afterwards as though the day had been an occasion. Because nobody knew what she would say next. She got cross and argued. They thought it was funny the way she remembered things that none of them had seen. And she took it for granted that they remembered those things too, which was really what was funny. It was only a farm, up there, when she lived there, at one time. Before they started blasting the mines under the hill, and she heard them. Just grass and trees, then. Animals, and sheds with lamps.

She would walk fast, farther than they ever walked, through the streets that had been fields and pastures and woods, on a snowy night before Christmas, with a shirt held out flat, in tissue paper, for a present, and a cake baked for somebody, and her cakes were famous for being bad. She never let anybody know she was coming. She would not go in. I won't come in. She stood there with the door open. She never stayed to talk. She was so thin that they compared things to her, and she wore an old overcoat and a round hat pulled down to her eyes in a way that people showed each other when she was mentioned. In years to come, some would know, without being told, that she was dead, and some would realize that it must be hard for people to re-member her name, even the few that were left who had known her.

She referred the passing weather to the great disasters. She spoke of the blizzard, when it snowed. It never snowed like the blizzard. Did it? Not like the blizzard, though. And she meant eighty-eight. Or eighty-five, whichever it was, they said to each other once again. When nobody was born but one or two. And in the snowstorm she saw the church burn, in the terrible cold. The whole spire catching, and the snow on the ground shrinking back in a widening circle, and them crying. Then the bells fell out onto the stones and smashed like glass, so that she always heard it. That was the year of the flood too. It came after.

When the bells fell, that was the worst, she said, since the burning of the Great Union, and they agreed. They said it themselves. They had heard it said. They knew it. What was the Great Union, and where? Nobody told. They looked away. Some nodded without meaning yes, and some shook their heads without meaning no. Even she had not seen it, whatever she might say. Unwatched by anyone alive, the immense white columns had bathed in flames, and dropped to their knees and faces in fire, reflected on all sides. The thousands of white candles hanging in rings of gold and crystal had melted and flown down through the high burning halls, onto the green marble, and the gilded roofs had hung for a moment in the heat like wings made by humans, and then had sprouted flames along cracks the shapes of lightning, and sagged and tilted, to shatter across beams and rafters, and splash into the piled fire. There was nobody to know whether it all sank in land or water. It must have burned all night, all day. Night and day. There was nobody for it to belong to. The farm had not even been thought of.

Vanity

One night we decided to camp in the hills beside a series of water-falls, and had to speak a little louder than we usually did in the woods. It was later in the day than we would have liked it to be, when we got there. It had rained all day and the grass and bushes were dripping. Just up ahead of us there was a small bridge over the stream. When we had eaten we got ready to sleep in the car. It was going to rain some more.

When it was already night we heard voices. Deep resonant voices of men. The summer nights there are twilit for a long time. We could make out a big old truck parked not far behind us on the same level patch, with its lights out. Some figures were using flashlights to get things out of the covered back of the truck.

If they peered in on us, we said to each other, the tops of bottles glinting in the dim light looked like the ends of gun barrels. They would think we were armed. We laughed. We lay whispering about them, rehearsing what we had heard about local people, and describing the place to each other, the sound, the light, the colors, the past day, in which we had come a long way.

One of the men, who looked very large, in a long raincoat, came over toward us. He looked like a farmer. He wore a sweater and a knitted hat. A big crumpled and swollen face, a protruding chin. He put his face up near the window. After a while he must have seen us. He said "Hello."

So we answered. We said "Hello."

He said we looked as though we weren't from around there.

"No," we said.

Well, he said, he wasn't either. He named a place he had come from, and asked whether we were acquainted with it, but neither of us had heard the name he had said, and so we answered no.

So he started to tell us about it. How far away it was. Its population. What the winters were like. What sort of people lived there. He shined his flashlight into the car and said it looked as though we really lived in there, and he admired that.

He asked us if we were going on in the morning, and we said yes.

"So is we," he said. And he asked us if we had heard of the Bible Meeting at another town whose name he chewed and swallowed, and we answered no. So he started to tell us about that. The road there, what it was like at different times of the year. What an event it was for miles about. How they sang hymns he had never heard. He said he was going there to preach. He liked to preach there. He went every year.

He said he hoped we wouldn't mind their staying the night beside us there. He said he had a young man with him who was not right in the head but he wasn't no harm, nor nothing like that. Just so we wouldn't think anything wrong. They would just be getting ready for bed, he said.

He turned away and took a few steps.

Then he came back.

He asked us whether we would be interested to know what text he was intending to preach on. So we said yes.

He raised his hand, and then bent down to the window to stare in at us.

From the Book of Ecclesiastes, he said. Two, five. He nodded his head. "Do you remember that one?"

So we answered no.

He shook his head, and gestured in the air, and rolled his words, and recited: "*I made myself gardens and parks and planted in them all kinds of fruit trees.*"

"That's it," he said. "*All kinds of fruit trees.*"

"Well, so good-night," he said.

So we said good-night, but he had already turned off the flashlight and was on his way back to the unlit truck and his companion.

So we laughed.

A Fable of the Buyers

A man walked down the street with three dreams for sale. Of course he would not tell anyone what they were. He even said that he couldn't, because the dreams wouldn't be the same for them. He couldn't tell them anything about the dreams at all. They were there like straws to be drawn. Everyone hopes for better dreams than his own, and people bought them. The dreams were to be opened in private, the buyers were told. They were printed on exactly the same paper, which was made to dissolve as it was read, or to dissolve anyway if someone tried to keep it without reading it, like a talisman, so that it might produce its dream that way, as everything can do if the right spirit approaches it. A little later they would return to sight in the man's hand.

People who bought the dreams sometimes met each other later and tried to compare which dreams they had bought. Very suspiciously, at first. Very cautiously, with hints back and forth. Everyone found out after a while that the other person seemed to have bought a different dream. But then it turned out finally that there were too many of them in the same room for them all to have had different dreams, and they started arguing with each other. For they had all seen that there were only three dreams in the man's hand.

But with each person each dream clearly had been different. And still the buyers wanted to know which of the three dreams they had had. They tried everything. They classified by means of every triad they could think of. They divided each other into three factions, which never seemed accurate enough. They kept changing sides, and never forgiving each other. Eventually, in order to check, two of them tried to read the same dream at the same time, and it disappeared at once, entirely, and never reappeared in the man's hand. That happened again and the man was left with only one.

"Now won't the others come back at all?" he was asked.

"No," he said. "But it doesn't matter. They were all copies of the same dream."

"Will you sell us that one?" they asked.

"No," he said. "I'm going to give it back."

"Which one is it?" they asked, almost in unison.

For none of them had learned anything at all. What can you learn from a bought dream?

A Miser

A man was able to get hold of all the laughter in the world, and he packed it tightly and locked it up in his house and hid the key.

The trouble was that nobody missed it.

He had to tell them what they were missing. Nobody knew what he was talking about. Nobody believed him. Nobody thought that what he was talking about was real. Who could believe that, after all? Would anyone believe it if someone came up and said that they had all the laughter in the world locked up somewhere? Would anyone believe it, even if neither of them laughed?

He tried to describe laughter to them. He showed them how it was done. He showed different ways in which different people could laugh. He told them all the things that made people do it, everything he could remember or invent. People falling down. Filth. People making terrible mistakes. People unable to control themselves. Misfortunes of all kinds. People with something the matter with them. No interest.

He told them that it would be good for their health, and that he would not make it expensive for them. No interest.

There were many things about it that he didn't even know, he said. No interest.

It had been called divine, he said. No interest.

But the man kept on trying. Because at least at night he could always go home and take out the key and open up some and have a good laugh to himself. But then one night he started to laugh at himself, and that made him lonely.

He tried to invite somebody else in to laugh. But it was very hard. He even said he would give the laughter away.

At that somebody else laughed.

So that person remembered how to laugh. So that person was on his side. They were laughing together. Somebody else was laughing with him.

But that meant that somebody else had some of the laughter in the world. So he started making plans to steal it.

But the other kept giving it away.

Speech of a Guide

The things that you lost by the way were guiding you. And you tried to replace them. Which do you think you will see again, them or their replacements? Unless you lost the replacements as well, which sometimes happens. And sometimes you had grown to like the replacements better. But sometimes they were hung around your neck in a bag, and taught you and taught you and taught you, like your own soul, and you grew as deaf to the one as to the other. Then sometimes what you thought you had lost turned up again. Even in the bag around your neck. And it was still guiding you, still crying "Repent," from a wild place. But you did not know how to follow it any better than before. You did not attend to the fact that it knew its way in and out of your life better than you did, even knowing where to wait for you, which you would not have known. You did not even consider its having a destiny of its own, woven through yours. Eventually disaster again separated you for an unknown period which neither of you might survive without changing lives at least once. And if you lost it and never found it again, as is most likely, it was something that was never yours to give away, it was a foretaste of total disaster, an absolute nakedness that you could never have conceived of and arrived at without so many guides. But some need only one. Some lead the guides.

So you went on losing and losing, as the rain loses, the mountain loses, the sun loses, as everything under heaven loses. You came alone together and here you are.

The Chart

Taking advantage of what he had heard with one limited pair of ears, in a single and relatively isolated moment of recorded history, in the course of an infinitesimal fraction of conceivable time (which some say is the only time), he came to believe firmly that there was much he could not hear, much that was constantly being spoken and indeed sung to teach him things he could never otherwise grasp, which if grasped would complete the fragmentary nature of his consciousness until it was whole at last—one tone both pure and entire floating in the silence of the egg, at the same pitch as the silence. Next, by measurement and invention he came firmly to believe that there were high notes which the dog could hear that remained inaudible to his own ears, and which the dog had been hearing for longer than he himself had been hearing anything. Therefore there must be something in the nature of the dog which the dog had never understood, for it had not been meant for the dog alone—something however which he himself would now understand better if he could ever come to hear it, since it was for understanding that he had sacrificed hearing. So he domesticated the dog. But before he learned to hear the high notes he came firmly to believe that there were lower notes which the donkey, the bull and the cow could hear and he himself could not, and he domesticated the donkey, the bull, and the cow. Still higher notes, and he domesticated the porpoise, the bat, the bee, the ant, and kept all the surviving species of birds in cages. Still lower, and he domesticated the elephant, the cat, the bear, the rat, and kept all the remaining whales in stalls, trying to hear through their ears the note made by the rocking of the axle of the earth. Because by that time, by measurement and invention he had defined a relation in which they stood to each other solely with regard to the frequencies of their limits of hearing, and he had drawn them, according to their frequencies, on a chart, in orderly progression, like a calendar going forward and backward but not in time, even though time was the measure of the frequencies, as it was the measure of every other thing (therefore, some say, the only measure), and across the chart he had drawn lines at the outer limits of what he believed each could hear, tracing a river flowing both ways. And from the chart he could calculate what each of the other existences could hear, though not what it could be: the owl could hear a head turn. Turning his head he tried to imagine what it would sound like to an owl. The bat could hear a hand held out. It took shape in the bat body. All he could not imagine was the bat. The elephant could hear the roots of a tree, and slept without moving its feet. But the chart did not teach him to hear anything or even how to listen for it. The flattened paper became one more of the promises of knowing for which he had given up fragments of his hearing. Furthermore he had to admit that the animals certainly did not hear the same things, tamed or in cages, that they had heard in their free state. And beyond—and in fact among—the last known animals living and extinct, the lines could be drawn through white spaces that had an increasing progression of their own, into regions of a hearing that was no longer conceivable, indicating creatures wholly sacrificed or never evolved, hearers of the note at which everything explodes into light, and of the continuum that is the standing still of darkness, drums echoing the last shadow without relinquishing the note of the first light, hearkeners to the unborn overflowing. The lines projected off the chart, out into the night. Even from the squares that were occupied by creatures with ears limited like his own, no sound rose. He pressed his fingers against the white panes of the paper, and he thought the vestigial ears in the skin of his fingertips stirred for a moment, but he still could not understand anything they heard. He straightened and turned out the light and listened to the rain.

Clear Lake

The bottom of the lake is standing on its side. It is made of oaken boards planed and varnished. You can tell that there is a slight, steady breeze, for the current of the oaken grain flows slowly up the varnished boards in lines of light. The wood is cracked here and there. A crack is a root, and every board contains memories of roots, and understands, while resisting. The lake hardly delays the light enough to be seen, until one is at a distance. Then its surfaces begin to shine above the already unseen boards, along which the light is flowing in lines, in another world. The eye can never perceive the movement of those lines, and yet it sees that they are in motion. They flow on, to join everything else.

The water is deeper than it looks.

Nearby the waves are echoing against an empty shadowless boat, and the heart listens.

Echoes

Everything we hear is an echo. Anyone can see that echoes move forward and backward in time, in rings. But not everyone realizes that as a result silence becomes harder and harder for us to grasp— though in itself it is unchanged—because of the echoes pouring through us out of the past, unless we can learn to set them at rest. We are still hearing the bolting of the doors of Hell, Pasiphaë in her byre, the cries at Thermopylae, and do not recognize the sounds. How did we sound to the past? And there are sounds that rush away from us: echoes of future words.

So we know that there are words in the future, some of them loud and terrible. And we know that there is silence in the future. But will the words recognize their unchanging homeland?

I am standing on the shore of a lake. I am a child, in the evening, at the time when the animals lose heart for a moment. Everyone has gone, as I wanted them to go, and in the silence I call across the water, "Oh!" And I see the sound appear running away from me over the water in her white veil, growing taller, becoming a cloud with raised arms, in the dusk. Then there is such silence that the trees are bent. And afterward a shock like wind, that throws me back against the hill, for I had not known to whom I was calling.

The Vision

As they grow, out of pure devotion, before long the festivities come
to blind us to their occasions, as the middle blinds us to the begin-
ning, when if we could see the beginning we could see the end, where
they sit together and nothing is hid between them. We keep remem-
bering something different from what we celebrate, to commemorate
a glimpse that we have forgotten, as a stone slab may commemorate
a resurrection. There were golden wagons moving without wheels
over the desert in a little cloud, with four tall torches lighting the
way in the mind of one who saw and tried to tell us. And we listened
and made wheels.

Chronicle

The bells in the savage mountains make such a tinny clangor because
century after century bells had to be brought up the mountains, hand
over hand, many sleeps on the way, over huge rocks and steep slopes
of naked stone, climbing stepped gorges, threading cliffs, crossing
deep ravines. And to have bells that were big enough, they had to be
thin. Trains of Indians and mules, both of both sexes, and both
slaves, and eating as slaves, hauled in the mountains bark cables
twisting and groaning, the shoulders of mules and heads of Indians
harnessed to fraying ships' hawsers dragging sleds to each of which a
heavy bell was bound with drying jungle creepers. They moved up-
ward in the white mists before the sun came out, the dark gorges
aflap with shrieking birds. And they stopped only when the sun had
set, painting their faces or their backs red as it went. They slept by
the trail, most of the humans attached to the propped sleds, each by
a long chain that led over the bell and through a ring in the collar of
one of the sentries' dogs. Around them like a second wave of sound,
unattached, slept the ones recruited in each village on the way, as
volunteers, sent by the elders of the villages by way of tribute, to pay
for the safety of the villages. Martyrs. They all slept under the black
trees, around the bells onto which leaves, acorns, pine cones, un-
known forest objects, fell in the night. The bells echoed waterfalls
too far to be heard. The long processions dragged the cavernous
heads behind them up into the neck of the rain-forest, down the
other, even steeper, slope, across a rugged plateau, and up again into
the high basin, to be beaten in the tragic sunsets, blending happily
with the old hammering on iron wheelrims of different sizes which
had been brought up before there were tracks for wheels or clearance
for sleds, and the even older army cauldrons with leather-covered
wooden clappers. Some of these survived and still bear the dents that
were struck when the first bell was rung in celebration of arrival, be-
fore the dogs had finished the bones of those who had died that day
in the gang hoisting the bell with ship's tackle into the crossed beams
of the patient tower. Even the slaves, in their way, had felt enthusiasm

for the end of the achievement, and had stood waiting for the fierce sound hammered out of it in the name of the greatest of silences, henceforth to tell the sun where he was. The bells survived the bearers many times over. When they crack and it does no good to beat them any more they are taken down and stood on the floor, where candles are lighted in front of them, the smoke of myrrh swirls around them like clouds on the mountains, and names are whispered, with different intonations, into their broken places.

What They Say in the Villages

A cross is a door of the dead. It was always so. Before there was any-one living, it was waiting to bring them into the world. It was the shape it is because of the way each one would be, thrown down or lifted up. Already the cross's shadow was reaching out over the ground, because they come up through the shadow. They always did, to be born, and to be born again. We sit at the threshold. Our shadow be-comes part of the shadow reaching out over the ground. There are steps going down inside the shadow, beyond our shadow, but they are not for the eyes of the living, they are not for our feet now. We sit here, and when the dead come up, the first step into the new life is inside us. We sit here whenever we can.

When we die we will walk down into the cross's shadow. Each of us will part three ways. Each of us will come to the end of being seen. We will have gone. Each one's shadow will stay here. No one will see it then. One by one, when we find the turning we will start to look for the others again. It will be dark. It is a larger world than this one, and as empty. But each of us will be looking for the same thing, the same shadow, in the dark of that world, which lies behind the dark of this one. When one of us finds the cross's shadow we will wait for the others, and when they come the three of us will become one, and start to climb. We will come out into a world that we never saw, even though our first step may fall inside the living, who will not see us. Our own shadows will not know us, but we will not need them any more. We will leave them and go on. That will be the life without shadows.

It leads through us.

We feel it. We feel it!

Walls

The mountains are there in every direction. Already we are high up.
They are higher, wherever we look. Sometimes the sun goes down
behind one, sometimes behind another, depending on us. The
mountains rise too steeply to climb, in most places. As far as the
mountains, on all sides, there are little courtyards, and tiled roofs,
with trees rising out of some of the courtyards. Dogs bark and bark.
Balls fly into the air and drop out of sight. Voices of children flutter
over the roofs. Roosters who never see each other, answer each other.
Immortal storms break around the mountains. There are caves in
the rocks. The clouds come down into the gardens at night. For hours
at a time the streets are removed. They are folded up and the houses
heal together over them. Then if you lay your ear to the heavy walls
you may hear a heartbeat.

Meanwhile the streets are put away in the caves in the mountains.
They lie there in the dark telling everything they know, without a
word, and it is washed away, and they are returned, wet, and ready to
go on watching. They are returned, a little washed away, but otherwise
the same, and to many the difference is not apparent. In the under-
ground streams everything becomes transparent in the darkness.
The only sound is that of running water, and only the streets can hear
it. When the streets are returned, the houses stop breathing, which
they can do for long periods of time without its being noticed.

The children who are born when the streets are away remember
their own silences. Formerly, in order to rule in the country, a child
of the blood royal had to be born at such a time, and so the royal
midwife was accompanied by an assistant who remained with an ear
to the wall throughout the entire delivery, praying for the streets not
to return, not one, not even for a moment. Nowadays this is no
longer considered important.

The caves do not listen to the streets, they merely wash away the
stories. They know that the streets will not come to them forever to
hear the sound of water, and that one day the houses will not heal,

and both the streets and the walls will die their next death, which is of the body. Then the water, silent at last, will wear away nothing but faces long since transparent, leaving only the eyes.

At Night

Those who work at night are one body, and sometimes they are aware of their larger self. There are watchmen, helmsmen, surgeons, purveyors, thieves, bakers, mothers, beginners, and all the others. Together they are alive under the presence of the spaces of night, and it seems as though their veins might go on growing out of them into the dark sky, like a tree. They hear a fire differently. There are those who work at night, alone. Only alone. When they work it becomes night, and they become alone, they alone are awake. All places become the same. The worker may be one of the fingers of night, one of the ears of night, one of the veins of night. Even one of the eyes of night, as the eyes are the eyes of day. He or she may be the mind of night, in which all those others are, and their days with them. You forget so much of yourself most of the time, they all say to me so that I can almost hear them. So much of yourself you know nothing about, and never will know anything about, they say. So much of you makes you uncomfortable. Some of yourself you are clearly ashamed of, they say. Well, you know. Anyway, what is wrong with working at night? You have the bellfrogs. You have the owls in the walnut trees. You have the sound of a well. You have the sleepers, with their dreams moving all around you. There are even dreams of you working at night, sometimes. You dream of it yourself. Do you really work in the dreams alone? Do dreams help you to work at night? Do anyone's dreams have any effect? Growing alone into the night all around you.

A Tree

A tree has been torn out and the blind voices are bleeding through the earth. Wherever the roots tentatively learned, the voices flow for the first time, knowing. They have no color, except as voices have colors. They do not even have sounds. They are not looking for one. They come together like fingers. They flow out. They explode slowly to where the branches were, and the leaves. And then the silence of the whole sky is the echo of their outcry.

As I was a child I heard the voices rising. I sat by a wall. It was afternoon already, facing west, near a tree, and I had heard them before. All the roots of the earth reach blindly toward mouths that are waiting to say them.

Martin

You turn into a white dust road at the foot of a hill, and there is a man up ahead carrying a beam that reaches all the way across the road. He is walking in the same direction you are, but some distance ahead. Five minutes' walk ahead. Less. Three minutes' walk ahead. Keeping the same distance, never seeing you, though the road winds a little, following the water in the bottom of the valley. There is no one else on the road. There are cows and horses far off in the flat pastures. There are donkeys. There is laundry on thorn bushes grown for it. There is a dome of a church over a hill. There is a cloud of blue smoke rising from behind another hill. There are black birds. There are little white clouds over the mountains. There is water hurrying silently in a stone trough. There is the light of the sound of brass. There is wind. There are feathers blowing.

He never sees you because he never turns. He never turns because he is carrying the beam that stretches all the way across the road. He is carrying it behind him, with his two hands and with a strap slung across his head. The beam is balanced on his back, on the strap from his head, and he goes on walking. He is taking the weight on his head, his neck, the slope of his shoulders, his feet, the backs of his heels, the backs of his legs, his lungs, some little part of it in his hands. He is wearing a coat the color of the road, down to his knees. The long ragged hem keeps whipping in the wind. The long hair on the back of his head is all that ever faces you. But he keeps the same distance.

Though he set out so long ago.

He was born five minutes before you.

If he had not nearly died of sickness when he was three, he would be far ahead of you by now, out of sight, with the beams already in place.

If his leg had not mended, when he broke it in his fifth year, he would be far away now, begging.

If his mother, who was two years dying in pain, had lived another fifteen minutes, he would now be behind you. You would never have seen him. He was not born where you first saw him, and if any detail

of his journey, of his whole life, had been different, he would not
have been there in time.

If his name had been different, he would not have been there
in time.

His name is Martin, but you cannot know that.

If the saint had not lived the man would not have been there.

But this world is not made any other way.

The water is flowing back.

It is not one beam he is carrying, but two.

But he is not tired. He keeps the same distance.

You will not catch up with him to find out what he is doing. Not
in a country of beams, rafters, planks, tables, cupboards, benches,
chairs, beds, doors, gates, posts, sheds, fences, fires, in which every
piece of wood has been stolen.

Brothers

A man from Lode had not seen any of his brothers for a number of years, and as the country had suffered invasions and wars and epidemics he was afraid his brothers might have died, or might be in distress, and he went looking for them. After travelling and inquiring for some time, he was commended to a woman who read fortunes, who told him to take the road to the city of Simburad, in the fen country far to the north. The man from Lode had no reason not to follow her instructions, and he set out for Simburad, though he did not know a word of the language of those regions.

Not many people take the road to Simburad, beautiful though the capital is reputed to be. The road is barely a road—a track over sand, or over marsh, crossing fords that can be dangerous even in mid-summer. From the time he passed into the country where the few inhabitants speak the language of Simburad, the man from Lode met no one else who was travelling there, and no one who was coming back. It was a long journey. He was alone, and he never saw any of the people who live in those regions, except at a distance.

He was less than a day's journey (by his own calculations) from Simburad, when he rounded a little hill one morning and saw that the track ahead of him descended once more into marshland, and half-way across a wide fen, among scrub trees and bushes, disappeared. It disappeared. Not only the track—he discovered as he approached it—but the ground on which it stood, for some distance on either side, had been swallowed into the earth. As he drew nearer, he saw that the track led to the sagging edge of a chasm. It was a country of waters, and he was not surprised to hear the sound of a river. He went nearer, to where he could see over the wet, slippery verge, and he saw, far below him, a piece of the road continuing along the floor of the other side of the chasm. It must have sunk in one piece, and remained that way, leading into the far wall of the pit. Nearer to him, on his side of the chasm, a stream was flowing, dark, green, with the heavy, murderous hissing of floodwaters. He saw the figure of a man down by the stream, bending and turning on the shore, as though

looking for something—the motion of someone picking over ruins
—and from time to time taking what looked like a piece of drift-
wood to a construction made of sticks, beside the dark stream. The
man from Lode could not tell whether the sticks were a shelter, the
beginning of a bridge, or the materials for a raft or a fire. The edge of
the chasm was boggy and treacherous, and the man from Lode lay
down to look more closely. He saw the body of an animal—perhaps
a goat—come floating down the stream, and the man below him fish
it out with a long stick, and roll it over and examine it, and then look
around, upstream, downstream, and up to the edge of the chasm, to
where the man from Lode was hidden by small bushes. Something
in the face of the man below made the man from Lode happy to
realize that the other could not see him. He reproached himself for
hiding; he could not explain to himself why he should hide from the
man below, but he was afraid to show himself, and he lay still. The
man below drew a long knife, and cut a piece off the animal and
began to eat it, just as it was, looking up around the edge of the chasm.
He turned away at last, and the man from Lode slipped back through
the bushes until he could not see the other man's head, and then he
sat up and thought about what he should do next.

He could think of no reason why he should be afraid of the man
below, but he seemed to be. Certainly he had no wish to stand up
and show himself. And even if the other had not been there, how
would the man from Lode have got down into the chasm, and crossed
the river, and got up the other side? All around the chasm, and on
both sides of the road that led to it, lay deep marshland, with mud
and water above his depth. He pondered the matter for a long time,
and at last decided that he could do nothing except turn back.

He returned the way he had come, and he met no one for several
days. Then one afternoon a man came toward him on the road, trav-
elling toward Simburad. The man greeted him in another foreign
tongue—not even the language of the country of Simburad. This
other was well dressed, and vigorous, and affable. They smiled and
bowed to each other, and after a few fruitless attempts at conversation,
laughed, and went on in opposite directions.

But then the man from Lode thought, "He thinks I've been to
Simburad and am coming back from there." And he thought he should
warn the other about the chasm, and perhaps spare him several days'

journey, for that road, after all, could no longer be said to lead to Simburad. So he turned and went after the other, and overtook him, and tried to explain about the chasm, and the river, and the man gathering sticks and carving up dead animals to eat, though even as he described it he could not explain to himself why he had hidden.

But the other traveller could not understand anything that the man from Lode was trying to say. He stood listening with an expression of polite indulgence that gradually turned to one of embarrassment, then one of boredom. The man from Lode redoubled his efforts to make him understand, speaking more and more simply, slowly, distinctly, repeating a few phrases over and over, with gestures whose emptiness he could feel as he made them larger and larger on the echoless air. He could see the other's patience give place to a suspicion that the man from Lode was the victim of some more or less acute mental disturbance, a suspicion that became a conviction when the man from Lode seized him by the arm to draw him back, away from the direction of Simburad. The other pulled himself free with a threat, and hurried on his way. The man from Lode ran after him for several minutes, repeating the same useless phrases and gestures toward the other's retreating back, and then he gave up for the second time on the road to Simburad, and turned back.

And the other travelled on over the sinking road, and came after several days' solitary journey, to the hill, and the marsh, and the chasm, and he crept to the edge and lay down and watched the swollen stream and the man below gathering sticks and bodies of animals, and the man's face frightened him, and he drew back to think of what he should do next, and decided to give up the journey to Simburad, and as he stood up and started back he remembered the man whom he had met, whom he had taken for a fool, and it occurred to him that all this may have been what the man from Lode had been trying to tell him. He wondered whether he would ever see the man from Lode again, and whether he would recognize the man if he found him, and whether they would be able to tell each other anything.

The Fugitive

The land of the fugitive is all around us. To someone each of these trees is a thing to hide behind. Each of these rooms is a place of concealment, judged essentially in terms of how well hidden someone would be in it, how long it would be good for hiding in, and how someone could get out of it. Each of these streets the fugitive watches with a view to passing along it unperceived. He would rather swim in a river than in a lake, and in the river and the lakes you can see why. He moves from body to body, and most of them admit him like a shadow, and a hollow is conceived inside their heels. The greatness of the flight does not depend upon the fugitive but upon the pursuer.

The fugitive never forgets the smell of dogs. And what is music to the fugitive? Above all things he hates his brother, the pilgrim, who walks on the ridges and rests under the trees, dissolves the rooms and the streets, and worships the rivers. The greatness of the pilgrimage does not depend upon the pilgrim. That is the family likeness.

To the fugitive a cave is a place of defense. A desert is only a danger. There are fugitives with children. The children are surprised at nothing. There are fugitives who collect animals, and tame them, and try to teach them to do everything that men can do. To a fugitive even a disease may be a place of refuge, since he was already hiding in his body. There is a picture of him as an infant, learning to walk, with his arms up as though he were trying to fly.

The sleep of the fugitive is all around us.

But it happens that he wakes into his brother.

The Good-bye Shirts

Daily the indispensable is taught to elude us, while we are furnished according to our wishes with armories of what we do not need. And like all armories, they wait. None of us needs a good-bye shirt. But which of us (if a man) is without one? The lack of one, to our eyes, would be a matter for pity ("Poor thing, not even a good-bye shirt") or for contempt ("Not even a good-bye shirt") or for the perfunctory expression of horror elicited by murders and grotesque accidents ("Not even a good-bye shirt") or for the prophylactic amusement used for saints ("Not even a good-bye shirt"). So in each of our cupboards there it lies, no doubt, or will lie, and we do not even know— we may never know—which one it is, any more than we knew which would be the meeting shirt, though we may have tried and tried to choose it. And what guides our hand at last? If we could be said to know what we were choosing, would we ever put on the good-bye shirt at all? Or would we put it on at once? Have we in fact already worn it repeatedly, through the casual farewells of days that have faded out, one behind the other? Are we wearing it now?

When two good-bye shirts meet each other, at the laundry, or on the bodies of their wearers, what lack of recognition (as far as we can tell) even at the moment and in the very gestures of routine parting! But then, are we ourselves prompt to recognize those who share our calling, our fate? And the shirts, the real good-bye shirts, can be certain of sharing only two things: they have owners; and they can be emptier when worn than when waiting in the cupboard or hanging on the line in the sunlight, waving.

Poverty

When I went to sleep among the late very poor, as a virtue, I took with me only what I considered indispensable. Everything else I had sold, as we have been commanded to do, and the proceeds had been given to the poor. The old poor, the poor of all ages and of every kind I could recognize. I made a study of the poor—from the standpoint of financial superiority—and by this time I had with me a single suitcase, and a book I was reading, about birds. I saw that all the cubicles opened directly off the hall and each was painted a shade different in color, the shades in orderly procession. But the spectrum of colors was not complete. The other end was not red, but just where the red should have begun was the wall of the shower room: pink. The light was on in the shower room. I saw, where doors were open, as we passed, that the cubicles had no windows at all, which I thought was important. I saw that they were painted the same color inside that they were painted outside. Of course they were small— hardly wider than the door—and I thought that was important too. I saw the soles of shoes, socks, and feet. I was given the room at the left, on the end, next to the shower. It too was pink. I had already paid. They had probably already locked the outside door. Old men were in the shower, taking showers. They were telling long stories of their childhoods that they had remembered only as they were coming down the hall, and the more they told the more they remembered, continuously without listening to each other, with the showers on. I did not want to shut the door, and I did not want to go into the shower room in the middle of the old men's shower. I sat in the pink cubicle, on the edge of the cot, and waited for them to finish. It was the longest shower I had ever heard. Each of them kept remembering other long stories out of his childhood and taking his time getting the facts right. I could hear about one word in five, which sometimes kept recurring and recurring. Only one of them sounded as though he had his teeth. They would get to laughing and start coughing, and then all take up coughing for some time, and then have a pause, and remind themselves of something and start off again with after-coughing voices, and sighs, through the sound of tropical downpour, while the roaches ran into the beam of wet light under the door.

I had had the foresight to relieve myself before I went in, and for the time being there was no urgent reason for me to leave the cubicle. The only light in there was a tiny bulb embedded in a heavy wire cage, that would not turn on at all with the door open. When it was lit it was so faint that the book had to be held up almost to the wire, for the print to be made out at all. Furthermore, the light was at the level of my knee, at the edge of the cot, on the end wall: I had to hold the book down and peer over the bottom of the page. The light made a small ivory circle that did not reach from one margin to the other, and the book had to be moved back and forth. I came to a picture of a night-blue bird, but the light would not show the whole bird at once, and I had to move the book in all directions, around and around, trying to remember the rest of the bird as I went, and never managing to visualize it all, while the noise of the old men in the shower came through the closed door just as though it were still open. If I shut my eyes the voices grew louder. Then there was the noise of people running down the hall and flinging open the shower door with a crash, greeting, some of the stories starting off again, and suddenly loud argument for a while, and then the sound of someone being sick, and the others shouting instructions and comments in the rain. I went out into the hall and could see the bodies moving slowly in the foggy glass. The light was out in the window of the office, near the other end, and the door at the far end of the hall was open. I walked quietly back along the colors, each of them like a shadow of the one before it, while the light from the shower room threw my own shadow the whole length of the hall, and my head and shoulders disappeared in the dusk at the far end. As I walked I saw empty cubicles, nothing in them but the cot. And I looked in — nothing. The noise from the shower room grew fainter and the air seemed better — cooler at least — as I got farther away. All the cubicles with open doors, with no one in them, were empty of belongings: there was just the cot. No one seemed to be in the dark green office, but there was another of the faint lights in the wire armor, burning above a table inside the window. The last cubicle of all, deep blue-violet, was vacant. I went in and sat down and it was like having a room near the sea at night. The noise from the shower room was like the breaking of an occasional wave. I lay down and shut my eyes and then thought I must ask if I might have this other, new, cubicle. I wondered whether it was being saved for somebody: the first one inside the door, on the left as you came in, opposite the lockers. I had not put anything in my locker, yet. It occurred to me that the deep blue-violet cubicle might be used by somebody connected with the management: so near the office and the outer door. Someone who had odd hours. I looked to see whether anything had been pinned to the walls, signs of prolonged occupancy, but it was too dark to tell. With the cubicle door open, and the door at the end of the hall open, I even seemed to get a little breeze there, stirring up the stale air, and that seemed important. I thought I had better go and ask at the office before I fell asleep in the dark blue-violet room, and I got up and as I went out thought of leaving the book to claim the place, and then laughed at myself and realized how tired I must be and how late it probably was by then, and I went out and stood in front of the office and peered into the dark green room with only that bulb like a reflection on an ornament, and what little dim light from the shower room came that far. After a while I could see that the desk was locked with a bar and a heavy padlock. There was a massive lock on the inside door. I wondered how I should go about waking up whoever was on night duty, and then I realized that there might be no such thing. I could see that it might not be easy to rouse anyone from the other side of the locked inner door. No light shone around it. The voices were still going on in the shower, with no change. I thought of giving up and going back to the pink cubicle, and then I thought that would be silly. When there were other empty cubicles where I stood a chance of sleeping, getting a night's sleep like everybody else. I stood listening to the old men's voices pulsing steadily down the hall. Finally, when I had almost forgotten what I was doing, I tapped lightly on the window. Nothing happened, and taking courage I was about to tap again when from an inside window that I had not been able to see, beside the inner door, a flashlight was shone onto me, and I thought I saw a thin man in a bathrobe. I tried to explain with gestures what I wanted to know, and for a while the flashlight shone on me steadily. Then another very small light was switched on inside, and I saw the man: long unshaven, a tattered dark maroon bathrobe, pale blue rumpled pyjamas. And he held up a long finger and made a negative gesture, probably meaning that the desk was closed, and that he would not speak with anyone at that hour. Too late, too late. In that case no one else should be coming for rooms; it might be all right for me to take the blue-violet cubicle, unless it was occupied by someone to do with the administration, and I thought I had better just make certain about that, so after a moment's bracing myself I tapped on the window again. Nothing happened. I raised my finger to tap again, feeling a welcome impatience, when the flashlight beam leapt out at me again. But as soon as it had picked me out, before I could make a single gesture, it went out, and I was left with my mouth open, about to pronounce the words silently for him to lip-read. But when the light went out I just uttered out loud—I did not shout—the word "blue." The light did not come back on again, though I went on gesturing for a while. And when I looked down the hall I saw that several of the doors had heads sprouting out of them, watching me.

"What did you want?" one of them asked. I could not see which one it was. The voices in the shower were going on just as before. The heads in the hall were outlined against the light of the frosted glass door of the shower room. I ignored the question as well as I could. Then someone else asked it, and then another. It sounded as though they were all asking me, and more heads came out, and doors opened.

"Nothing," I said.

"It's down there," one of them said, pointing toward the shower, and some of them laughed.

"Do you know whether anyone uses the room by the door?" I asked calmly, addressing myself to the nearest head, in its own shadow.

"Which room?" somebody asked.

"The last one. The dark blue-violet room."

"Blue what room?" somebody else asked.

"That room." I pointed.

A voice said "Purple" and then other voices repeated it with faint echoing satisfaction.

"Is anybody using it?" I asked again.

"Why do you want to know?" one of them asked.

"I'd like to change my room," I said.

"Why?" they asked.

"It's quieter up here."

"Have to ask," one of them said, and others agreed.

"They won't talk to me," I said.

"Too late," several of them said. The flashlight shone on me again, and then went out. I turned and gestured again. When I looked back down the hall, most of the heads had gone back into their rooms, and others disappeared as I stood watching. I decided that I might as well simply take the purple-blue room. If someone to do with the administration came in later and found me in his bed, he could always wake me then. By that time the old men in the shower might have gone to sleep, even if I had to go back to the pink cubicle—or I might find yet another empty room somewhere in the greens and yellows. Of course my key would be to the locker that went with the pink cubicle, but that would make no difference. I went back down the hall quietly, with no one paying any further attention, and into the pink cubicle. My suitcase was gone. Nothing else had changed—the sound of the pelting shower, the voices. I sat on the cot. I looked under it: nothing. I went and looked out in the hall. No one. In a moment of helpless rage I stepped to the shower door and pulled it open. There must have been eight or ten of them in there, but only two or three were in the shower stalls, in the steaming showers, their bodies hidden by slabs of echoing white marble, only their gray heads and occasionally a thin soapy arm appearing over the top. The rest were sitting along the wall and against the showers, wrapped in towels, in the steam. They were shouting back and forth. It was the one place where the light was any good and they could congregate. They all stopped their stories to look at me, in my clothes.

"My suitcase has been stolen," I said.

"Suitcase," one of them said.

"Just now," I said. I heard the word repeated behind me, and turned to see that the heads had sprouted again.

"My suitcase, yes," I said to them all.

"Should put it in your locker," one of them said.

"Didn't you get a locker key?" another asked.

"What did you have in it?" another one asked, and I wondered whether he didn't know. It seemed to me that nothing could have happened without them knowing it. But then I told myself that all anyone had to do was to walk into the open cubicle and pick up the suitcase and walk out with it as though coming back from the bathroom. I let the frosted glass door shut, and heard the voices begin to laugh, and then the stories begin again. I shut the door of the cubicle behind me. I still had the book in my hands. I turned on the light and tried to make out a sentence or two. I gave up and turned the light off and opened the door a little and lay looking up in the shady pink light. There was supposed to be ventilation. I thought I could hear it, over the noise of the shower. Then I must have gone to sleep, because I was wakened by someone opening the door of the cubicle —which must have closed—and gray daylight coming in. The man who opened the door was one of the people who ran the place, but I had not seen him before. I supposed that he was on the morning watch. The shower was off, dripping. The daylight came through the frosted glass. I got up and went out, and along the hall to the office.

The window was open and another old man, in a collarless shirt, was at the desk.

"Good morning," I said.

He returned the greeting without looking up from his paper.

"My suitcase was taken last night," I said.

"Suitcase?" he said, still not looking up.

"Yes, I had a suitcase. Everything I had was in it."

"Should have put it in the locker," he said.

"Perhaps somebody took it by mistake," I said.

"What do you want to do, press charges?" he asked, looking up. No expression at all, pale eyes. I looked down the hall. One or two men in towels, going back and forth to the shower room.

"It's only that there were things in it that I needed," I said.

"What?" he asked.

I did not answer right away. "A toothbrush," I said. He reached into a drawer and got me a new one.

"They're given to us," he said. "Complimentary."

"Thank you," I said. "But there was my razor too."

He got out a complete little shaving kit with a razor and blades and soap and brush.

"Thank you," I said. Then after a moment: "But there was my sweater too." It was cold outside.

"We've got some things here," he said, and reached over to a box of clothes by the inside door, and dragged out a big sweater fresh from the dry-cleaner's and threw it at me. I stopped asking. I went back and sat on the pink cot for a while, thinking about the other things that had been in the suitcase: underwear, socks, shirts, papers. I discovered that my virtue had ceased to be important to me, and I got up and went out to continue my study of the poor from a different point of view, no longer knowing what was important, and aware that there were aspects of poverty that I had never dreamed of. All that I had was a book about birds, the clothes I was wearing, not all of which I had chosen, a new toothbrush, a shaving kit that I had decided not to use, and whatever was in my mind.

Hunger Mountain

Who has been to the top of Hunger Mountain and seen what can be
seen from there, and returned? The view of The Promised Land.
Most who have come to tell went only part way. Many have died part
way. And even they have seen things that no one else ever saw, things
they could not describe, too hard for the words, and then too hard
for them, the witnesses. But certain ones who never forgot and who
never sleep gave us their words to eat. They buried their words in us
and went away, leaving us hungry, part way.

The Entry

When he has been walking for so many years why is his sack so
heavy? And in those woods which he thought he knew so well. But
he is older, and lost. The paths have gone. He does not know where
he is at all. At last he comes out on a rise above a railroad track.
Down there between the banks the snow is still drifted. It is spring,
but the snow is still deep there. More spring snow may fall tonight.
A train comes by, southbound. Passengers look at him. Some point
him out. He looks at himself. The train has gone. He walks on, along
the tracks, northward, until he sees a station ahead of him. The ties,
from which the snow, here, has melted, look like a flight of stairs
going neither up nor down. He does not even know what he has in
his sack.

A Suitor

There was a boy in a country now much changed who had a very curious and shrewd nature but could not imagine his own faults.

There had never been a road between the place where he lived and the capital. Little was known of the capital, and that little was rumor —no one where he lived had ever been to the city. But they had all heard of a girl there who was more beautiful than anyone they had ever seen.

It was decided, where the boy lived, to build a road to the capital, and men labored like ants, cutting through the forest, making ditches and bridges, passing places that they had lost, making mistakes, leaving blind alleys cut into the mountains, bridges half finished or collapsed, turning back, setting off again—because none of them knew the way to the capital. It was a long and tortuous road, and it was finished at last, but that is not the story.

The boy had decided that he would marry the beautiful girl whom they had all heard of, in the capital. When the road was finished, even before it was opened, he was the first to set out on it. He travelled day and night, and survived all the mistakes, and found his way back from the blind turnings, and one night when he was utterly exhausted but was almost in sight of the capital, the moon rose, and as it did someone ran past him going the same way, and was soon far ahead of him.

As soon as he thought about it, he knew that the other must also be going to the capital to court the beautiful girl, and would arrive long before him, and tell about him, tell everything about him, and win the girl before he himself even appeared, ragged and late. He began to imagine what the other would tell. For the first time in his life he began to envisage his faults one by one, starting with those that were not real, and then going on from there, little by little, because he could not stop. He walked along in the moonlight, at first crying, and then laughing.

The Crossroads

I have come to the crossroads twice now. In the end there is no way to name, as though to fix forever, the way the light can differ totally between one time and the next, in the same place. The difference is eternal. I can only imagine the future of light as something like the light I have known, when in truth it will be totally different, of course. If, as it may be, there is to be a third time.

The first time there was the green little boy. I came alone and when I stopped at the crossroads he emerged from the dark woods on my right. The sky was dark to show that he was not real yet. An effigy made of moonlight. But he knew me, and was expecting me. He would guide me in the dark, but he had no features. He needed my eyes. He would have to be a sleeve and I would have to be a hand going to wear him, groping. The hand of a child.

The second time there was the red little boy. It was daytime to show that he was not real yet, emerging in the same place, out of the green foliage. An effigy made of red cloth, the same shape as the first. He would take me to where I was going, but he had no features. He could not even stand up. He needed my life, to go into him like a body into an image, and go with my threadbare hands in front of me. The life of a child.

Each time the crossroads, as I later realized, was a day of my existence that I could not account for. And I did not even know what part of the day I had forgotten, that had let all the rest drain out—its number, its name in the week, its season, its saint. But each time I entered it and passed through, by what apparently was the only way. As a child. Even so, if I reach the crossroads another time, I do not think that there will be three of me, but only one, again, in totally different light. And of an unknown color.

A Cabin

The cabin is set into the huge treeless slope, facing west, toward the yellow evenings. From below it appears to be almost at the top. From above it appears to be less than half way. The sunlight enters through the open door and falls on the rough table and earth floor. It rests a hand on the ashes of the fire against the dug-out eastern wall. In the spring, late in the day, light is reflected from the slope outside onto the blackened beams. Then the cobwebs light up the corners. And then for weeks the sound of the stream at the foot of the slope reaches to the door. The wind rides over it, tramples it, but it keeps on, climbing, with the words brought from the ice, the clear consonants. In autumn there are whole days of stillness, in which voices from unseen throats drift in the air, calling sheep. The only neighbors live far out of sight on other slopes. When they pass they stop at the door. Their faces are red from the wind. Their hair has been mown. Everything about them is broad. They stand on the sill and laugh, describing the unlikely mind of authority, telling of involved triumphs of their own which never happened, raising their voices because of the wind. They leave, pronouncing invitations that are pure formalities.

Port of Call

Finally the day arrives when I watch myself coming back after years abroad.

By that time I am living in a little blue house of my own, up on a hill overlooking the harbor. There is a pergola of grapevines outside the back door that faces east, up the hill. Nothing a stranger would call beautiful: the pergola is a structure of plain iron struts set into the stucco house wall and threaded with heavy wire, from which in late summer the grapes hang. At the outer ends the struts rest on the posts of angle-iron that hold the heavy galvanized chicken wire of the garden fence. More grapevines in the garden, and beyond them tomatoes, peppers, eggplants, endive, leeks recently watered, beans both for drying and for eating green. The area outside the door itself, in the perpetual shade of the vines, is cemented over: a place for a long table and benches, painted gray. A few books and pencils on the table, the less precious books left out even at night, much of the year, in that climate. On the far side of the cemented area, a cemented wall a yard high, separating it from the garden; the wire fence rises from the top of the wall. On the wall, along the fence, there are pots full of flowers—some of which have been there for years, and have been cut back and re-potted in black earth, in the same pots. Bushes of basil in old square tin cans. Broken knives, spoons, forks, a wine glass without a stem, a pair of broken scissors lying on a rust mark shaped like scissors—a shadow in an eclipse—tucked among the pots. A ball of string, reposing in a little ring of spattered dust. Nasturtiums clambering on the wire. Sun dazzling on the vine leaves. The garden gate a framework of bent galvanized water pipe covered with the same heavy chicken wire as the fence; rusted hinges that screech when the gate opens, a rusted latch that clangs when it closes, and both sounds are parts of the gate, as anyone who knows the gate can tell. A white rag, thrown over the top of the gate, is rotting there. The yellowish gray wall at the foot of the fence is covered with the grain patterns of the planks that framed the space when the cement was poured. A long fading map of one section of a bewildering mountain region. The boards themselves have long since fed some fire. Empty bird cages on the wall, left by a former occupant, and kept, obviously, for no reason, as though there might be some other use for them. Resident spiders and lizards in the wall. I spend more time out there, as it happens, than I do on the other side of the house, on the roofed terrace facing west above the harbor. Every room of the long narrow cool house looks out to sea.

In the mornings the sun is welcome, slanting under the vines of the pergola, outside the kitchen door. And in the afternoons, when the day is hot, it is pleasant to sit out there with the sun beating on the other side of the roof, and the vine leaves sifting the glare, until the shadow in the garden suggests that it is time to begin work there.

Inside, everything is equally simple. Few possessions have survived the years, and those few are either useful or have their age and origin to commend them. A patchwork quilt that I remember from childhood. What would it mean to me if it were seen again only now, after the lapse of many years—half a life? Would it mean anything to me at all? Would it even be familiar? What enzyme of experience might have dissolved it in my mind? The books are more recent. And I no longer have the devotion to them, the individual objects—as though they might be pieces of a raft that I had in my early youth. But it is hard to imagine myself not knowing each one of them, never having seen any of this. I will never be able to explain it.

A steep path leads up to the house above the vineyards. There are no houses above this one. Beyond the garden is the dry hill: thorny bushes, and then the open pasture rolling away to the mountains of dark oak trees and gray limestone. What would it look like to someone who perhaps had grown to dislike walking? Horses wander up the path in the evening and chew at the wiry bushes, which continue to spring and thrash from time to time in the first hours of darkness. I try to imagine what a city must be like now. It is no use. What kept me?

And the others who have come and gone in this house since I came here to live. Women, a series of friends, whole lives, and my lives with them. To know nothing of all that, all those years on the other side of the planet, where it was night when it was day here. What can be told of such things, to one who never knew the people but only the names? What do pictures mean to those who never saw what they represent? What judgment can the ignorant contribute?

What will anyone know of all this in the future? What will they be judging except themselves? How do I know, for what can I know of them, and what pictures they may have kept? I am trying to imagine myself, on the basis of ancient, unsorted recollections, approaching the coast, on the last day of the voyage, after many years. What was it that I never thought I wanted, that kept me away there for half a life, promising to come back but not coming, perhaps believing myself happy? Was I?

It is a long voyage, and all morning the ship can be seen from the terrace on the hill, making its way across the metal sea and into the channel behind the breakwater. Half a day, all afternoon, for the men with cables and winches on the sea-wall to ease it up the narrow twisting channel, conceived for nothing larger than fishing boats, turning it around the eddies and pockets made by the tides, into the wide still harbor. It is almost evening, the hour of the first coolness in the shadows and the first premonitions of the long blue-and-yellow twilights, before I start down to the harbor, leaving the door unlocked, but then turning in the path outside, after I have closed the gate, to put my hand on it again. Well, I have done that before.

Then I go down the lane slowly, to the place where it becomes cobbled, past the weavers' houses with lengths of woven woolen cloth, brown and ivory, hanging out on wires—which nearer the houses also bear grape vines—and chickens scratching under them. And the houses of old women whose vineyards are tilled by the neighboring families in exchange for most of the wine, so that the old women look at the vineyards in the daytime as though they already belonged to someone else, but at the ends of the day they look at them still as the vineyards of their infancy, peopled with all the figures of that time, over which the old women now stand much taller, and much lighter, beginning to rise and fly away. Past the houses of those families of half shepherds and half fishermen, some of them taking turns, where I go more and more often to listen to the stories. After all my own travels, from which I always came back. I go on down to the cobbled steps, the marble cobbles, worn smooth, scratched by the horseshoes. Down past houses with hens on the balconies under hanging laundry, and doorways into leafy court-yards, where water is running.

I arrive at the open space along the harbor as the last cables are warping the vessel to its berth, in time to watch the late sunlight on the crowd waiting to see the ship dock, though they know no one aboard. It may fall to me to be the only one getting off here, I don't know. I feel cool, and as though with all my youth, standing in the shadow of an old tree by the harbor, watching the ship in. But it may not be so with me after the days of confinement on the ship, with its dull woodwork, its alien paint, its carton cabins. No one has been able to get in touch with me for a long time. The voyage has been good for me, the days of silence. What was it that held me so long, and will it call me back again to the shrieking of metals held in the hands, and the days like stammering? It was part of me. It sent me here, which is not to say that it will leave me here. It never left me anywhere before. Eventually the horizons were aching to part again. There was the expectation of some absolute encounter. The thought of women. To whom has it all been calling? What will it be like here? What will I be like? Knowing nothing of so much of my life, and the lives of others that have been woven into it. How can I ever know anything about them from words and a few photographs? What do I remember, at this moment, about myself?

Everyone knows who is coming. There will be no delay at customs, and the trunk, which is said to contain little besides a few clothes, books, notebooks and photographs, will be taken to the one hotel, with its columned lobby full of palms, and its glass reception desk. Neither of us was ever a frequenter of cafés, but there in the café of the hotel we will sit, with a bottle of wine, in the evening light, looking at the harbor, trying to come to know each other as we are now, after all. To know each other well enough to judge, as tentatively as possible, whether it would be better for me to come up the hill at once, and have the trunk (which I remember, laughing) brought up in the morning, or whether it might be as well for me just to stay at the hotel for a while, and we would then have dinner, and after dinner I would go back up there alone.

The Roof

They turned, on the roof, and noticed each other, and each wondered
whether the other had come up here first, and had been up here all
along, but not seen, not noticed, around behind the black cabin, per-
haps, where the stairs emerged from their well through a door that
was tarred on the outside. Or whether the other had come up later,
stepped through the doorway without being heard, approached on
the fine gravel fixed in tar, and stood there looking, for a long time.
Two men, both of them young, though not in their first youth. Both
thin, and unhasty. Then the taller, darker one, in the old jacket, found
that he was seeing the other, who was blond and in a red sweater, as
a little boy, sullen and hoarding himself. The face still preferred to
look down. And the one in the red sweater noticed that the other
one had been observing the new tomb. Then the taller one, in the
jacket, smiled, and greeted him.

The one in the red sweater asked him if he was looking for some-
thing. Up here.

The other one answered that he was the sculptor.

The first one said oh that was all right. He said he was the gardener.
And that he was surprised they had not met.

Each moved slowly and hesitantly to shake the other's hand, and
looked away. The afternoon was over. People were on their way
home from work. Some were home already, sitting down in the first
chairs. The gardener gave a laugh and said you could hardly call it a
garden. Small cypress trees in sooty tubs. Long boxes containing
cropped evergreen bushes. He explained that the Fire Department
would allow no more, and added that he was amazed they allowed
any of it. He asked whether the other had come to look at the sculp-
ture, though he already knew the answer.

The other nodded, as though smoking a pipe.

The one in the red sweater would hardly have called it a sculpture,
either, until that moment. But, as he said, he didn't know anything
about those things, and they didn't interest him. Just the same, he
wouldn't have called that a sculpture. Standing on the new tomb.

The sculptor said he had come up to see it at this time of day. They both stood looking west, over the city. A saffron light was filling the sky, and a few clouds were passing over, like silent trains.

The gardener asked him what they thought of his sculpture, and the sculptor said nothing for a moment, and then asked him whom he meant. The gardener simply pointed down beneath his feet, so that the sculptor could only have guessed whether he meant the inhabitants of the apartment building, the officials of the cemetery, the immediate family of the person whose body was in the new tomb, or the general public. Not the older dead, at any rate, behind plaques in the parapets of the roof. The sculptor shrugged and said he guessed they thought it was all right. They were going to have an unveiling, he said. Or they'd talked about it, anyway. But it had been so long since they said that, and they'd all seen it by now, he wondered whether there was any point in having an unveiling. He'd thought of taking a picture. He didn't have a picture of it. The gardener asked him whether he had come up to take a picture, and the sculptor said no.

The gardener asked the sculptor how they had heard about him, and the sculptor said he wasn't sure. They said they'd seen something he'd done.

The gardener asked whether they had told him what kind of thing they wanted on the tomb, what they had in mind, and the sculptor said no.

"They just let you do what you wanted," the gardener said, and nodded, to himself, to show that he was familiar with such liberty.

The tomb stood out from the wall like a marble bed. The first stains had appeared on the white stone. At the far end of the tomb, against the parapet, was a headstone of slate with edges uncut, irregular. Blank, no name on it. Behind it, the city: higher buildings, bridges, pigeons in the smoky sky. On the marble pedestal formed by the tomb was a life-sized baby carriage. At first it did not appear to be fastened to the marble. One of the gardener's objections to it, to begin with, was that he thought it looked real.

He said he had been surprised when he had heard that they were actually going to bury somebody up there. Nowadays. He said he sometimes came up just to have a look, too. At the view. Three years, he said, he had been working there.

The sculptor asked him if he'd done all that, pointing to the tubs, and the gardener said he had. There had been nothing there. It took three of us to move some of those, he said. Up all those stairs. You have to be careful where you put them. Over the joists downstairs. On top of structural walls. Otherwise the roof wouldn't take it, he said. He was afraid the Fire Department wouldn't allow it, but they never said anything. Of course it always *was* a cemetery, he said. But not for a long time. And it was one thing in the old days, but he'd never thought they would actually bury somebody else up there, now. He asked the sculptor if they just came and asked him, like that.

"They called up and came around," the sculptor said.

The gardener asked him whether they had told him anything about the individual he was to make the sculpture for, and the sculptor said they hadn't.

The gardener asked him when they paid him, and the sculptor said it was all right; they did.

The gardener asked him whether he had designed the whole thing, or just the monument part, and the sculptor said just the monument and the headstone. The tomb was already there when he came up, the first time.

Was he going to put the name on the stone in time for the unveiling, if there was one?

"No," the sculptor said.

Wasn't he going to put it on? At all?

"No."

The gardener turned away.

What did the family have to say about that?

The sculptor said he hadn't asked them. "They know who it was," he said. And if anybody else wanted to know, they could start inquiring, and that way it would mean something to them. He asked the gardener if he remembered names from cemeteries, and the gardener said nothing.

The gardener had objected to the fact that the baby carriage was painted, all bright colors. They spoiled the effect of the whole roof, he thought, every time he came up to tend the plants, and sweep. He asked whether the sculptor had a key, or what, and the sculptor said he did.

"They just come up here on week-ends," the sculptor said. And the gardener said yes, and maybe birthdays and like that.

"Or else the Board of Health," the gardener said. He had thought they might have to take the whole thing down again, tomb and all. He had never thought they would allow a funeral up there in the first place. Those others, in the old days, that was when the laws were different and people didn't know so much about things like that. As it was now, they must have had to have all kinds of special vaults or something to satisfy the ordinances. Or a lot of pull. But how long would that last? He guessed they wanted to keep them in their own building, he said.

But he kept thinking the Board of Health could change their minds even yet, and make them move it out of there, and then the Fire Department might make them get rid of everything else.

"Maybe," the sculptor said, and asked him where he worked, and the gardener named the richest addresses.

He had wondered whether it was, in fact, a real baby carriage, and since he was alone with it the first time he saw it, he had gone over to inspect it, and had touched the push-bar, and the springs had not moved, the carriage had not rocked. He had decided that it was bound to fill up with water in the first rain, but then he had looked inside and seen that the blankets and pillow were all molded and painted, and that there was a drain in the corner, that ran down under the carriage.

"I even heard somebody wanted to tear down the whole building," the gardener said. "Put up something else. Higher."

"They're always going to do that," the sculptor said.

The gardener said he wondered if they thought of burying any more up here.

The light was going out of the sky. The colors on the carriage were darkening. The sculptor turned his back on the tomb and said it was nice up here. He said the gardener must have really made a difference.

The gardener said it had just been a garbage dump.

"I've been up here in the morning," the sculptor said. "First thing."

"I always knew this place up here," the gardener said. "They called me up, one day, and said somebody told them about me, and they needed a gardener. A gardener, though. As soon as they told me,

I knew what they meant. But I like it. I come when I want. I believe it's the family themselves," he said. "The owners. Decided to fix it up and use it themselves."

"I guess so," the sculptor said. "They said it was their building. When they were around to see me. I just came up here once to look at where they wanted it put, with a couple of them. They were relatives."

"I think they have some kind of pull," the gardener said again.

The sculptor nodded. "Did you see that thing about it in the paper?" he asked, and laughed. The gardener said he hadn't seen it.

"I did it in the studio," the sculptor said. "And I want to see it in place, different times."

He looked around again, at the roof, the tomb, the lights coming on, the sky growing dark, and started toward the door to the stairs. The gardener picked up his tool bag and followed him. They stepped over the high metal-covered doorsill, onto the tiles, and the gardener turned on the light inside.

"You always want to lock it behind you," he said, as he locked the door, before they started down the stairs.

The Watches

One of the people I have come to know since I have been here is a priest in the small town. We speak with difficulty, in his language, very slowly. We sit at his kitchen table over herb teas that he brews, and stale tea biscuits, or over bread and fresh cheese, depending on the day of the week. His mother lives with him in the bare presbytery. They say little to each other; speech scarcely seems to be necessary between them. He has read a great deal, carefully, and kept his good humor. He tells me stories of the region, a detail at a time, with much questioning on both sides until I understand each part. Laughter, and moments of blank fatigue. Comprehension of a stage of the chronicle is a thicket opening slowly in the woods. Told in this way the stories begin to take on the momentous intangibility of legends; episodes echoed from an unknown sacred text; parables. Sometimes it is hard for me to understand what he thought was funny. Sometimes he appears to be a little foolish.

I mentioned the acquaintance in a letter to a close blood relative of mine, who I knew was interested in the church. I suppose I did so partly to boast of such an association, particularly as I knew that she had always considered me irreligious. She spoke of it, perhaps out of similar motives, to a priest of the same faith as my friend, who was known to her circle. He got my address from her. He was about to take his vacation. He came to visit me.

He was blond; bald but still young; tall and sonorous and assured. He spoke the language much better than I did. He was affable. He was wearing a neat well-cut gray suit which scarcely indicated that he was a priest. He went to the hotel to change into a cassock, for our visit to my friend, at the church.

We found him in the sacristy, at that hour, at a table under a shelf loaded with empty jars and volumes of old registers, receiving visits from his parishioners, like a country doctor. And in fact, in the recital of their misfortunes they asked for his opinions on medical matters, rather than send for a doctor. They left the three of us alone, and I introduced the stranger.

My friend the local priest welcomed him eagerly, broke out an ancient half-empty bottle of homemade peach cordial, and when we had touched our glasses to each other and sipped, brought from the depths of his cassock an old silver watch, on a silver chain, and held it up. I had never seen it before. It was embossed with flowers all over the back. A white enamel dial, with Roman numerals, like columns. The silver flowers and leaves on the case were worn down, as on the face of an old coin. He handed the watch across the table, to the visiting priest, with a speech about presenting it to the other world.

The visitor accepted it gracefully, admiring its age. Then he bowed slightly and took from his pocket a silver watch, the twin of the other—as I saw when he held it up—and with an identical chain, both of them new. And he handed it across the table with a smile, and they shook hands.

After that we sat down on the benches, facing each other across the table, and there was a brief, stiff conversation, comparing church conditions. The visitor said that he would not be staying in the town. He was on his way south. He became somewhat hearty. We got up to go. As we left I thought him affected. When he had changed back into the gray suit again he seemed more so: the way he held his head, with the large nose and puffy eyes; the way he talked about his travel plans, and all the places where he had been.

The Invalid

Through spring evenings when others find reasons to walk out under the trees, and through summer afternoons when almost everyone dreams of lying by a river, and through each season and each hour in turn, the invalid sits preparing his case. He is dying. Everyone knows it. But he has been dying, and apparently at the same pace, for some time now. For a number of years, in fact, as we realize occasionally, always with an astonishment which indicates, as much as anything else, that we have come to take his situation for granted, and it has become a habit of our own. Yes, he is dying, but neither he, nor the doctors, nor anyone seems to entertain a precise notion of how much faster than the rest of us he is dying, and whether his present prospect of life is to be thought of in terms of months, years, or decades. Some prefer to express the matter another way, and say that his life has been shortened, quite definitely it has been shortened—but this is scarcely a more helpful way of putting it. It appears to imply that he, and everyone, has, or may have, two distinct fates, a possible one and an actual one, and that the former is somehow measurable, a function of averages, perhaps, of norms, and that the actual thread of existence can be held up and measured against the so-called possible one, in advance, and found to be shorter, and for a known reason. This way of putting the matter, like the other one, makes it clear that what the invalid has lost may be no more than a particular, but unmeasurable, expectancy, or some right to it that had never been altogether beyond dispute—a nebulous treasure, as the successive rounds of the invalid's case have emphasized again and again.

Still, it is generally agreed that he is dying faster than if it had never happened to him—the little mistake which he claims was no necessary part of his life. And apart from the mental anguish caused, as he maintains, by the loss of his expectations, what is left of his life has otherwise been severely curtailed. He is full of discomforts—some of them severe, sleepless, worsening—that might not otherwise have been his. He is the victim of a catalogue of incapacities which he insists were not his before. And those pursuits of the flesh which are still open to him are now empty, in a way he had not noticed, of ease, and contentment, and joy. But the defense maintains that he cannot prove that he ever possessed most of what he declares he has lost, but that these things are illusions, of which, in many instances, he cannot even claim to be the author.

The event on which the argument turns is not even dignified—a plea which the invalid has not, so far, had the wit to put forward. He was born in another country and brought here by his parents (since deceased) in the first years of his adolescence. It was a painful change for him, one which he does not seem ever to have accepted wholly. Three decades later he still speaks with an accent. He was always shy, frail, poorly coordinated, and a hypochondriac. He is intelligent, received a good education, held a series of well-paid and responsible positions, never married, lived alone, talked (whenever he spoke of himself, which was seldom) of the country in which he had been born as though his homesickness had never healed at all; but though his financial and business circumstances would have made it easy for him to return there, he never went, but put it off. And so for years, until his life seemed as set as the sizes of his clothes; and everyone who knew him was startled when it became known, several years ago, that he had gone back, for the first time, on a visit to the old country.

Perhaps he would have been reticent about the visit itself whatever had happened. As things turned out, it was quite effectively eclipsed by what it led to. As he was returning to this country after a month or so, the customs officials became suspicious of the assortment of medicines in his baggage. In the first place, there was a surprising variety, for an apparently healthy individual. And then the quantities. He had taken from this country a large supply of certain medicines he was in the habit of using, so that he need have no fear of running out even if he were to stay considerably longer than he had originally planned to. Some of these he was bringing back, of course. Several large bottles had not even been opened. Then, while he had been in the country of his childhood he had rediscovered remedies which had been administered to him, or had held his attention, in his early years, and he had tried a number of these, and laid in stores of a few of them. Furthermore, he had tried a series of remedies from the land of his origin, for the ailments that were uppermost in his mind, and had been pleased, in some instances, with the results, and happy to think of taking back with him a provision of those restoratives. Finally, he had consulted several doctors in that country, had thought highly of a number of their prescriptions, and had taken the precaution of procuring quantities of these, against future complaints. When the customs officials began to question him on the subject of this collection, they were not reassured (to judge from the sequel) by his behavior. A hypochondriac can scarcely be expected to plead hypochondria, and he was no doubt evasive, contradictory, nervous, perhaps even irritable, in his replies. They detained him while the bottles were taken away for laboratory examinations. He was not put under arrest and was not allowed to call a lawyer, and his state of nerves while he waited probably did little to allay their suspicions. When at last he was released it was without apology, rather curtly, with a few impertinent remarks about his collection. He had grown accustomed to better manners, in the country of his birth.

It was not surprising that by the time he reached the place where he was living he felt that several of his chronic and recurrent complaints had been inflamed by the incident, coming as it did on top of the fatigue and strain of the journey. He was convinced that he felt crises of more than one of these complaints approaching, and one of the first things he did, before opening windows or mail, was to give himself full doses out of the appropriate bottles, with a little for good measure in each case, because of the circumstances, and then another little bit extra to spite the government officials, with their grossness, and their rude remarks inferring that his medicines were not only unnecessary but afforded him some eccentric pleasure.

The symptoms which began to appear almost at once were not those of any of the habitual ailments, nor of the side-effects to which he was accustomed in the use of some of the medicines. They were new, and alarming. A hot pain blared suddenly in the pit of his stomach, echoed very shortly by another in his head; and this latter was followed by a darkening of his sight, which increased until he could not see out of one eye at all, while the other was filled with flashes and a dim blur. He suffered from nausea, and an extreme weakness of the legs. Between bouts of vomiting he managed, despite his impaired vision, to call a doctor, who was some time in coming. By the time the doctor arrived the symptoms (a racing pulse, and chills, had joined the first manifestations that all was not well) were still more pronounced, and there were moments when the patient swayed on the brink of consciousness, and felt himself drifting out over the abyss. The doctor wasted a few more minutes trying to fit these signs of trouble to what he knew of the patient's medical history, and his subject was rapidly growing fainter before he stumbled onto the right track and began to examine the bottles carefully. The customs men, whether in the laboratory or outside it, had evidently put several of the medicines back into the wrong bottles, and the patient, as a result, had taken the wrong doses of at least two of them — doses dangerously large, and of specifics that should never have been taken together.

For some days the patient's life was in doubt. The sight of one eye was never fully restored, nor the patient's former strength and vigor. The invalid continued to be subject to frequent attacks of vertigo and palpitations, to a complex of shifting pains in the abdomen, head and legs, and his digestion scarcely merited the name. He was unable to go to the office, and though it was possible for him to perform some functions of his old job at home, he had to be content with this, and with a reduced salary. And he, and those who knew him, were led to understand that he could never recover from this new condition, and must expect to die of it.

Of course he brought suit for damages, high damages, and though the first round was contested with considerable callousness (possibly with a view to recording arguments that might forestall appeals later) he was awarded part of what he sued for. It was more money than he would ever have been likely to earn, but he was not satisfied. He brought suit again, for still more money, declaring that his health and his former expectations of life were beyond price, and it was then that the case turned brutal, and the defense maintained not only that it was impossible to establish that the medicines had been put back in the wrong bottles by the customs officials, but also that nothing which the invalid claimed to have lost had ever really been his. And now he spends all his money on lawyers, and in devoting what time remains to him to proving that he was deprived of health, and the prospects of longevity, and the infinite possibilities of existence, by the agency of other people; that these things were once really his; and that he had known them and enjoyed them and realized that they were worth a great deal, even at the time.

Path

Water laid out the streets of the gray capital, and day after day the rain falls into place along the pavements, and follows a design that is known to it, natural to it, and older than the first buildings, preserved now as bones in reliquaries, inside stone monuments built over them against the weather of the latter days. North of the mountains and the inland ocean with its long seasons of low skies, the city began, doubtless, as a margin of driftwood huts gradually outlining the shape of a hand or hands, where a river meandering through wide marshes chose many ways to the sea. Ricks of branches. In time, rafts. Eventually the shore-haunters brought stone down the river, for building in the color of the winter sky, and the flecked hewn granite began to wander at the water's edge like hems of the light.

The original settlements along the water line, huddled in the dark winters, must have been the stick-nests of clusters of hunters who pursued the retreating glaciers northward, killing along the new-born pastures. Deep in the ice a goddess of spring kept moving toward them. They called her with drums. They listened for her heart and heard soft hoofbeats in their sleep. The surviving legends all tell of journeys, leading out of earlier journeys, between hidden skies. The oldest lyric fragment that has come down to us, in the principal archaic language of those regions, likens the dome of heaven to an upturned boat in which we will embark once again, at the end of time. But that is a relatively late production. It is clear from the legends that the first arrivals came on foot: the travellers in all the ancient stories walk. There are reflected glimpses, in those narratives, of other roofs, by former shores: suns remote forever, older rivers, perhaps even the Nile Delta with its seven mouths, seven fingers, seven candle flames.

The stone facades still float in the rain. In the course of my visit it fell incessantly, beating on its temporarily buried places, and the days shortened, one by one, with a measured suddenness. I was beginning to think I had learned all I could learn, for the time being, of the nomadic legends of that region, and their recurrence in the later levels of the language. I knew more of the dominant archaic tongue than of the current local one, but I knew neither of them well: it was a rare phrase, from any period, that seemed transparent to me, and I was more conversant with the words' transformation than with their sounds. But the directors at the national library behaved toward me as though my interest, in itself, were a contribution to their archives: they put their entire collection, and all the means of consulting it, at my disposal, and the most celebrated philologist and literary historian in the capital, who spoke my language as his own, guided me through the centuries of what I thought of as evidence. As sometimes happens when one is helped lucidly but without interference, his response to my interest, the material he produced, the order in which he provided me with it, and his own commentaries, gave me a sense of our having worked together before. It was plain from the start that he understood what I was looking for—grasped it, perhaps, more clearly than I did, since he held in his mind, in detail, the whole extant body of texts, whereas I had only an intimation of what I believed must be there. And despite the difference in our ages (at least a generation, and probably more), years and exact learning had neither raised an insuperable barrier between us, nor rendered him brittle: he could not only guess what would amuse us both, in the morning papers as well as in the ironic turns of the recorded past, but from our first session onward he was able to put in my way, one after the other, resemblances, associations, traces, clues, the components of recognitions, which fed and warmed my enthusiasm.

We had almost finished going through his compilation of the old documents which he considered most relevant to my interest. We had proceeded in an order that was roughly chronological, and had come to the last of the materials he had set out, several weeks earlier, for me to study. I felt the weight of the approaching winter, and was looking forward to leaving and taking with me the mass of notes, to try to find out what they meant to me, when I had got them back to where I was living. One morning, as a gesture of anticipation, I went to the center of the city, to get my travel ticket, just to have it, even though I meant to leave the date open for a few more days. I walked, though it was raining even harder than usual. The traffic splashed and roared along the winding avenues, metal-boxed processions hurtling through smoke, hesitant chain-saws in water. I tried to keep to the back streets where there were almost no vehicles, though I risked getting lost, since none of the streets ran parallel, but branched off from each other—systems of veins. The closer I drew to the center of the city, the emptier the back streets became. Some blocks were closed to all motor traffic, with vertical lengths of iron pipe rising at intervals from the asphalt. In one such curving passage two waiters under a bare awning frame were carrying stone table-tops indoors. Down the middle of the narrow street an old woman was moving like a dark mollusc: her back was the same shape and color as her umbrella, and her legs appeared to have shrunk into the rest of her. She was carrying a patent-leather shopping bag. The rain ran off her and dripped at her feet. She was walking so slowly that I imagined, at first, that there was something the matter with her. I thought I was remembering her but could not recall having seen her move. It made me feel that I was walking too fast. The rain travelled down her coat and shopping bag rapidly, pausing but indifferent, as on a pane of glass: the gait of a mumbled rite. I was anxious to get to the travel agency, and then on to the library, but I felt reluctant to splash past her as though she were not there. For an instant it seemed that I should do something for her, yet I knew the next moment that the impulse was vain and absurd: she was certainly not helpless; there was no plea in her bent carriage, no despondency in the shuffle of her boots, nothing in the set of her that would have recognized pity. I slowed down, as I passed, and turned to nod to her. The waiters had gone in; we were alone on the street as on a country road. I looked, for a moment, under the umbrella and the dark hat-brim, into a face weathered with age, brown as wood, gaunt and merry. Bright blue eyes. She looked at me, smiling, perhaps laughing. I had assumed that she was doing her shopping; the sight of her face made it seem more likely that she was simply taking her usual walk, in-specting part of her estate, as she had been doing for longer than anyone there could remember. I was about to greet her, but hesitated and said nothing: I had been looking at her out of my own language, and suddenly was overtaken not only by the awkwardness and em-barrassment with which I spoke the language of that city, but also (as I realized only after I had gone past, and left the street) by an uncertainty as to what phase of the language, from what age, was properly hers and would be correct, if I were to address her. As I nodded, I heard the rain, above the sounds of the city.

I was late getting to the library. For the past week and more my mentor and I had been meeting in what was called the refectory. The materials that he had assembled for me to study had overflowed his own marigold-yellow office in the interior of the rambling edifice. We had moved to a table by itself at the end of a reading-room, but we could not talk freely there. One day we were invited to the director-in-chief's office, a spacious eighteenth-century room with huge windows of square leaded panes evenly filled with the gray light above the harbor: that side of the building faced onto a margin of shrubbery and a quay where a large warship was moored. The director sat with the light behind him. I had met him at the beginning of my visit: he had been amiable, helpful, and lofty. His manner to me, when I entered his office, was deferential and friendly, as though in the interval we had seen a great deal of each other. Another man was sitting beside him, near the desk facing us, in the light, wearing a gray-blue gabardine overcoat and a hat. He was introduced to me as one of their best-known authors, a man whom the director had particularly wanted me to meet, he said, because of my interest in their literature, on the one hand, and because, on the other, his visitor had recently acquired a reputation as a song-writer. The man was cordial, featureless, his voice toneless, his questions and remarks—I thought —unlit. Neither of the reasons given for our introduction seemed to account for it. I wondered whether we must resign ourselves— whether I must resign myself—to being interrupted by a series of such well-meant (perhaps) but pointless diplomatic encounters; my friend the philologist thought not. He explained to me, in his glancing but incisive fashion, as we returned along the corridor, that I had been repaying a favor. My friend had told the director-in-chief that we needed more room, and had suggested the refectory, which was not in use. The director had hastened to comply—he was more or less bound to do so with any request coming from my friend. But the invitation to his office had been (simple sociability apart) a re-establishment of the director's position of authority, after the favor he had granted. It had served to remind me—and consequently my learned friend—of my obligation. It had allowed the director—who also occupied a high post, and entertained further ambitions in the Ministry of Culture—to put on a small show of his own importance for the popular author, while seeming to flatter him. My friend did not think that the performance would be required twice, and (in exchange) we would have the refectory to work in for the remainder of my visit, and we would have it to ourselves.

He was waiting for me there, when I arrived, by taxi, with my dateless air ticket. I hurried through the reading room, in my wet coat, and through the small Gothic door at the end of it, and shut that behind me, in the huge somber hall, with a long deep breath and a moment's sense of homecoming, such as I had not felt in the place—or had not noticed—before. The high windows, here, were made of much smaller panes than those in the director's office. They were narrower and longer, the frames rising into stone trefoils and sharply pointed arches. Just above them were the massive transverse beams, the lowest level of the elaborate nest of rafters disappearing into the darkness of the ceiling. Neither the function of the hall nor its history were clearly defined. Part of the building, apparently, had once been a monastery, which had been almost wholly demolished. Sections of the library, much later, had been built in imitation of the earlier structure—or rather, in imitation of drawings, themselves ancient, of its ruins. A row of venerable, faded, ragged flags, on long poles, projected over the room from the stone pilasters between the windows. They were older than the hall and retained a stillness of their own. The polished surfaces of the two enormous parallel tables flowed out of the shadows at the far end of the hall, to fill with the cold light of the northern morning, and appear to be made of it. At the near end of the table on my left, fixed and bathed in that same light, were the piles of papers and folders that my friend and I had been using—I was startled to realize how much of my own unfinished work I had left, day and night, in that relatively public place. Yet not so public, either, I reminded myself, thinking of the locked door, the key in my pocket, and my friend sitting there waiting, reflecting the glassy table and the spread-out papers. He appeared not to have noticed that I was late, and I did not have a chance to ask him how long he had been waiting: he brushed aside my apologies, smiling about something else. He said that there was something he had been preparing for me, and for which our work until then might be considered a background. He referred, in a rapid summary, to the particular circumstances of historic scholarship in the last century—at the end of which he had been born. I had considered, and in fact remarked at one point upon the irony of our studying the early texts and the older reverberations reaching us through them, in the echoing hall that had been built, in emulation of the Gothic age (a time far more recent than the oldest of our texts), at the very period when the surviving motifs from the Gothic era and earlier were vanishing, just as interest and inquiry were first revealing how swiftly and completely they were receding. He referred me to some of the most ancient neo-nomadic fragments and travellers' songs, and read a few passages aloud to me several times so that I would catch the cadence of the archaic meter—the foot, the cadence itself, he insisted, even though, as I knew, the meaning of a number of the words, in those fragments, was now lost, probably forever, and the actual pronunciation was, to an uncertain degree, conjecture. He left me studying the texts that he had just read aloud, and a commentary on certain of their allusions, and told me that he would be back later. I was used to working alone in the high empty hall, where the shuffling papers, the pencil on the table, and my breath, echoed and re-echoed, and I paid no attention to how long he was gone. The clock in tower was striking as he opened the door again, but I had not noticed when it began to strike, and so could not count the strokes. There were two small boys with him, whom I could not at first tell apart, except that the one was slightly more blond than the other.

They came in without speaking, and the boys stood looking up into the rafters, even after my friend had told them to come to the table and take off their coats. They did neither. One after the other he led them over to me, the blonder of the two first, and introduced us, in their language, of course, and they held out their small hard hands. I could read no expression in either of their faces. They remained between me and the windows. My friend told them to sit down wherever they pleased, on one of the benches, near the piles of papers. The one whose hair was darker sat down in front of me, with the table and the open books and notebooks between us; his eyes ran over them, and over me, my hands, my pencil, my face, with the same detached alertness. The other boy sat down at a bench beside the far table, nearer the windows. He was turned toward us, but still looking up at the shadows in the ceiling, and the files of flags retreating into the darkness.

They were twins, my friend explained to me rapidly, in my own language, and he instructed me to sit still and say nothing. He began to talk to the boy opposite me, courteously, respectfully—as he addressed everyone, and as he would have spoken to someone of his own age. He told the boy that he had been thinking a great deal about the poems that the boy had told him (the word "tell," in that language, means both "recount" and "chant") at their last meeting and that he was as interested in them as ever, and would be grateful if I could hear some of them. The boy said nothing, but looked at me.

My friend asked him whether he remembered those poems, and the boy said that of course he did.

And others? Yes, the boy said, there were many.

Would he tell us one about the dark traveller?

He was in all of them, the boy said.

Tentatively, as though pronouncing the first phrase of a foreign language to a native, my friend quoted a few words, an opening. Something to do with the echoes of a foot on ice. The boy sighed, looked up past us at the wall opposite the windows, and began to hum and pat the table with the palm of his hand. Then he started to recite. His voice was pitched like a string on which the words were played at intervals. He hummed between them, and chanted them as they came, shaping them to fit a pattern that was recognizable but never quite predictable. The poem was a ballad of some kind, or so I thought, though it did not seem to keep to the metrical form of any ballad I knew in that tongue—or in my own. Missing many of the words, as I did, there were whole passages that I could not catch, but felt as though I were following at a distance; then a piece of narrative would emerge, and disappear again—someone walking in a mist— and I could not be sure whether the sense kept escaping me because of my inadequate knowledge of the language, or because of the boy's pronunciation, or because the poem itself was difficult. As it was: full of sudden turns, knotted phrases, kennings, allusions to episodes and characters unknown to me. The story, or the parts of it that I could catch, told of the dark traveller's encounters with a series of lights and a gleaming otter, on the marshes; of his arrival at a frozen fortress, with a fountain of ice; of meetings with helpers (the otter may have been one of these) and a fight with the first of the ice-giant's dogs. The traveller relied on the help of spirits some of whose names he did not know, some of whom he had encountered on earlier occasions, in human shape. He transformed himself, for protection, once into a cloud, once into something whose name I did not understand, in which he was frozen for some time—and there again I lost the thread. The idiom of the poem was contemporary—as nearly as I could tell. I could detect neither archaisms nor literary usages—in fact, it seemed to me that the language was not, in the usual sense, even literate: I could make out certain ungrammatical "incorrect" locutions of the current street languages and bits of recent slang. Once or twice I thought I heard echoes of a popular song a few years old, but I was not certain of that. I would have been interested in the performance however crude it had been, but in fact it was presented with pure authority, and from the start two things about it impressed me above all. First, the poetic power of the words, even when I did not understand them. And then, through the poem's sound and urgency, the distant but unmistakable beat of those same ancient fragments which my friend had been reading aloud to me earlier in the day.

Excited and alien, doubting even what I thought I understood, I must have been told it in a number of different ways before I grasped the fact that the dark traveller, the central figure in the apparently endless poem, was the second toe of the left foot, who had been called The Black Toe ever since he had been frozen. But whose left foot? The other twin listened, without a sound or a change of expression.

The recitation came to an end—or a pause. My friend thanked the boy and asked him whether that was the end of the poem. The boy said no, it was just where he wanted to stop for a while.

I saw that my friend had been taking rapid notes, in a phonetic shorthand partly of his own invention: I recalled, as though noticing a coincidence, that it enabled him to write the sounds of the language at each known phase of its development, and I found myself glancing across at the symbols, trying to see whether I could read them. He saw me looking, pushed some of the pages toward me, and brought a small tape recorder out of a shoulder bag. He began to explain its purpose and operation to the boy, who looked at its operation without obvious interest. My friend demonstrated the use of the machine, talking into it, playing back his own voice, distant and hollow in the echoing hall, and both boys laughed. He recorded their laughter and played it back, the last seconds of it: a tail vanishing through a doorway. He asked the twin who had been reciting whether he would tell a poem into the recorder, and the boy said nothing, stared at him, picked up one of the pencils and began to copy one of the shorthand symbols over and over on the margin of the page of notes. The other twin looked across, from the far table, and watched; though they were not facing each other, both of them laughed at the same moment.

My friend told them that it would take him a minute or two to prepare the tape recorder. He said it as an invitation, as though the operation of the machine might be something that they would like to watch—and they did, but they kept their distance. They began to talk to each other, not whole sentences, but phrases, allusions, half of them in whispers, making each other laugh. I understood little of what they said, and in my own language asked my friend what they were talking about. He told me that most of it escaped him too, as the boys meant it to. It was a semi-secret language, which apparently they made up, in part, as they went along. But he said that in any case they were alluding to things which they alone knew: family circumstances, street games, school. The machine did not seem to be running satisfactorily, or my friend had not mastered its controls. It clicked and whirred and burst into passages of frantic gabbling— glimpses of treble multitudes in panic-stricken flight, old haste of dry water—and while he stopped it and started it he spoke to me rapidly in my language, as though discussing the recorder, explaining to me that the twins came from a mountainous region farther north —he avoided saying the name of the place, so that they would not know we were talking about them, but I noticed them listening to the strange words, while they continued to make a game out of their own.

Their mother had been a young woman from that region who had come to the city as a child, with her parents, during the war, and had returned to the country some years later, with a man about whom not much was known except that he had been a legendary figure in the resistance. He had died, there in the mountains, before the twins were born, and their mother had brought them up by herself. No one had yet determined their exact age, but they were thought to be about nine. Their mother, too, had died, some years before our meeting, and the twins had been housed for a time at a farm of some relatives of hers, in that same region, but at a distance from their earlier home; later they had been brought to their maternal grandparents, in the city. There they had lived for a year, without being sent to school: fed and clothed adequately; allowed to run in the streets—until their existence came to the notice of the authorities, who looked into their situation and set about resolving what they described as the problem of the boys' education. The twins had a rudimentary ability to read and write, picked up at home, from their mother, and from observation of their elders: they were quick and alert and remembered what they chose to. But they were several crucial years older than the other children whose formal education was no more advanced than theirs. The authorities waxed anxious over the boys' associates: they wanted to make sure that the twins would be able to find friends of their own age. They feared that the differences of background, of sophistication, would isolate the boys and further retard their assimilation. They need not have troubled themselves. The twins were soon running what amounted to a gang of their own—posing new problems for the anxious educators. Their schooling required a special arrangement: the twins sat through an hour or two, every day, of the ordinary classes, never called on for answers, though much of the teaching, whether or not they were aware of the fact, was directed at them, as at a pair of silent judges. And a tutor was found for them, ostensibly to help them catch up with the studies of the children of their own age—or what their age was assumed to be. He was a man acquainted with the region where they had grown up—a student of it, indeed, who had been spending his summers there for over a decade—and he understood the dialect, which the twins still spoke with their grandparents. He got along well with the boys, was more interested in them than in their schooling, and it was he—among those responsible for the boys' education —who had first heard the poems. He had thought them remarkable, and had brought them to the attention of some of his learned and literary acquaintances, who had shared his enthusiasm; it was in this way that my friend the philologist had first heard them. He told me that the boy had at one time made poems in the regional dialect as well, but apparently had not done so for some time, and no one was certain whether he remembered them.

"But are they really his own?" I asked.

My friend gave me an oddly blank look.

"Does he make them up himself?"

"We don't know that," he said. "We don't know at all."

"And the meter, the ballad form, the rhythm, those echoes of the ancient poetry?"

My friend shrugged. He said that none of those things had been encountered by the folklorists in that region—or anywhere else. He wanted to record whatever he could of those poems, he said, before the twins were fully literate. There would be time to analyse them later.

He seemed to have the recorder working to his satisfaction, and he asked the twin who was sitting at our table whether we could hear some poetry, with the machine listening. The twins had been laughing and whispering together; now the one who had recited sat back again, looked up into the darkness, took a long breath, and began to hum. My friend switched on the recorder. The boy started to pat the table, sometimes with the palm of his hand, sometimes with his fingertips. Then the words came, the chanted beats, in a voice deeper than the boy used in talk. It was the same landscape as before—a low sky, an ice fountain. Far away on the horizon, a fire, under the night: the house of a planet burning. The Black Toe still unfrozen, in this poem; not yet named, calling toward the fire. A water-flame coming to help him, out of the sky. The boy stopped.

The philologist stopped the recorder, re-wound it, and started to play back what he had just taped. We heard a crackle of static—perhaps scratches on the tape. Then echoes from the room. Then the humming, but deepened and overwhelmed with reverberations: a series of hollow beats like steady thunder—the boy's hand on the table. The poem began, beyond the rumbling and the echoes, as though coming through water. The words—to me, at least—were incomprehensible. But the boys were laughing, both of them. They laughed as loud as the noise of the machine, slapping their legs like old men. My friend turned it off. He tried to explain to the boy that the machine was not working as it should. He asked the boy whether we could hear that part again, when he had it running properly, and had moved it off the table.

"No," the boy said.

My friend asked him whether it was just that he didn't want to say that poem again, and the boy, in a caricature of the scholar's gesture a moment before, shrugged, and the twins laughed.

Would he say another poem for the listening machine?

"No," the boy said.

Didn't he like the machine?

The boy shrugged again, looking at his brother, who shrugged too.

My friend began to explain the purpose and mechanism of the machine in greater detail, and how it should work, if it were running properly. He asked the boy what he objected to, about the machine. The boy said he didn't want to be turned into *that*.

"Into what?"

"That noise," the boy said, pointing to the machine. "What came out of there."

"But you laughed," my friend said.

The boy shook his head.

"Don't you want the poem to be there?" my friend asked.

"No," the boy said.

"Why not?"

"I won't go in there," the boy said.

My friend put the recorder away.

"What if you forget the poems?" my friend asked.

The boy looked at him without expression for a moment, and then smiled—an impudent, ironic, mocking smile—and took a deep breath again, looked up, began to drum on the table. It was a different beat, more intricate, with syncopations, rhythmic pauses, and after a minute or two I became aware that the other twin was patting the other table, in those pauses. Between them, on the two long polished surfaces, they were beating out a single rhythm. Then the other twin began to hum. I glanced at my friend the philologist, who looked as surprised as I was. I saw the other twin's lips begin to move, and the voice came, lighter but more urgent than his brother's, and with the same power of feeling, the same unquestionable echoes of the ancient rhapsodic diction. His landscape was brighter, but the story was as fierce, full of teeth and blades. The second twin's chant paused, and the first took up the recitation in the name of The Black Toe, running on ice; the boy's words trailed off into lengthening, distorted syllables, and a long wail of loneliness like three descending wolf chords. Then his brother continued, and I understood that his hero was the second toe of the right foot, The White Toe, so called because he raised his face out of the dust, out of the shadow. In one of the episodes he was disguised as a cripple, and his brother rescued him; it was implied that the rescue also happened the other way round. There were calls of warning, triumph, incitement, between the two voices. When the second twin also had ended his words and his humming, and both of their hands were still, the two tables went on echoing, vibrating—strips of gray daylight running into the darkness at the end of the hall.

The Box

One day an old man was digging in his garden when he turned up a
rusty iron box. It seemed frail with age and he tried to open it and as
the lock gave a little he pried harder and harder and suddenly found
that the lid had come away in his hand and that there was nothing
under it, and that his other hand had disappeared. Then he heard
the box shut and he was at the end of his garden, and the sun had
not yet gone down, and the spade was hanging up, and both of his
hands were on the gate.

Late Capital

Many of the family tombs are neglected. Iron doors stand ajar, rusted into their quadrant tracks, rust flaking from lower panels molded with reliefs of wreaths resting on crossed arrows. Hinges solid as sculpture. Snow of rust on the echoing floors. Nothing to steal. Broken vases. Dry flower stalks, held with green wires. Portable cement wreaths with the word *Regrets* running around them. A quiet which is neither of the city nor of open country. The few sounds, such as the barking of an old spoiled dog, seem to be coming from farther away than their visible sources.

Small groups of people, all of them past middle age, cluster on benches, talking. It is the day of rest. It is clear that many of them meet here every week, weather permitting, after visiting the family tomb. On some benches those at the ends, of either sex, sit forward and talk across those in the middle, which makes them all look as though they were laying plans, in the shade. It also makes them broader. They wear warmer clothes than the day requires. On other benches everyone sits back and faces out across the walk and among the tombs, even when someone is talking, which is not always the case.

One woman, plump and merry, comes with a small bright-colored bucket containing scraps from her dinner, which she feeds to the cats that appear at the sight of her, like gods. Then she takes the bucket to the faucet, rinses it out, and brings back water for washing out the tomb. She keeps a colored brush behind the door. She has dyed red hair and no hat. She is younger than most of the others. She jokes with the cats. Two other women who have come with her, in hats, sit on a bench and wait. They all know many of the same words.

Beyond high walls, gray streets with movie houses in session, papers blowing past them in the light before rain in the afternoon. At the intersections of the avenues, army trucks are waiting for anyone. Going to other intersections. More trucks come in along the avenues, and stop, and let people off who were coming to a particular intersection, and other people, who were going away, get on. The green cloth sides of the trucks have been rolled up and tied. There are benches running from front to back, as in the old days. The passengers climb up steps and walk along the benches as though they were on stages, treading the boards, about to receive prizes, and some who are passing stop and watch. The passengers sit facing outward over the heads of the passers-by. Pairs of knees all along. They don't know the neighbors to right or left. Not a word. Umbrellas. They read papers, or stare at the glare of the avenues, keeping the faces out of focus, waiting, gazing past the new buildings innocent of life.

The Inheritance

On a mountain whose name had been forgotten, a shepherd found a book in a cave.

He had been gathering stones to make a wall across the cave mouth, when he found it. It was under the last stone of a pile in a corner of the cave. He had never seen a book before. He had never heard of such a thing. He was frightened and crept back a few steps toward the cave mouth, watching it.

He wanted to see whether it breathed. Whether it was a thing that breathed, and if it was, he wanted to see how long it could go without breathing. The first and second things he wanted to know.

He wanted to see whether it was really dead, or only pretending to be dead. He had seen animals pretending to be dead, looking like that but shaped differently, crouched together or coiled up underneath. He had seen men pretending to be dead, looking like that but shaped differently, lying there with weapons hidden under them. He had seen, worst of all, beings that looked like men, and even looked as though they were breathing, suddenly turn into stones or logs or shadows, and pretend to be dead, only to follow him later until he was unable to tell whether he was asleep or awake. But they too were shaped differently, like logs, or stones, or shadows. Even if it was alive, this was none of those things. It must be something else. So he wanted to see what it was.

Then he wanted to see whether it was a door. He had heard of doors, like doors into real houses, but doors into the floors of caves. This, if it was a door, was a door like an old lost garment of something, gone stiff now, and strange to everyone, smelling of unending darkness, and hostile to the infant present. It had been lying alone in the darkness too long, the only book.

If it was a door it was a door like food, lying in front of him, submissive but alien. It had a few rows of patterns pressed into it. Tracks.

He bent forward and put his ear to it and listened.

Things might be asleep in those tracks now. Those might be their beds. The things might be out now, hunting, and come back to their beds, and he would be there. There would be many of them. He had heard of them, small people.

Maybe not, though.

He had heard of boxes. He began to want to know whether the thing was a box. He had even seen boxes. He had heard that some of the boxes still in the world had been found in dark hiding-places, in caves. Some of them had had valuable things in them, and some had had terrible things in them, and death itself hiding under the lids. Against these last, he knew, no human weapons gave protection. But he pulled his staff closer. The sun was going down. There was no fire.

It was almost dark. He was afraid to touch the thing now with his hand. He was afraid to touch it just before night. But he was afraid to leave it. But he wanted to send the dog to bring the sheep up to the cave. But he couldn't bring the sheep in the cave now, with the book there. But already he could hardly see it. But when he moved forward, his own shadow, which for some time had been nothing but a shapeless cloud of darkness, moved forward also and covered the book. But he heard the sheep rustling and coughing outside the cave, lambs crying, not near enough. But he listened for the dog. But he could not hear it. But he thought of the night coming. Outside, in that part of his mind, stars were walking forward toward night until their lights were visible, and they came on walking, and stopped in their places, and then night carried them toward the mountains.

He listened for the fox.

He listened for the wolf.

He heard the wind that came after sundown and then went away by itself.

Then he wanted to hear whether he heard breathing in the cave, that wasn't his own breathing.

But then it seemed to have stopped.

He was listening. He was watching the place where he had last seen the thing, trying to remember exactly what it looked like.

But he kept thinking of wolves. There was one wolf he had seen many times, and he wanted to know whether it was the same wolf every time. Wherever he was, it always came alone, just at evening. He had never seen it come. Each time he had looked up and it was there, watching somewhere to one side of him. Each time he had fixed his eyes on the wolf, kept them there, almost stopped breathing, only to see, some time later, that he was watching a wolf-shaped patch of darkness, from which the animal had gone. He thought now that he must still be watching the wolf.

When the first light came into the cave he could see nothing at all in front of him. Then he felt his cheeks. They were wet with tears. Then he saw the book, and without waiting he crossed the cave, and bent down, and touched the book, and made his hand stay there. He felt a small animal, a small lightning, run up his arm, but it was not painful. He moved his fingers over the tracks. Then he straightened and put the fingers of his left hand into the palm of his right hand, and folded the fingers of his right hand over them, to comfort them, to talk with them and ask them. With one hand in the other, that way, he went out of the cave and down the slope.

The sheep were scattered. When he called the dog, he felt the tracks stir in the fingertips of his left hand. They stirred every time he called the dog. When the dog came it seemed to be afraid of him.

When he had the sheep together again, and the dog watching them, up by the cave, he went in to the book, and with both hands lifted an edge. When the book fell open, he knelt to look at the tracks. Many animals seemed to have passed there and he did not know any of them. When he tried to lift again, pages turned and the tracks went on. He came to the empty pages at the end. He knocked to see whether the bottom page was hollow. He lifted it and the whole book came up and he carried it out into the sunlight.

After that his life changed.

He stared at the book for hours every day. He wrapped it carefully in his sack when he changed pastures. He began to be able to remember some of the tracks. He thought there was a secret in them that he would discover. He looked for them in the world and sometimes he saw them, but alone, or in a different order, so that he thought the others must have disappeared. He began to remember the order in which the tracks came on the pages, and some of their repetitions, some of the groups in which they travelled together, some of the companies in which some of the groups travelled.

He thought he was coming closer all the time to learning the secret in the book which was making the book change his life.

But the book had infected him with a new fear—of losing it. He guarded it carefully. He avoided other shepherds. They became suspicious of him. They spied on him. They followed him. They saw the book. They saw him open it, stare at it, kneel, staring at it. They stole it from him. They killed his dog so that he would not be able to follow them. They tried to kill him. He got away at night. He went on until nobody knew his language. He was beaten. Everything else was taken away from him. He was found in a marketplace, begging. As he sat there he tried to trace some of the lost tracks in the dust, to remember them. He was seized. He was taken away and tortured, while they kept asking him questions he did not understand. The tortures were stopped and an old man led him away to a tent and gave him food and had him washed and dressed in clean clothes. The next morning they set out, and he with them. They travelled for days, into the mountains. Everything got older. They came to ancient rocks, ancient trees, a huge ruin. A man even older than the first one seemed to be the king there.

They led him to understand, with gestures, that they wanted him to trace the tracks, in the dust. The old king came to watch him make the marks, and stared at them, and asked the shepherd questions no word of which the shepherd understood.

They tried to teach him their language so that he could explain what the tracks meant, because the old king had heard of writing. They tried to learn the shepherd's language, in case the meaning of the tracks could be expressed only in his native tongue. They learned to trace the tracks themselves, to be ready for the day when he would be able to tell their meaning.

He showed them the tracks again, here and there in the world, and he saw that they treated each other, afterwards, with care and reverence. He never came to understand their language, nor they his, but they listened to him, they bowed to him, they followed him, they waited on him, they gave him a place next to the king, nodding to him as though he were a mute. And to please them he went on trying to remember more tracks, till the end of his days, forgetting even so, getting the order wrong, forgetting more and more, and supplying it as best he could, from mere habit.

But he never tried to tell them where the cave was. No one ever knew. No one even knew what mountain it was on.

Refugees

My little friends, my trusting friends, my thin friends, little ugly girls, both of you, with whom I have been a child, it is forbidden here. It is forbidden to be a child here, and see, we cannot leave. It is forbidden to run here, and we have run, through the dark, empty, echoing green halls. It is forbidden to laugh here and we have laughed, in the empty rat world, as we ran. Whatever is forbidden is funny. Where there were stairs we ran on the empty stairs, the cement stairs guarded with signs and posters, and our breath ran with us hand in hand. Before long we had forgotten how it began, and when we had met, and what day had been before us. Such a long time we had not known each other! It was already late. No one was looking. We started to run.

You followed me, both of you, and of course we are lost. But when we discovered it we were still laughing, in the last dark corridor. The doors were locked long ago. We came down the last hall to the green wooden stairs, above which the light was a little better, hoping to get out. We ran up the wooden stairs to the last landing, and stood, still laughing, at the top. We tried to hold our breaths and listen. We heard our hearts. We put our hands to each other's hearts. Someone was coming.

We heard him coming through the sound of our hearts. There are no doors on the landing. Nothing but boxes. We piled them up so that we could reach the dirty skylights full of wires, where we hoped to get out. But they would not open, they were locked, and he was coming.

At last we saw him, in his thick shoes and orange shirt. He is old, but strong. He had caught us. He hates us. His heart is a secret. He started up the ladder. We were still laughing. We saw his glasses, reflecting the skylights, dirty and thick, and his eyes watching us over the tops of them, as he came up the ladder slowly, hating us step by step as though he had known us and had been watching for us. I took hold of the top of the ladder and pushed it over backwards, and he fell.

But he is scrambling, putting it back. He will come up again for us, watching us over his glasses.

My little friends, how did it begin? Why did you follow me? Where did you come from? Who are your parents? You have stopped laughing, but you are still trusting, thin, ugly. Where were you hoping to go when you got out?

Listen, it will be all right. He will not take us anywhere. I will go down the ladder and throw him off it again. Perhaps I will break his glasses, as though they were the skylights. I will take away his keys. Climb down behind me. Keep away from his hands. We will get out and throw the keys away. You will escape. And I will never be a child again.

Treasure

As we begin to dig we find that we are not the first. For all our knowledge of history, we are surprised. Others have dug before us. Did they find it? Did they take it away? How did they hear it was there? Was it there? Was it ever there? Why? What was it, really? Is it still there? What happened to them?

And that, again, is history. Which leaves us in ignorance.

We continue to dig. No one has been before us tomorrow.

And we dig alone. The true present is a place where only one can stand, who is standing there for the first time.

The Secret

A carpenter and a woodpecker met in another world. No one in that sphere needed comfort or shelter; neither the worm nor the hunger for it was to be found there; and in any case there was no wood in that world, so the carpenter and the woodpecker had found themselves deprived of those callings which each had thought he could not live without. Each remembered his former life only a little more clearly than we remember ours, in this world. Each felt that he himself might be anyone, and was willing to learn. When they met, each thought there was something familiar about the other, and each bowed and tried to speak.

But at first their languages flew past each other without meeting, and the carpenter and woodpecker stood staring across the space between them without understanding what had happened.

"What did you do?" the carpenter asked. It was the only way he knew how to put the question, and he tried again. "What did you do, before?"

The expression in the bird's eyes did not change. Then the woodpecker, in what it remembered of its language, asked the carpenter the same question, but with no better success. However, with the loss of what they had thought of as their purposes, the sense of time and its urgency had left them too, and neither of them was in any hurry. They repeated their questions over and over. At last, in its eagerness to comprehend, the bird began hopping on one foot, whereupon the carpenter remembered an ancient pain in his thumb, stuck his thumb in his mouth, and beamed at the bird, with eyes full of the delight of sudden understanding. They embraced each other.

They repeated their first lesson over and over, with growing excitement, taking turns at asking the question, dancing on one foot, sucking a thumb or a wing-feather.

A wind sprang up, and the woodpecker was moved and made signs to remind the carpenter of the sighing of leaves and the bending of big trees. The carpenter understood the woodpecker to be extolling the satisfaction of planing a piece of wood, and he danced around and around with his thumb in his mouth. In the sky there was a drift of mackerel cloud, and he pointed to it in order to go on and describe the grain of the wood emerging under his hands, and the woodpecker looked and remembered the patterns made by insects under the bark, and it danced on one foot, and they embraced each other.

They became close companions, and little by little, out of evocations of what each knew of the nature of wood, they contrived something which they used as a language. Everything they saw or heard found a place in it, and it became for them the key to a treeless world. They even invented what they thought of as a song in the new idiom. It was composed as much of hopping and stroking and head-beating as it was of syllables uttered with a voice, but the carpenter and the woodpecker went along singing it happily, lone sharers of a deepening secret.

Crusade

Peter the Hermit woke in a cave above a cold valley. Rain. He was a hardier man than I am, though I profess to be hardier than I am. What did Peter the Hermit profess, hardy as he was? Sometimes he slept standing.

From soft spring meadows, from fishy streams and shade, and forests full of creatures before tapestries he called those who were born to all that round life, the oppressed and oppressors of that moment, maker and taker, and made them listen, after a long time, though at first they ignored him. Either their beasts were fat, and they themselves happy at table and in bed, and hoping to get richer. Yet fearing for what they had—fire, imminence of disease, suddenness of death, urgency of life to come—and at the same time bored and believing that there was something else. Or they were full of black bile, hacking and hewing at each other. Or both. He persisted in drawing their attentions to their own pain, joy, and hope. And linking what they dreaded to what they concealed.

When they came to him, he told the men to leave everything, the women to send the men away to set free a city that not one of them had ever seen, which had been theirs for a thousand years, and in which they would all live forever once they had died. He convinced them with their bad dreams, he invented visions of bliss which they did not want to deny were theirs. They followed him through deliberate sleep, not daring to wake, contriving new theories of possession, imagining new fortifications, carving a long wet red road for the ox-cart of knowledge, it is written, they who could not read.

Some came back and were buried at home, having seen the city.

Nobody knows much about him. Either you believe or you don't. There is only the cave he is said to have slept in. Nobody called him Peter. Nobody woke him. He may never have slept at all.

By the Grain Elevators

This afternoon in rolling, partly wooded country, still green, though
the summer is far gone. Here in the north they are still harvesting.
All day yesterday the harvesters maneuvered like tanks across the
grain fields, under dark heavy clouds, racing with the menace of
rain. Sound of their throbbing echoing along hillsides, their clacking
and rumbling, all for one species that numbers its days. Last night
they harvested long after dark. I listened, imagining the nocturnal
animals of the soil, with a light not of the sun dawning for them.
And the animal heads of the wheat, being harvested in their sleep: a
sudden blinding light, suddenly going out around their closed eyes.
I thought of those who would eat the bread that was harvested at
night, that night, in haste, late. I listened to the night harvest, the
approaching and receding noises of machines in the dark, and the
syllables of human shouting, woven across the nearer cries of owls,
waking the magpies and crows, drowning out the crickets, and the
cheeping of mice, among the roots. I watched the beams advancing
slowly across the blackness. It came into my mind how suddenly my
father had become an old man, wanting to be old. The wheat was
green, then, and it was another year. Last night I honored the change
better than at the time. We are taught not to grieve, but having felt it,
I slept peacefully. I woke once and it was over. They had gone home
from the unlit stubble, taking the grain. It must have been the dew
that made them stop. The night was still.

Today they began again as soon as the sun had burned off the
lower mists. The lines of the woods were dark on the hills and be-
tween the fields. A few cattle in the woods. Brick farmhouses, and
little streams crossing pastures, reflecting crows and the low gray
rushing sky.

A sign said FERRY, and I took that road, not to cross, but to see
the river. Ahead of me were trucks and trucks of grain, going north.
They converged from side-roads, ahead and behind. Together with
them I left the open fields and entered the woods. The road was
narrow. Barbed wire was stretched among the trees, higher than

someone could reach. The road drops steeply to the shore. Many of the trucks continue across the ferry. They sit in lines and wait, for hours. Few still go at all to the grain elevators built from fortifications of the last war. The year it was declared, for some time their fathers went right on, just the same, with the harvesting, through week after week of perfect golden autumn days, many of them with horses or oxen. Then there was only the day harvest.

The Fair

The streets are changing color. Small, narrow streets curving to cling to the sides of hill after hill. I came up here hours ago. Walls along the streets painted white, ivory, blue. Faded. Gardens spilling over the tops, here and there. Cobbles and mud. Passing steep cross streets that drop straight from the mountain to the harbor, a long way below. Each one a cold, shadowy draft. Looking down through them, much of the city out of sight, every time. Behind the houses, and beyond hills.

Now it is evening and the colors of the streets are deepening. It is almost time for me to go and call the tall dark young woman who came to bring something back, this morning, to the big house at the edge of the city, where I am staying as a guest. She is an old friend of the family. They left us together. I had something to mail. She brought me into town.

Under a stained-glass roof projecting from the front of a blue grocery shop fortified with lettuces and eggplants, a large, bald, overweight, dominating man in a translucent, starched white shirt, with rings on his fat fingers, is telling a small group of shorter men, in suits, with their hats tilted back, about something that happened at the Fair, in town. The International Industrial Fair. Big money, big money. He says what they say down there.

An older man, to whom they all listen with blank respect, returns to the subject of the British tent, which was put up today. He is flanked by men of his own age, sitting on produce boxes, in their Sunday clothes. He tells what a brilliant tent it is. Red and white stripes. He says it came in an Australian boat. He was a sailor, and he has been there. He tells them about Australia.

It was the British tent, the same one, that the young woman and I watched going up, as we walked through the Fair, before lunch. We stopped as the red and white mountain climbed itself, leaning, swaying, the stripes unrolling and straightening. New, bright pavilion. Shining white ropes. Inside, the pipe railings and scaffoldings newly painted white. There were Australians among the crew putting up the tent.

There was a brown tent like that, which I then remembered having seen once, that had disappeared in turn to reveal a baseball field that had not been there before.

I had seen that tent put up in a lot at the outskirts of the town where I was a child. I had been coming back from a short trip with my father, in the first car. A circus tent. My father had talked about carrying water for elephants, though there were none to be seen. Later, an ageing soprano tried to make a come-back, in a tent on that same lot. Her dressing room was a smaller tent inside the big one. She came out in her blond wig and stood behind a box of tulips whose petals were the shapes of her body, and sang about how she was alone.

One time when there was nothing on that lot but grass, we had driven past all together, and my mother was talking about peaches and apricots so that I imagined them growing among their leaves.

The city is full: hotels, restaurants, cafés. People have come from all over the world to the Fair. Turning down the next cross street, I see the group still standing in front of the grocery store, gesturing. Radios out of upper windows, instead of their voices. Advertisements for soft drinks, between bursts of music.

The New World

Possibly it occurs to others among us, from time to time, and perhaps even to more than one of us at the same time and within sight of each other, to look up, for some reason afterwards as irrevocable as a dream, from the gestures and entire labors that will never really seem natural to us, now in our lifetimes, and remember the queen as she was when we were there, rather than as we have come to imagine her. Then instantly, for all of our polishing of the handles with our palms, we may feel, each of us separately, a roughness as though the wood were unpeeled and our hands were back without the calluses again. At such moments we seem to have straightened too suddenly. We are dazzled. We are overcome. We hope no one notices. What has betrayed us, or what have we betrayed? The gestures from which we look up belong to labors that we have chosen deliberately and even wilfully, and apparently we had imagined that our choice had put us beyond doubt or even surprise. But when we came to choose those labors we were no longer children, and childhood is the time to learn things so that they become shapes of the growing body. Once that is no longer possible we have entered upon age, with its fragments. By the time we were old enough to choose, we could not help but doubt.

The ways we perform our present labors are not even the ways of our own country, for that matter. What we have learned that is of use here we have garnered from foreigners, illiterates whose names we can scarcely pronounce, watching them every day as though they were new, and picking up, with what appeared to be the essence of the actions, the local and personal idiosyncrasies, rehearsing the combinations awkwardly, feeling foolish, but going on, having to get the job done before the end of its unpredictable season. Certainly they are not gestures that we were born to—whatever that means— and it is something that we have come to question more and more often, though this too only to ourselves. It is hard to think of anything in our childhoods preparing us for these actions, and yet it is always this adult that the child was busy making. It is true that in those days we had not met the queen. For some of us she was not yet born.

We look up, then, touched by some impulse that is indeed ours but which we do not recognize and cannot later retrace, from a labor upon which we are voluntarily engaged, and which we have undertaken in her name, though she is aware of it only distantly if at all. It is some work that we have learned to do in the course of doing it: our different awkwardnesses have settled into habits, we have ceased to pay attention to our imitating and have developed primitive variants, original mistakes and graces that in due course were repeated, and entered upon destinies of their own. And suddenly we are overtaken as by a chill, or a dizziness on standing up in the sun, by the strangeness and lateness, the improbability of each of our movements and of the whole enterprise. And in that moment of awareness of the alien nature of what we are doing, it seems that we cannot have begun it for the reason we imagined, but must be working for something else perhaps inadmissible and even unknowable. All at once how unlikely, how preposterous it seems that she could ever set foot (that foot like painted china) in these muddy paths, and spend her days among these raw fields beside the river of hard water yellowing its stones, these caked and matted animals, and these attempts to repeat the shapes of palaces in logs which we have hewn ourselves—all of them things that have come to seem beautiful to us.

Smitten by the oddity of our efforts, and face to face with the unlikelihood of her ever inhabiting the place that we imagine we are preparing for her, it is then that we glimpse her for a while as we knew her—and ourselves as we knew her—and remember how silly she sometimes seemed to us, how ordinary, to tell the truth, and how undignified; on occasion, how capricious and shallow; how ignorant her accent sounded in certain of the stone rooms, so that we tried to avoid her there. But also how we managed, in those days, to refer to such things among ourselves, and to laugh at them even though we had been brought up to regard the person of the sovereign as beyond reproach, like one of the elements. Now, of course, we scarcely dare credit such thoughts, even when we are alone. No, we accuse the sudden lucidity itself of being a disguised temptation to surrender, if only for a moment—a disloyalty to the entire undertaking and to the hope that was behind it, and in time we find ourselves examining that hope, also. But meanwhile we are here, and the winters come sooner than we remember, and there is no one to prepare for them but ourselves.

And yet those who came here first, and chose the place, were right. She will not be able to stay on where she is, where we were children. She will be forced to leave, even to give up everything. She will bring it upon herself, perhaps by those very frivolities that we have managed to escape at last, here, and—it seems—almost to forget. A place must be made ready for her, and its preparation has become the abiding and cheerful purpose of our lives. A place that she will have read about, but in which we will have learned to survive. Some of us brought our families—but it must be said that others, even some of the founders, have gone back, in spite of everything.

Most improbable of all, at moments, are the decorations, which we have fashioned in the winters, without experience or skill, from strange materials, but according to her taste as we remember it, or after drawings of objects that she is known to be fond of. Baskets of flowers cut into the log walls, wooden wreaths pegged to the cow barns. A set of carved steps painted with her flower and her initials in a crown, which we plan to use in the great throne room, when we have time to build it.

A Voyage

Many times when I was a child we had driven past the octagonal stone school building that had not been used in my lifetime nor in my parents' lifetime. It sat out in a field, by then, and the plow went past the door, drawn first by huge white horses, then by tractors, crossing the place where the path had been, and the one where the privy had been, and crops of wheat and corn grew, and rattled around it and were harvested. Whenever we passed the building, it meant, if it was on the right, that we were going to visit my parents' relatives—but my mother had none. And if it was on the left, that we were coming away from them again. Each time, if we had been gone for a winter or so, we would say we hoped it had not been torn down.

And there I stood inside it when both parents were gone. It was larger than I had expected. Long rays of the afternoon sun came through the narrow stone windows. It was later in the afternoon than the children would have stayed. There were shelves around the walls, with nothing on them. The plaster had been an ivory beige. Corinthian flutings, painted white, around the windows.

As I stood inside, listening to the dry stalks in the field, everything was looking past me. I felt a tall heavy wave wash over me and go on to break somewhere else, and then I was there without it, casting a shadow in the beam from the window, looking at the shelves, thinking of the alphabet, and through it.

Perhaps the building's proportions made it seem larger inside than it looked from outside. With the years it had sunk into the ground. The wooden floor was rotten in places. Abroad, in Europe, in France, I had seen an octagonal dovecote, somewhat larger across, and much higher. As high as a castle tower or a church belfry. Wagon spokes of rafters. The walls speckled with light, but most of the shaft in shadow, lined with thousands of square stone niches built into the masonry, and beside each opening a recess to the left, and another to the right, for the nests. A few wild pigeons flapped in the rafters and on the stone window grilles.

The light on the patches of plaster behind the shelves was also reflected from an angled bay of the central reading room of the British Museum, some years earlier, with the reference dictionaries of language after language arranged alphabetically around it. Coastline, horizon, zodiac. Except for the doors.

The small panes that remained intact were pearly. Like the tall slender octagonal glasses, from which some had once expected to drink *aquavit,* on that ship which the Swedes had launched to be the pride of the new navy they hoped to build. Many of those who sailed out on her had studied all through their childhoods, in uniform, for that moment. I think the Swedish rulers were hoping to challenge the English, as the Spaniards had done. To hold the Baltic, first— some such idea. They were years building that ship, but not a toast was ever drunk on board. There were many gun decks, many rows of gun ports, much gilding—since the vessel would be a flagship. Many statues of ancient gods, deities from languages no longer spoken by children, auspices made of wood. Golden carvings representing sea spirits and players of music clambered over the high curling stern, which was black, as I recall. The launching was a royal occasion. Someone would have been to Venice and seen a doge marry the Adriatic, and heard the music. What animals did they eat, that day, from the points of their knives? Every Swede can still tell you that they christened the giant ship-of-the-line the *Wasa,* which now means the same thing, to start with, in every language, as soon as it is known.

It sailed down the coast with all its flags flying, its band playing in answer to the band on shore, everyone in full dress uniform, officers and men lining the rails or aloft in the rigging or manning the guns at the open gun ports and looking through them at the sea rushing past, the light of the northern day reflected in the spray. Everyone on shore watching, waving, shouting. Puffs from the cannons on shore, then the sound of the royal salute reaching the ship many seconds later, across the water. The vessel rounding the headland under full sail, in the brisk wind, and all its guns answering the salute. And then, so suddenly that the watchers on shore rubbed their eyes, to which tears had not yet arrived, the great ship sinking with all hands. Perhaps the sea flooded the open gun ports. Nobody knows for certain how it happened.

After three centuries light returned to the wreck, swimming
down to it with air-hoses, peering in. Everything was preserved by
the water there, and by the mud, the darkness, the newness of the
objects themselves, when they sank. It was said that everything was
just as it had been—as though anyone knew.

The crowns of Sweden had changed heads many times. The school-
house was already standing empty.

A proposition was put forward to raise the wreck intact from the
sea bottom, and the king approved and subscribed royal hands for
the enterprise. It took years to lace a harness around the vessel, in the
mud, and hoist it, with pneumatic equipment, inch by inch toward
the ultra-modern sections of floating drydock, on the surface. There
was a royal celebration on the day when the ship first broke the sur-
face of the water, from below.

Meanwhile, samples had been brought up and examined in labo-
ratories. A method of preserving them from the air of our age had
been devised. It included, for many of the materials, a chemical
treatment to embalm the tissues not only of wood but of fabrics:
clothing—much of it never worn—and sails, rigging, wet flags. And
it assumed the construction of a hangar: a vast hall built to house—
as eventually it did—the whole of the *Wasa,* indoors, in a controlled,
surprisingly warm, temperature, cradled in a delicate scaffold-work
of beams, with jets of tepid sea water playing over it continuously to
keep its moisture at a measured level, black hoses winding through
it, lights inside the hull showing the dripping interiors, while a
swirling cloud of steam rises constantly around it toward the trans-
lucent ceiling—the new surface. Replicas of the original misted
octagonal glasses from the ship are sold at the door, packed for
travelling. A raised decorative band runs around the nacreous sides,
like scars of shelves. I could check the facts, but this is something
I remember.

The Ship from Costa Rica

At the edge of the city of towers a narrow park runs for a mile or so along the river. When I lived nearby I would often walk there in the afternoons. Bridges for pedestrians, bicycles and baby-carriages cross the heavy traffic of the expressway at regular intervals, and ramps descend from their river ends into the park. Thin branches of slaty trees reach toward the suspended slopes, surround them, and wait, always expecting something else. The park is bounded by a railing, a barrier of the utmost simplicity, next to the expressway, within arm's reach of the hurtling traffic. That railing is never touched, and is evenly wrapped in smoke. The gutter outside it is never swept by anything except the wind of the passing cars. Another railing follows the main pathway along the top of the river wall. It has been bent, here and there, and broken, in places. All the way along, the top has been worn smooth by hands, so that it shines. After heavy rain, or a mid-winter thaw, the scattered spots of rust never last for more than a day. Leaning on the railing, one can look straight down the dark masonry of the river wall: granite blocks perpetually wet with the heave and slap of the polished leaden water, and exhaling its leaden smell. Wakes of tugs and barges unfurl up the dank wall, and fall away, leaving their shadows on it, drying. Coming and going, the tide clings to the wall.

Between passages of hands, gulls watch the water from the cold bright rail. It has an age of its own, a function of the lives that have touched it, slipped along it, held on to it. It is older than the ore it was made of. Its icy curve reflects dimly, in the manner of frozen surfaces. Objects loom and vanish there as amorphous shadows: drifting gulls, the vast bridge high overhead with trains flickering slowly across it and traffic on it creeping through the sky above the river—all are there, but only their watery motions, their changes, are distinguishable. The far shore itself is mirrored there: its smoking factories, gas tanks painted like checkerboards, warehouses and wharves, are reduced to an indistinct margin on the unworn outer edge of the iron. They merge into a horizon of solid rust.

There is a silence in the park that always seems sudden, because of the din that encloses it. Trucks and cars roar beside it, trains rumble and clatter above it, horns blow, sirens and the whistles of tugs howl and blast along it, compressors, drills, tear at it—it remains there, they miss it, one steps down onto it. Yelping of dogs and shrieks of children drift through it like small kites, and float away. At each season it contains the others. It was mid-winter when I stood by the railing and saw my father on the far side of the river.

He had emerged from a high office in a rusted factory near the bridge: an edifice of many storeys, each of a different size and shape from the others, like the superstructure of a ship. A sugar factory. I had often stood and stared across at it. At that distance the buildings appear to have only one side, with nothing behind it. But even from so far away I could recognize him.

He was wearing only a shirt, in spite of the cold north wind. A fresh yellow shirt, the color of lighted office windows before dark. And no tie. He looked fatter than when I had last seen him, but the shirt was loose, and the sleeves fluttered in the wind. He stood leaning on the balcony railing, looking down at a ship, moored below, that had been unloading there for several days, its bow higher every day. It came from Costa Rica. I could not see what was being unloaded from it. I waved, but I was not surprised that he did not see me. He was not even wearing his glasses. At that time he still had nine years to live.

I waved again. What was he doing in the sugar factory, hundreds of miles from where he had been born and was living? I considered that if I were to walk to the nearest ramp, and away from the river, many blocks, to the bridge approach, it would be dark long before I even came in sight of the factory again. As I watched, he turned and went back in, and at once I began to wonder whether I had seen him at all. Of course I said nothing about it. And of course I knew he was far away all the time. Letters came from my mother, as usual. All was well. When I thought it had been only the day before yesterday that I had seen him, I realized that it had been longer than that, and then I tried to remember whether it had been Wednesday or Thursday, and was startled to think that it might even have been the Saturday before, and then for a moment I could not remember what day "today" was. I had been back more than once, and had not seen him. Then one afternoon he came out again.

I had stopped—as I had done each time I had returned to the park, since I had first seen him—for a long look at the factory. The same ship was still unloading, the stern almost as high as the bow. I thought it strange that they should take so long about the unloading. I wondered about the expense, and whether the factory owned the wharf. That same flag from the tropics flapping day after day in the wintry afternoon light. As I watched, the same door opened, and he stepped out, in his shirt-sleeves again, and put his hands on the balcony railing and stood looking down at the ship. I thought, as I had the first time, that he looked younger than he did at home. That, then, was the way he looked at the sugar factory—a life he never mentioned, a life of ships, distances, cargoes, easy-going gazing from balconies, without noticing the cold—whereas at home, in the life in which I was used to seeing him, he set the thermostat in the upper eighties and complained of drafts. Rays of the winter sunset passing between the piers of the bridge fixed the ship and the factory and the balcony in salmon light. I waved to him, but he was watching the ship, and even if he had looked up and across the river, he would have had the sun in his eyes. He straightened up, rubbed his arms—whose softness had always depressed me—and turned to look down the river, for a moment, before going back into the office behind him.

Seeing him a second time did not remove my earlier doubts; it exacerbated them, and awoke new ones. I wondered whether the man I had seen had been there at all. I wondered what that meant—in any sense—and why I had seen him, and how I knew that he was my father. For I knew that he was my father. Who I knew was living hundreds of miles inland, at that moment. The sun went down. The black puddles were frozen under the bridge. Why did I think I had seen him?

The bright weather of the first lengthening days continued, and the next afternoon I walked onto the long bridge across the river. The ship was still there, riding high in the water, again reflecting the sunset. As I leaned over the bridge railing, which was not polished, and reflected nothing, he came out again, on the balcony below me, and looked down into the empty ship. I thought that I could have called to him, but I knew that the distance was deceptive, and the traffic on the bridge was roaring behind me. The day was milder than the one before, and without wind. The tide was rising. I watched him for a long time, waiting for him to look up, and he did, but not toward the part of the bridge where I was waving. And then he went in, and I walked on, farther across the river, until I stood over the factory and could see the back of it, the trucks in the courtyard on the landward side, the chutes to another building, the open warehouse doors, the streets beyond. I considered going all the way across the bridge, and into the factory, and inquiring—what? Asking for my father? By what name? Asking for the man on the balcony? About what? There I was, older than my father had been when I was born. I looked across the bridge, downriver, at the navy yard. I recalled the way my father had used the term "navy yard"—a phrase evoking secret privileges, participation in some arcane freedom and authority, in another time. Yet I knew that the phrase, as he used it, did not refer to the place I could see, with its gray hulls tied in bundles, but to somewhere inexplicably different, vanished, on another coast, with two wars between. I had never been able to imagine him having anything to do with ships. When he had shown me, once, a photograph of himself and friends, on their ship, in the first war, he had had to point himself out to me: sitting cross-legged, grinning, in a knitted hat, on top of a big tube called a ventilator. What he said was their ship looked like part of a building: a floor. When he showed me the brown picture I thought someone else was speaking to me, from behind him.

The day after I had seen him from the bridge, the ship was gone. I knew that he was still in the factory, but he did not come out that afternoon. In the days that followed I found it hard to believe that I had ever seen him, and I never saw him there again, alive.

The Old Boat

When I took you out, that day, in the old boat, I meant for it to show
you something, and now I would not be able to tell you what that
was. I wanted for you to see it, not merely because you did not come
from the same place I did. But you did come from far away, after all,
from another country, over much water, with your pale flame of
hair. And I had come long before, in a smaller boat—but you already
know that. To tell the truth I had forgotten that voyage. Was it really
heroic? Was I? If so, I hope it did not show. The boat from the old
family boathouse, which is almost never taken out any more. Think
of the dangers of those other times. Think of the women with babies,
women who would never again see anything in the same light. Think
how I did not want to come. Think how cold I must have been, in
the winter. Guess, if you will, at the terror of my fires, and the temp-
tation to hate my life, the vacancy, long before you were born. But
that was not what I wanted to show you.

One time my mother took me out to the island to see the Statue
of Liberty. She thought it would show me something, and I thought
so too, though how could I say a thing like that? It must have been
ten o'clock in the morning, and I was wearing a dark beret; I was
somewhere between four and seven. I was never afraid when I was
with her.

As we approached the island we slowed down and came into a
harbor surrounded by stone walls. She had taught me the word
approach. The boat with its white beams turned to the right and
then swung to the left and ran aground with a heavy sigh. There was
excitement around us, and people rushed to the rail with cries and
exclamations, but my mother told me they were silly. She showed me
that we had run aground in soft black mud. She informed me that
we were a little early. She took a calm, knowledgeable interest in this
routine event which seemed to surprise others. She took me to see
our shadow on the green water of the harbor, in which the mud had
been rolled up—by us. Our own mud. Outside the shadow of the
railing our shadows waved back at us from the water, when we

waved. Fine spokes of light radiated from our shadows, as they did from the raised hand of the statue, in pictures, which I remembered. She showed me the gouge in the mud, where we had run aground, as the captain often did when he was early, because he was young. She pointed out places where the boat had run aground before, as people should have realized. The harbor had not been constructed with a view to this boat's being able to turn around in it easily. It was being enlarged, but until the new wharf was finished sometimes the boat had to run aground. She had taught me the word *tugboat* at an earlier time, and the word *ramp*. Later I was convinced that Venus and the Statue of Liberty had both been taken from the same model, and perhaps I was told that—it might even have been during the visit to the statue. But that was not what I wanted to show you, or wanted the boat to show you.

It was something to do with the boat itself, and not just with when and where it was taken. The curving of the ribs, did you see: an ancient shape akin to the waves, to the reflections of mountains, and to the courses of heavenly bodies? I made them myself, once. A little hull to show myself something I could not afterwards explain, something that cannot be kept in a boathouse under cobwebs each with its map of a need. Well, we went out in the old boat. It was past the middle of the day, and in a place I remembered I ran aground, deliberately, as though I were young or early, and we left the boat there with the tide going out, so that it would stand on earth near its drying anchor while the sun went down—I showed you that, as we walked away from it. You saw the gold earth rising out of the water, and on it the gold boat where we had been. Someone knew and would come for it, on the dark tide. As when the Ark grounded on Ararat, a little before sunset, and in the morning there was only the world that no one had spoken for.

On the Map

In a part of the country where my parents lived before I was born
the brick streets are wearing away. At the foot of steep walks often
iron railings remain. Beyond many of the railings, then as now, the
river. Out in the country, a few miles from there, the river was green.
Small fish of sunlight quivered in it without moving. My father and
mother went there on a Sunday with church friends, and after eating
they sat under a tree at the edge of the water, and someone who knew
them came with a folding camera and they turned their heads away.

The old one-room brick canal office, that harks back to before
the railroad, is closed now. It is a comfort to see it still standing,
unnoticed. A thin, white-haired widower, in starched shirt-sleeves,
collar and tie, looks after it, to occupy the time. He was born next
door and has lived in that house all his life. The canal passes out of
town at a different level from the river, with the railroad track on
one side, under the glare of a pearly sky that is redoubled in the pol-
ished surface. The canal is a long white beam. Light hides in itself.

White stone steps descend from the brick sidewalk to the water
every block and a half as long as there are the ends of gardens. Brick
walls. Fences. Tall stalks lean against each other, late in summer, on a
Sunday, forming seeds. In the next town there is still a central square.
There used to be a market there—some sect. But it was closed, of
course, on Sundays. A church, in the square, with a bell tower. They
marked it on their map, which they kept.

After the railroad turns away, the canal enters deep woods. Out
there is the old college where they once talked of sending me. The
name is familiar, from the beginning. The quiet of the woods, and a
spring coolness, even in the clearing that contains the one large
building and the smaller ones beyond. Curtains blowing from upper
windows. Archers in the dusk, young men and women in traditional
white, hardly speaking, smiling, shooting in turn, one at a time, into
targets under the far trees, and never missing, while the dew gathers
on the grass. The sound of the bows.

Ten

Ten o'clock, and nothing here looks like night. Nor like evening. The white sky is as light as at four in the afternoon — some hushed, overcast afternoon in summer. Summer: a past, a time remembered, a season buried in the antipodes. I recall with surprise that this, in fact, is summer; this too: the glassy air empty of birds, this blank unmodulated hour, this lidless night. The old woman might have locked the enamel clock face, with a half turn or a whole turn, and taken away the hour hand. But what she locked was the windowed front door, some time after supper. It looked like one of the mores of a close-fisted region: locking the house in the afternoon, against the empty woods. Now they are all asleep. They have vanished. There is not a sound in the low wooden house. The white curtain over the glass of the door gathers the light from outside and gleams more intensely than any part of the sky. It breathes, when everything else is still. It goes on breathing, far from the sea, and out of sight of the moon. The old woman put the key on a ledge of varnished wood, in the hall, and before she had gone it had been lying in that position for centuries: it had been removed in one piece — ledge, varnish, dust and all — without disturbing so much as its shadow, into the museum of summer. I cannot hear whether the tall clock with the enamel face, standing in the hall near the key, is going or not. I put my ear to the wooden case varnished the same color as the ledge. Yes: far away a dry leaf rocking. But it is slow, according to the silent alarm clock in the next room, standing on a table piled with old magazines. Ten after ten, in there. Hanging on the wall, in that room papered with the rusted vines, is a calendar ten years old turned to a month of spring, and a faded photograph of a field of daffodils, beside blue water, under a blue sky. At the foot of the calendar, a vase full of dusty plastic poppies.

The room on this side of the hall, the one that has been given to me — what was it before? It is hard to imagine that this building — squat, shapeless, a melting bungalow, on cement blocks, covered with green tar-paper shingles, some of them dog-eared and torn —

ever had a dining room. But the walls were once conceived differently: the patterned wallpaper has been thinly painted over and still shows through the ivory brush-marks. The linoleum on the floor has been painted gray. A partition has been set up, near the wall farthest from the windows. What for? A shower that was never installed? And four iron cots have been arranged in a row, with their feet to the windows: half ward, half nursery.

She did not come from here, she told me. Not from this country at all. The language they speak here is not her native tongue. This was her husband's place, though not his house. This region, these woods. He had wanted to come back, talked of it for years, but had never returned. After he died, she had decided to come, by herself, to live away from the city. She spoke vaguely of sons, far away, with families of their own. The house in which her husband had been born and had spent his childhood had burned down, and the big barn with it. This house had been built afterwards, and the shack, half barn, half garage, facing it. Everything had run down, she told me. The people around here knew nothing. "Ignorant," she said, standing a little stooped, with folded arms, in an old cardigan, her head in a kerchief: the eternally foreign owner. A short heavy man with a white face that looked flattened against a glass, was splitting wood on a stump, beyond the house, in the gap in the elder bushes where the overgrown hedge opens into pasture, as she spoke. Chunk. Chunk. A sound coming across water. When I next looked he had disappeared: there was no one standing in the gap, in front of the glow from the pasture. Rusted hay-rakes, rotting wagons, the chassis of a truck—ancestors in daguerreotypes—emerge from the high green nettles and brambles. I saw them as I arrived: half-buried flotsam washed out into the woods. I see them through the white curtain on the door. I could take the key and go out. Nothing is moving out there. These lilacs have finished blooming. Along the one bend of a stream motionless willow bay is in flower. The birches have grown around and up through the stone foundation of the burned house that was a farm in another century, and they have overflowed the foundations of the barn: the dark walls are becoming transparent before the woods that are at once older and younger than they. On the side toward the house a cement loading ramp rises out of the mid-summer growth and leads up to a mossy platform surrounded by nettle and elder leaves. The pile of split firewood gleams at the foot of bushes as tall as the woods. There are no shadows out there.

It is the only farm (if it can still be called a farm) in the woods. And the woods—they are the horizon, from a long way off, and I went on beside them and they came closer. Other farms in the region stand far apart on the plain: red houses with ladders against them, floating in hay fields in the long gold evening, while the dust turns slowly to mist the color of the sky. They must be anchored, for they do not move. And they too are asleep in the shadowless night. Once I thought I would never see this hour. The farm then would be black on its hill, against the black sky, with hulking great Theo asleep in his one shirt, in a black room, behind bare glass the color of the night, and his mother, whom no one else ever saw except from a distance, asleep somewhere else in the unseen house sagging toward its foundations. But I never saw it at this hour. That was the summer when I was ten, and I believed that the night was dark and not allowed. Theo had a huge white horse, and in the daytime, when it had rained, he would let me walk behind it with him, holding the plow handles. Sometimes he took his hands clear off them, when the plow was running easy, and I could hold them where they shone. We seemed to have the wind with us both ways; the cool furrows glistened along the slope, and I smelled them, and the horse, and Theo's shirt. Flocks of shrill birds wheeled around us, brushing us with their shadows, until Theo undid the links, at the end of the field, and we left the plow where it stood, and walked to the barn, with the horse dragging the traces, and their tails flicking over the ground, and I went home to supper, long before the yellow sun went down. The cold summer had turned, but the days were said to be long yet.

Out beyond the shining pile of kindling, in the pasture, a big white horse comes into sight. It sheds light like the curtain I watch it through. I think that it too may be transparent. I stand wondering how long it has lived, or could have lived. It moves slowly toward the house, never looking at it. It stops to gaze into fresh firewood. It turns and comes through the high elder hedge, nibbling here and there at a tuft of green. It passes the shed, on which an old ladder is hanging, and stands still in the space between the buildings, blowing at the ground on which it casts no shadow. Then it turns and walks past the loading ramp and the foundations of the barn and the house, into the woods. Still gleaming, it passes out of sight among the trees, like the white sun. Again nothing is moving, nothing has changed. I could take the key, and open the door, and go out and see, and no one would hear me.

A Parcel

One day a package of implements arrives in the mail, from a house I had known in my childhood. Most things from that house have been lost by then, or are not wanted at the moment. These things that have arrived are still useful. A few knives and spoons. It is a surprise to see wood, such as handles, after it has been put away for so long. The wood appears to be smaller, paler, or lighter or heavier than the memory of it. The origin of none of the pieces of metal and wood is known by anybody, now. Some of them belonged to my parents. Some of those pieces they had inherited. Some others were souvenirs, but not of places where my parents had ever been.

Here, far from where I was born, after I have lived in many houses, the late spring flowers are opening toward the southeast, and I do not know where any of these things came from.

I helped to dry these spoons in that one house where we lived together. I hear the water running in that kitchen. The clink of the plates at the draining board. A parade of refrigerator doors. A footstep on the linoleum, that I recognize as my mother's. We have all dissolved. I see the light in the kitchen, the reflections on the painted walls. There were places then, the same ones as now, where the silver of the spoons had been worn away, at the base of the bowl and where the handle rested. It was already so when the things were Margie's. The insides of the bowls were already scratched, so that they gave back no reflection. But I could hold two of them up to my closed eyelids and look, as though I were looking through them.

Then I took them down and went on looking.

The Ford

Slides of his travels. I thought oh yes, and dismissed the enthusiasm in his voice, that clearly was begging for attention. The lights were on, so the slides were faint and translucent on the wall. Brought out in a hurry, with a touch of shyness, much of it false. There were other conversations going on. I listened here and there, for a moment, and so I missed the beginning of what he said about the pictures. I turned back to them only at the mention of the horses, the tone of the voices agreeing, saying, "There they are," and the slight pause that came after that, an intake of breath, a wave falling back.

Pale yellow wall, half dissolved by a diaphanous section of lit sky, some other time of day, maybe a winter noon, or summer in the far north, reflected in a surface that must be water, a water, a piece of shore beyond it, a river bank, so a river, part of a river, part of what could be seen of it from one spot, at one instant in the past. The wall gone from behind it. And there they were, the horses. A line of them, crossing from right to left, all bays—the slides were in color. There were nine or ten of the horses, in water almost to their bellies, and it looked as though there might be others behind, out of the picture. They had flat white cloths on their backs—blankets, or thin packs, it was impossible to say which, as everyone finally agreed after asking each other. He knew no more than the rest of us did. The horses were following a large bay, several lengths ahead of them, who looked like a stallion, and had nothing at all on his back. There were no lines, traces, ropes, harness. The horses were travelling by themselves. Even on the wall they appeared to be moving, like smoke.

He said that he had not seen them when he took the picture. They weren't there, he said. He didn't see them. It was only after he got back, and had the rolls developed by the same special laboratory he always used, where they did good work, professional. Somebody asked the address.

He said it wasn't until he brought them home to look at with the projector that he saw the horses. It wasn't anything like a double exposure. There they were, wading the river, the legs out of sight in the water. Just in that one picture. Of the river. The only one of the river. He had thought he was just taking a picture of the river. Not even the river—that same building, from across the river.

"I know that place," one person said. "I asked about it once. All they had to say around there was that it had been there a long time. But it must have been something else. At one time."

I had scarcely noticed the building, on higher ground, looking no bigger than a single haycock, in the distance, to the left, well above the water and the horses. And as I looked harder, to make it out, the slide changed, and I saw the landscape across the river, no water, no horses. The landscape into which the horses would have been able to pass: stubble fields and unmown straw-gold meadows curving uphill into dark green woods, and in a clearing near the top, the same building, a little nearer but still small and doubtful. A cluster of roofs, and in the center a round tower, all the walls painted the red of barns, but darker, an ox-blood, dry blood, color—though it may have been the light at that time of day, or the distance, or the exposure, that made it look that shade. The slide changed again, and showed the wooden tower, much closer, with small windows on each floor. One roof, butted against it on the left, was clearly a habitation. Another wing, of corrugated iron, had been tacked against the tower at an angle, and was covered with tin, that had rusted. The dark red paint was peeling. The top of the tower rose in a point, like a hat. Another slide, taken from closer still, showed only the upper storey of the house, and the top part of the tower. The curving rows of small windows, in sight of which the horses would pass. The windows looked as though lights were about to appear in them.

"Somebody living there?" one of the spectators asked.

"That's as near as I went," the man who had taken the picture said.

"I don't think anybody was actually living in it when I was there," said the one who had told them he knew the place. "But that was a few years ago."

"I was just taking pictures of the building," the man at the projector said. "I still don't know what it is."

"Looks like a farm," one of them said.

"Maybe at one time," another answered. "But it's not being used as a farm. The grass is too high."

"I wanted to get one picture of it from across the river," the man at the projector said again, now that they would understand. "And I never saw—"

"You'll have to go back," somebody said.

But the man said nothing. And then they started talking about where the horses were going, and where they might have got to, by then.

Wagon

Mid-summer, not far from the sea. North. Long evening, everything finished, houses closed, cobbled streets washed and empty. Echoes prowling. Shadows horizontal. Upstairs in the hat factory there is a stuffed pheasant with a broken neck, and a large model of a seventeenth-century merchant vessel, with a light bulb behind green and red portholes, and a light switch that does not work. The stairs, the halls, parts of all the rooms and the bathroom, are piled with dusty hatboxes. Downstairs the doors are locked with polished locks. Everything smells of leather, felt, and pipe-smoke.

Starched white curtains on the windows. Full moon. It never really gets dark. The light bellies out on things. The facades in the unpeopled street remain white while turning green and blue in the moonlight. The white paint on the window frames gleams like teeth. Even with its colors, dawn at first looks duller than the moonlight. Nothing stirs in the street.

Well before the early sunrise there is a sound of distant thunder. It fades, and then is there again, nearer. It approaches. It becomes continuous. The rumble can be felt in the house. The street echoes. The doors and windows rattle. It is a cart, a wagon. Big iron-bound wheel-rims racketing, banging on the cobbles, rolling globes of the thunder sound ahead of them. Their roar is shot through, split, hacked and hacked by the massive slapping-together of the load of heavy sawn planks far too long for the wagon, and waving down behind, trying to touch. Looming and flapping closer, more than ever like thunder. Closer than anyone would have believed it could come, beating down every other sound, shaking every wall and painting, setting the dust adrift, and then passing, with no one look-ing out to see whether it cast a shadow or who was driving. Going by, high as the second-storey windows, and beginning to recede, and fading away until at last the heart is louder and the day begins.

A Street of Day

I know the morning is not over, from the way the light quavers on the face of the yellow brick apartment building across the street, and flows along the slack telephone wires above the far sidewalk. Sections of shadow, where the wires, as they swing, appear to cross, race back and forth between the poles, never touching them. The sections change shape, as the daylight changes. At breakfast they were long and liquid. Now they are drier, shorter, and they hurry. I have asked whether they are messages, and have been told that they are not. They are nothing. So they make no sounds. I know the sounds they do not make. Early in the morning, a violin bow on a saw. Then the sound of the breath of an animal running. While I watch, there are words passing through those wires. They are the messages. They can only be heard by the people they are going to. They know nothing of the racing shadows they pass through. Neither the mouths that are speaking nor the ears that are listening are aware of those shadows.

This is the view from the dining room. Most times of day it is a little dark in there, as though one had just come in from outside, because the shades are drawn on the upper halves of the windows, and the gauzy curtains film over the rest. It is lighter in the bay window, over the street, than in the depths of the room, but I have been told not to go too near the windows and be seen looking out. The dark oval table holds a reflection of window, a sleeve of a cloud. Once I walked under the table, and long afterwards I was told of having done it: a thing too dangerous to repeat.

Up the street to the right it is earlier. Where the sidewalk opposite passes a courtyard between garages with gates made of green-painted boards, topped with broken barbed wire, which have stood open for so long that now they will not close, and black dust dances tirelessly on the cement inside, it is the hour of coming home with the morning's shopping, pushing carriages, stopping to talk— one carriage facing one way and one the other. Past the corner with the butcher shop, out of sight of the dining room and into the next block, which is set back (for the street is wider there) several paces to the west, more of the morning is left. The children have been swallowed up in school: it has just happened, and a hush has filled the streets. The air is cool. There is still some blue in all the colors. The whole day lies ahead, with time enough for anything. A great space on all sides. It is the hour when aunts on visits take their walks. People are still buying morning papers at the tiny store in the middle of the block, and have not yet started buying ice cream or candy. And in the block beyond, where the street narrows again, breakfast is being eaten in the shingled houses, brick houses, stuccoed houses, upstairs as well as downstairs. That is the block on which something is always about to appear, like a streetcar arriving around the far corner.

But that far corner is not the beginning. The street continues straight on, rising out of itself, becoming visible—I have seen it happen. There are blocks that I forget each time until I see them again. They lie in the hours before the day has been claimed, as though they were not moving. And past them, in the twilight before dawn, at the edge of the darkness in which sirens wailed and the monastery burned into black silence, there is the big stone building like a barn or boat house, on the eastern side of the street, which I saw only once, and wonder whether it is still there. In that block the street runs close to the edge of the cliff, and behind the building I saw the seaport spread out far below in the first colorless hazy light, and the breathless polished river beyond the docks. The streets were empty and wet with dew—I could smell it. The huge doors of the building, giving onto the street, were wide open. Barn doors, firehouse doors: they had been folded back to expose a room bigger than a garage, almost as big as a church. I could see that it was not ordinarily disclosed to the gaze of passers-by, and that no one was expected in the street at that hour. The big room was darker than the sky outside; it was lit only by a few candles on tall silver-wrapped candlesticks. Near the doors there was a wagon with a bier on it. The body was draped in stiff white and gold ecclesiastical vestments, with a gold mitre on its head, and a long gold staff in its hands. The feet were toward the open doors. Over the body two young men in white brocade vestments, wearing gold birettas, were bending, one on each side, holding candlesticks, and arranging folds of the drapery. They looked up and saw me and appeared surprised. Then they went on with what they were doing, and I could see that to stay would be an intrusion. That seems a long time ago.

Going the other way, it is afternoon almost at once. An old wooden house, on the first corner, is lived in by some people who are never seen. Beyond it, picket fences. Tall bushes. Nodding flowers. A block of small brick houses with low black iron railings along in the sidewalk, where children come back from school in groups, with their mothers, and go in for something to eat. In there it is nice, quiet, musty, and the sideboards are old women. By the time one gets to the park, the day is growing late, as you can see by the way a ball drops from the air, and can hear from the echoes of voices playing tag, and of a rope striking the pavement. Urns at the tops of columns mark the way home to supper, in a cool breeze.

The street itself goes on, after the park, down the long viaduct, through the dusk, while the lights come on, and sounds of hymns drift from evening services. From the foot of the viaduct the street heads out through the night in the port, and comes to an end at the ferry barns, which are closed at that hour. The wide cobbled plaza in front of them is empty except for one car with its lights out and no one in it, parked at the foot of one of the ramps. All of the ramps have been closed with criss-cross iron gates. There are few lights around the plaza. The city to which the ferries go looks nearer than it does by day. But over there even now the stars are going out above tall buildings, the sky is growing pale, and it is already tomorrow.

Watching a Train

Through dusk on summer fields far from habitations a stone wind is heard rising through a cut in a hill. A long note and a short one.

The earth is still twilit after sundown at the time when the ray first appears, in high summer, bleaching the path ahead of it. Then the linked shadow full of lighted windows that sweep the fields making them darker, not reflecting them, follows.

Rows of lives are looking out of sound they no longer hear. They think it is night here, as they pass, with their minds in other places.

Sparked between hills, the windows are erased at their own speed. Then the sky is deeper, though there are no stars yet. And the rare crickets are clearer, as when the wind drops.

The Field

Every railroad station exists in a dream. There is no way to avoid that. Now we can even imagine the railroads themselves ceasing to exist. What will stand then where the stations are now? If there should be any people in those places by then, what would they dream, perhaps many storeys up in what is now air? They will not know that a station was ever there, the trains coming and going below them where they sleep. In a dream people still get on a familiar train, and the doors close, and they know where to look for the first field. When they see it, already the station is far behind, and each of them is in a different green afternoon.

Birds at Noon

Before mid-summer I shake out my pockets in the sun. The trees pay no attention. The long grass is young green, full of buttercups. The unknown key, worn smooth in my pocket: it seldom sees the light yet it shines. I reproach myself, in passing, for indolence, lack of faith, not knowing the key. Leaves are shining pieces. When I look at them I feel myself trying to remember. But we are new.

Over the wall, bird-cherry trees, plum trees with green plums, oaks, an ivy thicket. Smell of bird-cherry, *Prunus avium.* I can blame only myself for my age, and it is too late now to do anything about it. I feel responsible for what I have forgotten. Meanwhile, the sound of magpies, voices of stones in a river. I am words that I do not hear, but I grew up believing that I might. A photograph passes through three lives and the one in the middle never looks at it. In the flowering bird-cherry trees a flock of titmice have gathered for the first time of the year, as though it were already August. For the first time they make sounds that they were born knowing. The swallow and the goldfinch utter whole sentences of hard joy. How do I know? What is the first thing that I remember? It flew away.

Everything is flying. The sun is flying, and the trees; the living and the dead hand in hand. The jay flashes through the intricate thickets like part of a storm, but without crashing and without turning its head. It shrieks for the victim, so that the victim hesitates. I try to imagine the woods as they appear between the jay's eyes. The green dark woods unfolding through the head of a jay, at great speed, to that one syllable, and no choice. The needle jay.

The nightingale comes and sings in the shade of the bird-cherry, too deep for the jay. I see only the woods I can see. I am a foreigner, with this key. I watch. The jay is preceded and followed by a brief hush such as surrounds a wind skimming like a plate over the woods. A taut, invisible horizon. Approaching it, the messenger jay: *Change! Change!* When the echo has gone, the titmice speak again, about August.

White-throat, black-cap wren sing in turn in one oak tree. As each of them sings a whole branch lights up. The presence of singing. At moments the whole tree lights up. The nightingale makes the whole tree light up, in the middle of the day. Green light occurring as a skylark makes morning. When the singing stops I go on sitting with all that I remember, from there and from many distances, and with all that I have forgotten, in that grassy place in late Spring, after hearing something I wanted to know.

Pastures

The rain drives from the west into the opening thistles. The finches: spools on nails, vehicles on spools.

An old affection for thistles. I hid once in a hollow behind a clump of thistles. They were surrounded by a thick bower of ferns, the summer's growth, green above, and rimmed and written on below, mingled with the sepias of other years in that place. It was evening in summer: few trees in the enormous rolling west light. Hummocks rising on all sides, full of rays: a flock of buffalo shining in their sleep. The thistles their constellation by day. We were all hiding behind the hummocks. In the hollows where we lay, the grass had been cropped by cows. We lay among the buffalo. The hollows were filled with shadow, which made them softer and deeper. Part of the shadow came from above, part from below. I became transparent. The thistles were my friends.

These are hare thistles. Where the hare comes, in the middle of the day, loping, sniffing, sitting and looking and looking, and then going on. When he leaves he does not know he is leaving, nor that I go with him part of the way.

Those were fern thistles. Ferns do not grow here, nor the smell, half remembered, half invented: chestnut, apple, pine.

These are rain thistles. They were not part of the game.

There are no hollows behind the thistles here. Limestone and sheep, mother and daughter, and the hare going on through the ages of colors, among the finch-wheels.

Beyond those thistles was the lake. When the hollows were full of shadow, voices would call us, from the shore, and we would all emerge, feeling the dew, and smiling at having won.

Small Oak Place

Swallows glide hunting under the branches here, in the late afternoon. Rain flows east, when it comes. A dry ground most of the year, red, and shallow over stone. Every gray lives here, and changes like a cloud. The stones gather according to their kind. Waiting is here, no words, marjoram. Pink flowers of calamint, bees, seed-heads so small that a blade of tawny grass hides them. Straw is native, and the smell of heat, and cracked bark. The yellow thistles first opened to an evening in summer, and to them morning is always a surprise. The clipped sheep hurried past in the mist at sunrise, with dew on them full of light.

Mice flow out of crevices, shadows have rabbits, snakes leave their skins among the stones. At noon, underfoot, it is pure night, trembling with the same cicada sound as the day.

Long ago some human with an age came and thought to stay here, and decided where to put stones on top of each other, and which stones, and a roof over them. Nothing else is known of that person. Birth, name, face, death, friends. Above the stones there is the sky. In the summer, by the roofless house among oak trees, plums can be heard falling into the high grass a field away, hour after hour.

Promontory

The sea gleams all the way to the south horizon, on which there are two mountains, mirrors full of smoke. It is morning for all of us.

Lines of white foam are sliding in from the left hand. Breakers bright cerulean, and enamelled in some places. Curled porcelain, alive. Sun after ten days of storm. Large waves, green, suddenly shouldering out of riding swells, and running forward. In other places, slate of a long roof of breath passing inland. Invasions, ages, generations of bright foam proceeding at the same time over coral, to coral sand, after innumerable changes and distances, continue to arrive at no arrival at all.

Over the foam a haze of blown spray is rising and moving landward to join heavy clouds against the mountains of the coast, to the right, on the west: green ridges straight up and down, regular as statues, not statues of anything. Steep foothills marbled with red that is erosion, a skin parted and drawn back without a word. Valleys opening, filled, where they widen out, with palms and banana trees, foam of leaves. Valleys of sunbeams between dark cliffs. Rows of sharp buttresses, necks of stone horses running together, flecked with lichen. Water rushing in white falls between them. The word *palisade* has gone around the world, echoing.

Clear east, blue east, mother of loud unseen wind without beginning, without name. Clouds gather on steep mountains, deepen, and their shadows blacken on dark, sharp, carved cliffs. They float through clefts. They fill high caves.

Two flat roofs, below, one on either side, hide parts of the sea. Neither roof is finished. A new tin chimney, on the one to the right, splashed with tar, is already turning the color of mist, a tower in our time. At the pace of the sea the rain is taking the mountains. Hammer sounds seem at first to be separate. Saw sounds run together. Rain disappears.

Harbor

Rarely is the night so clear, on this coast, at this time of year. All day
we sailed in fog, floating through a pearl. The tide changed under us.
We felt it, at times. The light went out of the pearl and we sailed on,
through the back of a mirror, hearing the sound of a stream, which
was ourselves, in the darkness. But we knew where we were, as one
remembers parts of a story. We heard a buoy where it was supposed
to be, and we passed it according to the instructions published for
the season, which means us. Then suddenly the fog cleared, and we
saw the night: many stars, and ahead of us and on either side an
unbroken band of darkness. We were in the estuary. The sound of
our passing through the water swallowed up the last low tones of the
buoy behind us. Channel markers blinked, bells rang far off over
the water as we made our way in.

We had not planned to arrive at night, but it makes no difference.
I reach out over the stern and grasp the thick line that leads back to
the patent log trailing behind us in the night to tell us our speed
through the dark. I feel the pulsing of the line, the beat of the steady
fish that is our time, and I reel in the heavy cord, hand over hand,
stripping the water from it, hearing the metal fins break the surface
and flounder over it until they come to hang upright, swinging in
the night air, dripping into the babbling wake.

There are three of us: besides me there is the old friend whose
boat it is, and the young woman whom he scarcely knows, who came
with me. After the long passage we speak little, sailing up the estuary,
and when we do say something our voices are hushed and strained.
We come to the end of a breakwater, where a small light is blinking
on the top of a pole, and we turn into the stillness beyond it.

I remember the harbor in the evening, in another time: the glassy
enclosure reflecting the cool sky full of yellow light after sunset and
the one other vessel, a fishing boat moored alongside the looming
fish-canning factory—structure like an old colliery, of wood and
rusted tin, rising from the harbor's edge into the clear hour. One tall
wharf. Ten or twelve houses around the shore; small, pointed white

buildings from an age before any of us was born, with grass running down to the water, and some windows full of sky, some with drawn white curtains. Hydrangea bushes in the twilight, fading.

We move slowly across the still harbor. I can make out the tall black shape of the factory, and then the high wharf jutting toward us on its stilts. My old friend walks forward and we take down the sails and glide on, propelled by nothing but our own momentum, in a long curve that ends with the wharf a few feet away. I take a painter and wait until I see, moving slowly toward me, the black form of a long ladder. I reach out to it, and with the line coiled on my arm, start to climb. Step by step the pilings of the wharf sink under the stars.

We will hear our feet walk along the wharf and onto the echoing land, in the night. We will walk up the street between the few stores, past the speechless houses. Behind the curtains everyone is asleep. No one will know we are there. We will be standing in the street among the houses when the stars begin to fade, each of us seeing a different place. Unheard by us, someone will wake, on the other side of a curtain, and see us there, and not know who we are nor where we have come from.

About the Author

W.S. Merwin was born in New York City in 1927. From 1949 to 1951, he worked as a tutor in France, Majorca, and Portugal; for several years afterward he made the greater part of his living by translating from French, Spanish, Latin, and Portuguese. His many awards include the Pulitzer Prize in Poetry, the Lannan Lifetime Achievement Award, the Tanning Prize for mastery in the art of poetry (now the Wallace Stevens Award), the Bollingen Award, the Ruth Lilly Poetry Prize, as well as fellowships from the Rockefeller and the Guggenheim foundations and the National Endowment for the Arts. He is the author of many books of poetry and prose; his most recent volumes of poems are *Migration: New & Selected Poems,* winner of the National Book Award, and *Present Company.* For the past thirty years he has lived in Hawaii.

Copper Canyon Press is grateful to the following individuals and foundations whose extraordinary financial support made publication of this book possible.

Anonymous (5)

David G. Brewster & Mary Kay Sneeringer

Betsey Curran & Jonathan King

Vasiliki Dwyer

Jane W. Ellis & Jack Litewka

The Charles Engelhard Foundation

Kay & Joe Gantt

Mimi Gardner Gates

Stanley & Kip Greenthal

Cynthia Hartwig & Tom Booster

Phyllis Hatfield

George Hitchcock & Marjorie Simon

Steven Holl & Solange Fabiao

Mary Ingraham & Jim Brown

Peter & Johnna Lewis

Sheila & Jim Molnar

Walter Parsons

Cynthia Sears & Frank Buxton

Rick Simonson

Kevin Tighe

Jim & Mary Lou Wickwire

Charles & Barbara Wright

The Chinese character for poetry is made up of two parts: "word" and "temple." It also serves as pressmark for Copper Canyon Press.

Since 1972, Copper Canyon Press has fostered the work of emerging, established, and world-renowned poets for an expanding audience. The Press thrives with the generous patronage of readers, writers, booksellers, librarians, teachers, students, and funders—everyone who shares the belief that poetry is vital to language and living.

Major funding has been provided by:

Anonymous

The Paul G. Allen Family Foundation

Lannan Foundation

National Endowment for the Arts

Washington State Arts Commission

For information and catalogs:

COPPER CANYON PRESS
Post Office Box 271
Port Townsend, Washington 98368
360-385-4925
www.coppercanyonpress.org

This book is set in Minion, designed for digital composition by Robert Slimbach in 1989. Minion is a neohumanist face, a contemporary typeface retaining elements of the pen-drawn letterforms developed during the Renaissance. Trajan and Sirenne are used for the book and part titles. Book design and composition by Valerie Brewster, Scribe Typography. Printed on archival-quality Glatfelter Author's Text at McNaughton & Gunn, Inc.